Assyrian Discoveries

The Ancient Near East: Classic Studies

K. C. Hanson
Series Editor

Albert T. Clay
Light on the Old Testament from Babel

Albert T. Clay
The Origin of Biblical Tradition

Leonard W. King
Legends of Babylon and Egypt in Relation to Hebrew Tradition

Friedrich Delitzsch
Babel and Bible

George Smith
Assyrian Discoveries

George Smith & A. H. Sayce
The Chaldean Account of Genesis

Assyrian Discoveries

George Smith

New Foreword and Bibliography by
K. C. Hanson

Wipf & Stock Publishers
Eugene, Oregon

ASSYRIAN DISCOVERIES
The Ancient Near East: Classic Studies

Copyright © 2006 Wipf & Stock Publishers. All rights reserved. Except for brief quotations in critical publications or reviews, no part of this book may be reproduced in any manner without prior written permission from the publisher. Write: Permissions, Wipf & Stock, 199 W. 8th Ave., Eugene, OR 97401.

ISBN: 1-59752-624-X

Cataloging-in-Publication data

Smith, George
    Assyrian discoveries / George Smith; new foreword and bibliography by K. C. Hanson.

    The Ancient Near East: Classic Studies

    ISBN: 1-59752-624-X

    Includes bibliographical references, illustrations, and indexes.

    p.; ill.; cm.

    1. Bible—Antiquities. 2. Bible. O.T.—Antiquities. 3. Assyriology. 4. Cuneiform inscriptions. 5. Iraq—Antiquities. 6. Assyro-Babylonian literature—Relation to the Old Testament. I. Hanson, K. C. (Kenneth C.). II. Title. III. Series.

    DS70 .S73 2006

Manufactured in the U.S.A.

Series Foreword

The archaeological discoveries of ancient cities and texts in Mesopotamia, Egypt, and Syria-Palestine began in earnest in the nineteenth century and only accelerated in the twentieth and twenty-first centuries. A few of the most significant early explorations and excavations make the point:

- In 1838, Robinson explored and inaugurated the geographical study of Palestine, especially exploring Jerusalem, including Hezekiah's Tunnel.[1]
- Funded by King Friedrich Wilhelm IV of Prussia, Richard Lepsius discovered several monuments from the Old Kingdom of Egypt during his three-year expedition (1843–1845).[2]
- The earliest treasures of Assyria were excavated by Layard at Calah (Nimrud) and Botta at Nineveh (the Kuyunjik mound in Mosul) in the 1840s.[3]
- Sir W. K. Loftus carried out the earliest explorations of Ur (Tell Muqqayyar) in 1849. But it was Wooley

---

[1] Edward Robinson and Eli Smith, *Biblical Researches in Palestine and in the Adjacent Regions: A Journal of Travels in the Year 1838,* 3 vols. (Boston: Crocker & Brewster, 1841).

[2] C. R. Lepsius, *Denkmäler aus Aegypten und Aethiopien,* 12 vols. (Berlin: Nicolaische Buchhandlung, 1849–56).

[3] Austen Henry Layard, *Nineveh and Its Remains,* 2 vols. (New York: Putnam, 1849); idem, *Discoveries in the Ruins of Nineveh and Babylon* (New York: Harper, 1853); Paul Émile Botta, *Monument de Ninive* (Paris: Imprimerie Nationale, 1849–50).

who did the systematic excavations almost seventy-five years later (1922–34).[4]
- Charles Warren surveyed the topography of Jerusalem and the temple mount in 1867 and 1870.
- The ancient Egyptian sites of Tanis and Gizeh were ex-plored by Sir Flinders Petrie in the 1880s.[5]
- The University of Pennsylvania began excavations of Nippur (southeast of Baghdad) in 1889.[6]
- Under the auspices of the Deutsche Orient-Gesellschaft (German Oriental Society), Koldewey excavated Babylon (part of modern Baghdad) from 1899 to 1918.[7]

The remains of ancient societies often require decades to unearth, but much longer to interpret and understand. The methods of archaeology have progressed dramatically in recent years. Archaeologists have continuously refined their tools, methods, and techniques. Today archaeology is characterized by pottery identification, classification, and cataloging; disciplined excavation of "squares"; use of sophisticated electronics, such as GPS, infrared, and computer-aided design; and the integration of multiple methodologies, such as epigraphy, art history, physical anthropology, paleobotany, and climatology.

---

[4] C. L. Wooley, *Ur Excavations,* 10 vols. (London: Oxford University Press, 1927–74).

[5] W. M. Flinders Petrie, *Tanis,* 2 vols. (Egypt Exploration Fund, 1880–1888); idem, *The Pyramids and Temples of Gizeh* (London: Field & Tuer, 1883).

[6] Clarence S. Fisher, *Excavations at Nippur* (Philadelphia: Babylonian Expedition of the University of Pennsylvania, 1905).

[7] Robert Koldewey, *The Excavations at Babylon,* trans. Agnes S. Johns (London: Macmillan, 1914).

The interpretation of ancient Near Eastern history and cultures has also progressed. An increasing number of documents has been unearthed. The vast document collections from Tel el-Amarna, Nippur, Mari, Nuzi, Ebla, Ugarit, and the Dead Sea caves are just some of the more spectacular examples. These provide an enormous amount of detail about the royal administrations, business transactions, land tenure systems, taxes, political propaganda, mythologies, marriage practices, and much more. And things that sometimes seem unique about one culture at first look often fit into larger patterns of relationship when the surrounding cultures are better understood.

The Ancient Near East: Classic Studies (**ANECS**) reprints classic works that have brought the results of archaeology, textual, and historical investigations to audiences of scholars, students, and the general public. While the discussions continue and the results of earlier investigations are continuously re-examined, these classic works remain of interest and importance.

—K. C. Hanson
Series Editor

Select Bibliography

1. Language and Texts

Beyerlin, Walter, editor. *Near Eastern Religious Texts Relating to the Old Testament.* Translated by John Bowden. Old Testament Library. Philadelphia: Westminster, 1978.

Buccellati, Giorgio, and Robert D. Biggs. *Cuneiform Texts from Nippur: The Eighth and Ninth Seasons.* Assyriological Studies 17. Chicago: University of Chicago Press, 1969.

Budge, E. A. Wallis., and L. W. King. *Annals of the Kings of Assyria.* London: British Museum, 1902.

Clay, Albert T. *Documents from the Temple Archives of Nippur, Dated in the Reigns of Cassite Rulers.* Philadelphia: University Museum of the University of Pennsylvania, 1906.

Cole, Steven W., and Peter Machinist, editors. *Letters from Priests to the Kings Esarhaddon and Assurbanipal.* State Archives of Assyria 13. Helsinki: Helsinki University Press, 1998.

Craig, James A. *Assyrian and Babylonian Religious Texts.* 2 vols. Assyriologische Bibliothek 13. Leipzig: Hinrichs, 1895–97.

Dalley, Stephanie. *Myths from Mesopotamia.* Oxford: Oxford University Press, 1989.

Driver, G. R., and John C. Miles. *The Assyrian Laws.* Ancient Codes and Laws of the Near East. Oxford: Clarendon, 1935.

Fales, F. M., and J. N. Postgate, editors. *Imperial Administrative Records*. State Archives of Assyria 7. Helsinki: Helsinki University Press, 1992–.

Grayson, A. Kirk. *Assyrian and Babylonian Chronicles*. Texts from Cuneiform Sources 5. Locust Valley, N.Y.: Augustin, 1970.

———. *Assyrian Royal Inscriptions*. 2 vols. Records of the Ancient Near East. Wiesbaden: Harrassowitz, 1972–.

———. *Assyrian Rulers of the Third and Second Millennia BC (to 1115 BC)*. Royal Inscriptions of Mesopotamia: Assyrian Periods 1. Toronto: University of Toronto Press, 1987.

———. *Assyrian Rulers of the Early First Millennium BC I (1114– 859 BC)*. Royal Inscriptions of Mesopotamia: Assyrian Periods 2. Toronto: University of Toronto Press, 1991.

Hallo, William W., and K. Lawson Younger Jr., editors. *The Context of Scripture*. Vol. 1: *Canonical Compositions from the Biblical World*. Leiden: Brill, 1997.

———. *The Context of Scripture*. Vol. 2: *Monumental Inscriptions from the Biblical World*. Leiden: Brill, 1999.

———. *The Context of Scripture*. Vol. 3: *Archival Documents from the Biblical World*. Leiden: Brill, 2002.

Hunger, Hermann, editor. *Astrological Reports to Assyrian Kings*. State Archives of Assyria 8. Helsinki: Helsinki University Press, 1992.

Kataja, L., and R. Whiting, editors. *Grants, Decrees and Gifts of the Neo-Assyrian Period*. State Archives of Assyria 12. Helsinki: Helsinki University Press, 1995.

Kwasman, Theodore, and Simo Parpola, editors. *Legal Trans-actions of the Royal Court of Nineveh*. 2 vols. State Archives of Assyria 6, 14. Helsinki: Helsinki University Press, 1991–2002.

Lau, Robert J., and Stephen Langdon. *The Annals of*

Ashurbanipal (V Rawlinson pl. I-X). Semitic Study Series 2. Leiden: Brill, 1903.

Layard, Austen H. *Inscriptions in the Cuneiform Character from Assyrian Monuments.* London: Harrison, 1851.

Livingstone, Alasdair, editor. *Court Poetry and Literary Miscellanea.* State Archives of Assyria 3. Helsinki: Helsinki University Press, 1989.

Luckenbill, Daniel David. *The Annals of Sennacherib.* 1924. Reprinted, Ancient Texts and Translations. Eugene, Ore.: Wipf & Stock, 2005.

———. *Ancient Records of Assyria and Babylonia.* 2 vols. Chicago: University of Chicago Press, 1926–27.

Luukko, Mikko, and Greta van Buylaere, editors. *The Political Correspondence of Esarhaddon.* State Archives of Assyria 16. Helsinki: Helsinki University Press, 2002.

Meissner, Bruno, and Paul Rost. *Die Bauinschriften Sanheribs.* Leipzig: Pfeiffer, 1893.

Messerschmidt, Leopold. *Keilinschrifttexte aus Assur: Historischen Inhalts.* Vol. 1. Leipzig: Hinrichs, 1911.

Parpola, Simo. Letters from Assyrian Scholars to the Kings Esarhaddon and Assurbanipal. 2 vols. Alter Orient und Altes Testament 5/1-2. Kevelaer: Butzon & Bercker, 1970– 83.

———. *The Correspondence of Sargon II.* 3 vols. State Archives of Assyria 1, 5, 15. Helsinki: Helsinki University Press, 1987– 2001.

———. *Neo-Assyrian Treaties and Loyalty Oaths.* State Archives of Assyria 2. Helsinki: Helsinki University Press, 1988.

———. *Letters from Assyrian and Babylonian Scholars.* State Archives of Assyria 10. Helsinki: Helsinki University Press, 1993.

———. *Assyrian Prophecies.* State Archives of Assyria 9.

Helsinki: Helsinki University Press, 1997.
Piepkorn, Arthur Carl. *Historical Prism Inscriptions of Ashurbanipal.* Assyriological Studies 5. Chicago: University of Chicago Press, 1933.
Pritchard, James B., editor. *Ancient Near Eastern Texts Relating to the Old Testament.* 3d ed. Princeton: Princeton University Press, 1969.
Rawlinson, H. C. *A Selection from the Miscellaneous Inscriptions of Assyria and Babylonia.* Cuneiform Inscriptions of Western Asia 5. London: Harrison, 1909.
Reynolds, Frances. *The Babylonian Correspondence of Esarhaddon, and Letters to Assurbanipal and Sin-Sarru-Iskun from Northern and Central Babylonia.* State Archives of Assyria 18. Helsinki: Helsinki University Press, 2003.
Rogers, Robert William. *Cuneiform Parallels to the Old Testament.* 2d ed. 1926. Reprinted, Ancient Texts and Translations. Eugene, Ore.: Wipf & Stock, 2005.
Rost, Paul. *Die Keilschrifttexte Tiglat-Pilesers III.* Leipzig: Pfeiffer, 1893.
Starr, Ivan. *Queries to the Sungod: Divination and Politics in Sargonid Assyria.* State Archives of Assyria 4. Helsinki: Helsinki University Press, 1990.
Stephens, Ferris J. *Votive and Historical Texts from Babylonia and Assyria.* Yale Oriental Series: Babylonian Texts 9. New Haven: Yale University Press, 1937.
Tadmor, Hayyim. *The Inscriptions of Tiglath-pileser III, King of Assyria: Critical Edition, with Introductions, Translations, and Commentary.* Publications of the Israel Academy of Sciences and Humanities, Section of Humanities. Jerusalem: Israel Academy of Sciences and Humanities, 1994.
Thomas, D. Winton, editor. *Documents from Old Testament Times.* 1958. Reprinted Eugene, Ore.: Wipf & Stock, 2005.

Thompson, R. Campbell. *Assyrian Medical Texts from the Originals in the British Museum.* London: Oxford University Press, 1923.

Weber, Otto. *Die Literatur der Babylonier und Assyrer: Ein Überblick.* Der Alte Orient Ergänzungsband 2. Leipzig: Hinrichs, 1907.

Zimmern, Heinrich, and Hugo Winckler. *Die Keilinschriften und das Alte Testament.* 2 vols. 3d ed. Berlin: Reuther & Reichard, 1903. (Rev. ed. of Schrader 1883.)

2. History and Society

Bienkowski, Piotr, and Alan Millard. *Dictionary of the Ancient Near East.* Philadelphia: University of Pennsylvania Press, 2000.

Bottéro, Jean. *Mesopotamia: Writing, Reasoning, and the Gods.* Translated by Zainab Bahrani. Chicago: University of Chicago Press, 1992.

Frankfort, Henri. *The Art and Architecture of the Ancient Orient.* 5th ed. New Haven: Yale University Press, 1996.

Gordon, Cyrus H., and Gary A. Rendsburg. *The Bible and the Ancient Near East.* 4th ed. New York: Norton, 1997.

Hallo, William W., and William Kelly Simpson. *The Ancient Near East: A History.* 2d ed. Fort Worth: Harcourt Brace College, 1998.

Hilprecht Anniversary Volume: Studies in Assyriology and Archaeology Dedicated to Hermann V. Hilprecht. Leipzig: Hinrichs, 1909.

Liverani, Mario. *International Relations in the Ancient Near East, 1600–1100.* Studies in Diplomacy. New York: Palgrave, 2002.

Machinist, Peter. "The Fall of Assyria in Comparative Perspective." In *Assyria 1995: Proceedings of the 10th Anniversary Symposium of the Neo-Assyrian Text Corpus Project, Helsinki, September 7-11, 1995*, edited by Simo Parpola and R. M. Whiting, 179–95. Helsinki: The Project, 1997.

Olmstead, A. T. *Western Asia in the Days of Sargon of Assyria, 722–705 B.C.: A Study in Oriental History*. Cornell Studies in History and Political Science 2. New York: Holt, 1908.

Parpola, Simo, and Robert W. Whiting, editors. *Assyria 1995: Proceedings of the 10th Anniversary Symposium of the Neo-Assyrian Text Corpus Project, Helsinki, September 7-11, 1995*. Helsinki: The Project, 1997.

Rogers, Robert William. *History of Babylonia and Assyria*. 2 vols. 2d ed. New York: Eaton & Mains, 1900.

———. *The Religion of Babylonia and Assyria, Especially in Its Relations to Israel*. New York: Eaton & Mains, 1908.

Roux, Georges. *Ancient Iraq*. 3d ed. New York: Penguin, 1993.

Saggs, H. W. F. *The Might That Was Assyria*. Great Civilizations Series. London: Sidgwick & Jackson, 1984.

———. *Civilization before Greece and Rome*. New Haven: Yale University Press, 1989.

Sasson, Jack M., editor. *Civilizations of the Ancient Near East*. 4 vols. New York: Scribners, 1995.

Snell, Daniel C. *Life in the Ancient Near East, 3100–332 B.C.E.* New Haven: Yale University Press, 1997.

Van de Mieroop, Marc. *The Ancient Mesopotamian City*. Oxford: Clarendon, 1997.

———. *Cuneiform Texts and the Writing of History. Approaching the Ancient World*. London: Routledge, 1999.

———. *A History of the Ancient Near East, ca. 3000–323 BC*. Blackwell History of the Ancient World. Malden, Mass.: Blackwell, 2004.

Walls, Neal H. *Desire, Discord, and Death: Approaches to Ancient Near Eastern Myth.* ASOR Books 8. Boston: American Schools of Oriental Research, 2001.

Yamada, Shigeo. *The Construction of the Assyrian Empire: A Historical Study of the Inscriptions of Shalmanesar III Relating to His Campaigns in the West.* Culture and History of the Ancient Near East 3. Boston: Brill, 2000.

TO

DR. BIRCH, LL.D.

KEEPER OF THE DEPARTMENT OF ORIENTAL ANTIQUITIES,

BRITISH MUSEUM;

PRESIDENT OF THE SOCIETY OF BIBLICAL ARCHÆOLOGY;

PRESIDENT OF THE ORIENTAL CONGRESS,

ETC. ETC. ETC.

AS A RESPECTFUL TRIBUTE TO HIS LEARNING AND GENIUS,

THIS WORK

𝔍𝔰 𝔇𝔢𝔡𝔦𝔠𝔞𝔱𝔢𝔡.

PREFACE.

THE following work was written to give in a permanent form some account of the excavations undertaken in 1873 and 1874 on the site of Nineveh; and the principal discoveries which have resulted from these operations. The honour of having started this enterprise belongs to the proprietors of the "Daily Telegraph" newspaper, and at the close of the first expedition they presented the firman and excavating plant to the trustees of the British Museum to facilitate the renewal of the work. The second expedition was only to take advantage of the remainder of the time allowed by the firman, and I was directed to close the excavations within the period allowed by the concession of the Porte.

I have been working in the territory of the Turkish empire, and it is with regret that I have had to mention the unsatisfactory conduct of many of its agents. I have not made the most of this; I have omitted many incidents of bad conduct, and have stated those I have mentioned as moderately and slightly as possible; but I could not have passed the subject over entirely without falsifying my narrative. I have not the smallest doubt that in the government of Asia the Turks are not alive to their own interests, and particularly in the oppressive laws and persecution of the Christians. The American missions in Asiatic Turkey are doing a noble work in the country, but they can only be useful in proportion to the amount of official support they receive from England and America.

In the body of my work I have acknowledged the assistance I received from several gentlemen, official and private, in my expeditions. To these I must add the name of M. Pérétié, the French consul at Mosul, who was of great assistance to me in my dealings with the Turkish officials, and took as much interest in my affairs as if I had been a fellow-subject with himself. The presence of M. Pérétié at Mosul, and his generous attention to British interests, makes the want of a British consul less felt; but it is extremely unfortunate that in the wide extent of country between Aleppo and Baghdad there is not a single British representative.

CONTENTS.

CHAPTER I.—FORMER EXCAVATIONS AND DISCOVERIES IN THE VALLEY OF THE EUPHRATES AND TIGRIS.
Interest of subject. — Botta's excavations. — Layard's works.—Rawlinson.—Hormuzd Rassam.—Loftus.—Decipherment of cuneiform.—Grotefend.—Rawlinson.—Behistun text.—Hincks.—Oppert.—Later decipherers . page 1

CHAPTER II.—DISCOVERIES FROM 1866 TO 1872.
Date of Jehu.—Annals of Assurbanipal.—Eclipse, B.C. 763.—Pekah.—Hoshea.—Azariah.—Early Elamite conquest.—Religious calendar.—Sabbaths.—Early Babylonian history.—Chaldean account of the deluge.—Offer of the "Daily Telegraph" . 9

CHAPTER III.—FROM LONDON TO MOSUL.
Paris.—Marseilles.—Mediterranean.—Palermo.—Etna.—Syra. —Smyrna.—Alexandretta.—Beilan.—Hotels.—Pass of Beilan.—Afrin. — Robber. — Aleppo. — Turkish holiday. — Euphrates. — Tcharmelek.—Orfa.—American missions.—Christians in Turkey. —Varenshaher.—River Khabour.—Nisibin.—Rising of Shammer Arabs. — Sofuk. — Abdul Kareem. — Tellibel. — Djezireh. — River Tigris.—Khabour.—Zaccho.—Mule driver.—Nineveh . . 15

CONTENTS.

CHAPTER IV.—VISIT TO BABYLONIA.
Mosul.—The serai.—Turkish pacha.—French consul.—Inscription of Vul-nirari.—Raft.—Nimroud.—Kalah Shergat.—Rocks and cave.—Tekrit.—Baghdad.—Col. Herbert.—Babylon.—Babel.—Extent of walls.—Kasr.—Hanging gardens.—Birs Nimrud.—Seven stages of tower.—Ruin of Babylon.—Hymer.—Tel Ibrahim.—Cutha.—Arab encampment.—Road to Mosul.—Ervil.—The Zab.—The Ghazr.—Ferry 46

CHAPTER V.—EXCAVATIONS AT NIMROUD.
Toma Shishman.—The mound.—Tower.—Palaces.—History.—Temple of Nebo.—South-west palace.—Model of hand.—South-east palace.—Painted wall.—Winged figures.—Graves.—House building.—Arab entertainment.—Close excavations . . 69

CHAPTER VI.—EXCAVATIONS AT KOUYUNJIK.
Wall of Nineveh.—Northern gate.—The Khosr.—Great gate.—Nebbi Yunas.—Kouyunjik.—Palaces.—History.—Capture of Nineveh.—Library.—Hammum Ali.—North palace, Kouyunjik.—Law tablet.—Deluge fragment.—Discoveries.—Khorsabad.—Orders to close.—Syllabary.—Visit to Nimroud . . . 86

CHAPTER VII.—FROM MOSUL TO ENGLAND.
Backsheesh.—Mill stream.—Jebel Abjad.—Power of rivers.—Deluge mountains.—Stories.—M. Costi and Mr. Kerr.—Desert Arabs.—Nisibin.—Wounded Arab.—Orfa.—Abraham's pool.—Castle.—Biradjik.—Aleppo.—Turkish custom-house.—Deceit.—Alexandretta.—Antiquities seized.—Their release . . 104

CHAPTER VIII.—SECOND JOURNEY TO MOSUL.
Release of antiquities.—New discoveries.—Syrian robber.—Severe winter.—Tcharmelek.—Calah.—Dinasar.—Turkish conscription.—Abdul Kareem.—Irregular soldiers.—Nisibin.—Entertainment.—Dancing boy.—Derunah.—Post travelling . 119

CONTENTS. xi

CHAPTER IX.—EXCAVATIONS AT KOUYUNJIK.
Ali Rahal.—Turkish governor.—Redif Pacha.—New policy.—Turkish demands.—Temples.—Curious pottery.—Early palace.—Roman bottle.—North palace.—Ruined entrance.—Perfect bilingual tablet.—Inscriptions of Shalmaneser I.—Palace of Sennacherib.—Entrance.—Library chamber.—Fork.—Historical cylinders.—Difficulties.—Close of work 135

CHAPTER X.—RETURN FROM ASSYRIA.
Khan Balcos.—Mosul.—Departure.—Severe weather.—Stoppage.—Tel Adas.—Semil.—Discontent of soldiers.—Want of pay.—Durnak.—Crossing the Hazel.—Djezireh.—Circassian guides.—Their outrages.—Varenshaher.—Orfa.—Curiosities.—Biradjik.—Antiquities stopped.—Ride to Aleppo.—Difficulties with pacha.—Release of boxes.—Embarkation.—Return . . . 153

CHAPTER XI.—THE IZDUBAR OR FLOOD SERIES OF LEGENDS.
Chaldean account of flood.—New portions.—Izdubar.—Probably Nimrod.—Antiquity of legends.—Conquests of Izdubar.—His illness.—Hasisadra.—The flood.—Erech.—Conquest of Monster.—Zaidu.—Heabani.—Humbaba.—Ishtar.—Divine bull.—Death of Heabani.—Izdubar's sorrow.—His journey.—The giants.—Hasisadra.—Account of deluge.—Building the ark.—The flood.—Mountains of Nizir.—The birds.—Translation of patriarch.—Cure of Izdubar.—His lament.—Ghost of Heabani.—Comparison with Bible and Berosus.—Remarks 165

CHAPTER XII.—EARLY BABYLONIAN TEXTS.
Elamite conquest.—Sargon of Akkad.—His birth.—Concealed in ark.—Agu.—Temple of Bel.—Prayer for the king.—Dungi king of Ur.—Kudurmabuk.—Hammurabi.—Conquest of Babylonia.—Early bilingual text.—Turanian writing.—Semitic writing.—Riagu.—Text from Kouyunjik.—Kurigalzu.—Merodach Baladan I.—Royal grant.—Boundary stone.—Curses . . . 223

CONTENTS.

CHAPTER XIII.—EARLY ASSYRIAN INSCRIPTIONS.
Early pottery.—Text of Vul-nirari I.—Shalmaneser.—Temple of Ishtar.—Tugulti-ninip.—Babylonian wars.—Mutagil-nusku.—Assur-risilim.—Tiglath Pileser I.—Assur-nazir-pal . . 242

CHAPTER XIV.—INSCRIPTIONS OF TIGLATH PILESER II., B.C. 745 TO 727.
Annals of Tiglath Pileser.—Their importance.—Tablet from Nimroud.—Babylonian wars.—Eastern wars.—Arabian wars.—Syrian tribute list.—Building of palace.—Fragments of annals.—Azariah.—Menahem.—Rezon.—His defeat.—War in Palestine.—Pekah.—Hoshea.—Confirmation of Bible 253

CHAPTER XV.—INSCRIPTIONS OF SARGON, B.C. 722 TO 705.
Historical cylinder.—Median chiefs.—War with Ashdod.—Azuri.—Ahimiti.—Yavan.—Revolt.—Turning watercourses.—Judah.—Edom.—Moab.—Embassy to Pharaoh.—Egypt's weakness.—Advance of Sargon.—Flight of Yavan.—Seal of Sargon . 288

CHAPTER XVI.—INSCRIPTIONS OF SENNACHERIB, B.C. 705 TO 681.
Cylinder C.—Intermediate record.—Titles.—War with Merodach Baladan.—Conquest of Babylonia.—Conquest of Kassi.—Ellipi.—War in Palestine.—Elulias of Zidon.—Zidqa of Askelon.—Revolt of Ekron.—Battle with Egyptians.—Hezekiah.—Siege of Jerusalem.—Submission and tribute.—Second Babylonian war.—Letter from governor 295

CHAPTER XVII.—INSCRIPTIONS OF ESARHADDON, B.C. 681 TO 668.
New texts.—Wars with Tirhakah.—Bahal of Tyre.—March through Palestine.—Meroe.—Desert.—Want of water.—Long marches.—Conquest of Egypt.—Wars of Sennacherib.—Suzub.—Elamites.—Plunder of temple of Bel.—Babylonian dated tablet 311

CHAPTER XVIII.—INSCRIPTIONS OF ASSURBANIPAL, B.C. 668 TO 626.
Greek Sardanapalus.—Library.—Former publication.—Egyptian history.—Sabako.—Tirhakah.—Undamane.—Text.—Titles.—

CONTENTS. xiii

Campaign against Tirhakah.—Revolt of Egypt.—Death of Tirhakah.—Undamane.—Second Egyptian campaign.—Siege of Tyre.—Arvad.—Gyges of Lydia.—Psammitichus.—War with Minni.—War with Elam.—Revolt of Babylon.—Wars with Elam.—Restoration of Nana.—Arabian war.—Armenian embassy.—Restoration of palace.—Restoration of temples.—Brick from Babylon . 317

CHAPTER XIX.—INSCRIPTIONS OF BEL-ZAKIR-ISKUN, KING OF ASSYRIA, AND HIS SUCCESSORS.
Want of Monuments.—Obscurity of history.—Bel-zakir-iskun.—Cylinder.—Fall of Assyria.—Rise of Babylon.—Nebuchadnezzar.—Evil Merodach.—Nergalsharezer.—Method of dating.—Nabonidus.—Belshazzar.—Cyrus.—Cambyses.—Darius.—Trilingual text.—Artaxerxes.—Parthian date.—Important evidence . 381

CHAPTER XX.—MISCELLANEOUS TEXTS.
Hymn to light.—Translation.—Invocation to Izdubar.—His worship.—Babylonian text.—Prayer to Bel.—Inundation.—Seven evil spirits.—Their work.—Bel.—Sin, Shamas, and Ishtar.—Attack on the moon.—War in heaven.—Message to Hea.—Mission of Merodach.—Comparison of legends.—Character of deities.—Astronomy.—Four seasons.—Intercalary month.—Astrolabe.—Observation of eclipse.—Respect for laws.—Epigraphs.—Letter.—Deed of sale.—Date of Assurbanipal.—Sale of slave.—Syllabaries.—Bilingual lists 391

CHAPTER XXI.—FOREIGN INSCRIPTIONS.
Baghdad lion.—Egyptian monarch.—Ra-set-nub or Saites.—Founder of Shepherd power.—Tablet of Rameses.—Date of monument.—Hyksos.—Expelled by Amosis.—Worship of Set.—Type of lion.—Hamath inscription.—Seals at Nineveh.—Cypriote inscription.—Phœnician texts.—Contract tablets.—Pehlevi inscriptions.—Later texts.—Nisibin.—Destruction of monuments . . 420

CHAPTER XXII.—OBJECTS ILLUSTRATING ARTS AND CUSTOMS.
Larger sculptures already discovered.—Hand in wall.—Lintel.—Head of Ishtar.—Shoulder of statue.—Winged bull.—Assyrian

columns.—Crystal throne.—Crystal vase.—Name of Sennacherib.—Lamps.—Lamp feeder.—Assyrian fork.—Glass.—Roman bottle.—Glass seal.—Pottery.—Cypriote style.—Chariot group.—Commerce.—Personal ornaments.—Rings.—Beads.—Seals.—Later occupation of mound.—Destruction of antiquities . . . 428

CHAPTER XXIII.—CONCLUSION.

Difficulty of work.—Short time.—Good results.—Babylonian kings.—Assyrian kings.—New inscriptions.—Uncertainty of chronology.—Assyrian history.—Jewish history.—Pul.—New light on the Bible.—Origin of Babylonian civilization.—Turanian race.—Semitic conquest.—Flood legends.—Mythology.—Connection with Grecian mythology.—Astronomy.—Architecture.—Importance of future excavations 437

LIST OF ILLUSTRATIONS.

AP, Frontispiece.
2. Side of portal excavated by M. Botta at Khorsabad, to face p. 2.
3. Black obelisk, discovered by Layard at Nimroud, 10.
4. View of Nimroud, 49.
5. Terra-cotta winged figure, 78.
6. Photograph of figure of warrior on painted brick from south-east palace, Nimroud, to face p. 80.
7. Plan of site of Nineveh, to face p. 86.
8. The Jebel Djudi, or Deluge mountains, to face p. 108.
9. View of bay of Alexandretta from Beilan, 116.
10. Bronze lamp, 140.
11. Pottery from Kouyunjik, 141.
12. Procession of warriors, 142.
13. Roman bottle, 143.
14. Terra-cotta vase, 146.
15. Bronze fork, 147.
16. Bone spoon, 147.
17. Dead buffalo in water, 148.
18. Photograph of marble model of winged bull, to face p. 174.
19. Emblems of the gods on stone of Merodach Baladan I., to face p. 236.
20. Head from statue of the goddess Ishtar, from her temple, Kouyunjik, 248.

xvi   *LIST OF ILLUSTRATIONS.*

21. Photograph of lintel of doorway, great court of Sennacherib's palace, to face p. 308.
22. Photograph of terra-cotta bilingual tablet, to face p. 392.
23. Object with Cypriote characters, 423.
24. Model of hand found in wall, 429.
25. Bronze throne, discovered by Layard at Nimroud, 432.
26. Terra-cotta lamp, 433.
27. Terra-cotta lamp feeder, 433.
28. Bronze bracket, 434.
29. Bronze style, 434.

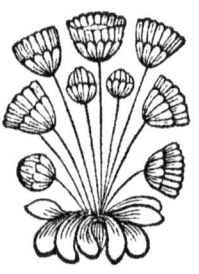

ASSYRIAN EXPLORATIONS AND DISCOVERIES.

Chapter I.
FORMER EXCAVATIONS AND DISCOVERIES IN THE VALLEY OF THE EUPHRATES AND TIGRIS.

Interest of subject.—Botta's excavations.—Layard's works.—Rawlinson.—Hormuzd Rassam.—Loftus.—Decipherment of cuneiform.—Grotefend.—Rawlinson.—Behistun text.—Hincks.—Oppert.—Later decipherers.

HE interest attaching to the valley of the Euphrates and Tigris is of the widest kind; and, excepting the land of Palestine, no other part of the globe can compare with it in the importance of its traditions, its history, and its monuments.

It is the home of man's earliest traditions, the place where Eden was supposed to have been; some of its cities are stated to be older than the Flood; it is the land of the Deluge and of the tower of Babel, and it is the birthplace of the great race of Israel which has played so important a part in the religious history of the world.

In Babylonia arose the first civilized state, and its arts and sciences became the parents of those of the Greeks, and through them also of our own.

Watered by two of the noblest rivers in the world, on each of these stood a great capital, Babylon on the Euphrates, Nineveh on the Tigris; cities which in the earlier period of history were unrivalled, and which even in their ruins have attracted the attention of travellers in all ages, from the time of their overthrow until now. M. Botta, who was appointed French consul at Mosul in 1842, was the first to commence excavations on the sites of the buried cities of Assyria, and to him is due the honour of the first discovery of her long lost palaces.

M. Botta commenced his labours at Kouyunjik, the large mound opposite Mosul, but he found here very little to compensate for his labours. New at the time to excavations, he does not appear to have worked in the best manner; M. Botta at Kouyunjik contented himself with sinking pits in the mound, and on these proving unproductive abandoning them.

While M. Botta was excavating at Kouyunjik, his attention was called to the mounds of Khorsabad by a native of the village on that site; and he sent a party of workmen to the spot to commence excavation. In a few days his perseverance was rewarded by the discovery of some sculptures, after which, abandoning the work at Kouyunjik, he transferred

SIDE OF PORTAL EXCAVATED BY M. BOTTA AT KHORSABAD.

his establishment to Khorsabad and thoroughly explored that site.

M. Botta's workmen had sunk a well at Khorsabad, and arrived at one of the palace walls. Subsequent excavations led to the discovery of many chambers and halls, faced with slabs of gypsum carved over with mythological figures, battle scenes, processions, and similar subjects. Long inscriptions in the cuneiform character ran along the middle of most of the slabs, and some of them were also inscribed at the back. The palace which M. Botta had discovered was built by Sargon, king of Assyria, B.C. 722 to 705; it is one of the most perfect Assyrian buildings yet explored, and forms an excellent example of Assyrian architecture.

Beside the palace on the mound of Khorsabad, M. Botta also opened the remains of a temple, and a grand porch decorated by six winged bulls, under which passed the road from the city to the palace. The operations of M. Botta were brought to a close in 1845, and a splendid collection of sculptures and other antiquities, the fruits of his labours, arrived in Paris in 1846 and was deposited in the Louvre.

Afterwards the French government appointed M. Place consul at Mosul, and he continued some of the excavations of his predecessor. Among other antiquities he discovered one of the gates of the city to which the palace of Sargon belonged. This gate was flanked on each side by gigantic winged bulls, and the space between them was spanned by an arch springing from the backs of the bulls.

Mr. Layard, whose attention was early turned in this direction, visited the country in 1840, and afterwards took a great interest in the excavations of M. Botta. At length, in 1845, Layard was enabled through the assistance of Sir Stratford Canning to commence excavations in Assyria himself. On the 8th of November he started from Mosul, and descended the Tigris to Nimroud. Next morning he commenced excavations, and soon discovered the remains of two palaces. Mr. Layard has described in his works with great minuteness his successive excavations, and the remarkable and interesting discoveries he made. At Nimroud he found several buildings, palaces, and temples; at Kouyunjik he found the palace of Sennacherib, and one of the great gates of the city; at Nebbi-yunas a palace of Esarhaddon, and minor monuments at various other sites. After making these discoveries in Assyria, Mr. Layard visited Babylonia, and opened trenches in several of the mounds there. On the return of Mr. Layard to England, excavations were continued in the Euphrates valley under the superintendence of Colonel (now Sir Henry) Rawlinson. Under his directions, Mr. Hormuzd Rassam, Mr. Loftus, and Mr. Taylor excavated various sites and made numerous discoveries, the British Museum receiving the best of the monuments.

The materials collected in the national museums of France and England, and the numerous inscriptions published, attracted the attention of the learned, and very soon considerable light was thrown on the history, language, manners, and customs of ancient Assyria and Babylonia.

The key to the reading of the Persian cuneiform writing had been discovered by Grotefend; but it was left to Sir Henry Rawlinson, in his great work on the Behistun inscription, to read the records of Darius and first decipher the accompanying Scythic and Assyro-Babylonian texts; thus giving a clue to the reading of the thousands of inscriptions discovered in Assyria and Babylonia.

The study of the cuneiform writing was carried on with great zeal and success by Sir H. Rawlinson, Dr. Hincks, Dr. Oppert, Dr. Norris, M. Menant, and H. Fox Talbot, Esq., and recently by M. Lenormant, Rev. A. H. Sayce, and Dr. Schrader. Other scholars have also assisted in the work, but have not taken any prominent position in deciphering the inscriptions. Beside the original discovery, the chief merit in deciphering the Assyrian inscriptions belongs to Sir H. Rawlinson, who in 1851 published the discovery of the capture of Samaria by Sargon, the war against Hezekiah by Sennacherib, and the names of many persons and places mentioned in the Bible.

In 1862 Sir Henry Rawlinson published one of the most remarkable Assyrian documents yet discovered, the Assyrian eponym canon, a chronological document giving the outlines of the Assyrian official chronology. This inscription is invaluable in the comparison of Assyrian and Scripture history.

In 1863 he published a number of discoveries, including the tablet containing the synchronous history of Assyria and Babylonia. Next after Sir Henry Rawlinson comes Dr. Hincks, a successful student both of the Egyptian and Assyrian, and on some points the close rival of Sir Henry Rawlinson. Each of the other scholars has contributed his share to the discoveries which have been made from time to time ; these are so numerous that it would take too long to do justice to them here, but the accounts of previous explorations and discoveries will be found in the following works :—

Botta. Monument de Ninive, Paris, five vols., 1849-50; Mémoire sur l'Écriture Cunéiforme Assyrienne, Paris, 1849.

Layard. Nineveh and its Remains, London, 1851; Nineveh and Babylon, London, 1853 ; Monuments of Nineveh, London, 1851 ; second series, 1853; Inscriptions in the Cuneiform Character, London, 1851.

Loftus. Travels in Chaldea and Susiana, London, 1856.

Place. Ninive et l'Assyrie, Paris, 1870.

Grotefend. Zur Erläuter. d. babylon. Keilschrift, 1840; Bemerkungen zur Inschrift eines Thongefässes mit niniv. Keilschrift, Göttingen, 1850-1; Die Tributverzeichniss d. Obelisken aus Nimrud, Göttingen, 1852; Erläuter. der babyl. Keilschrift aus Behistun, Göttingen, 1853; Erläuter. zweier Ausschr. Nebukadnezar's in babyl. Keilschr., Göttingen, 1854, and some minor papers.

Rawlinson (Sir H. C.) Commentary on the Cuneiform Inscriptions of Babylon and Assyria, London, 1850; Babylonian text of Great Inscription at Behistun, London, 1851; Memoir on the Babylonian and Assyrian Inscriptions, London, 1854; Notes on the early history of Babylonia, London, 1856; Orthography of some of the later royal names of Assyrian and Babylonian history, London, 1856; Cuneiform Inscriptions of Western Asia, vol. i. 1861, vol. ii. 1866, vol. iii. 1870, and numerous papers in the Journal of the Royal Asiatic Society from 1850 to 1864, and in the "Athenæum" from 1851 to 1867.

Hincks. Numerous papers in the "Athenæum," Transactions of Royal Irish Society, Journal of Royal Asiatic Society, Journal of Sacred Literature, from 1850 to 1866.

Oppert. Études Assyriennes, Inscription de Borsippa, Paris, 1857; Rapport au Ministre de l'Instruction publique, Paris, 1857; Expédition en Mésopotamie, Paris, 1863; Éléments de la Grammaire Assyrienne, Paris, 1860, second edition, 1868; Commentaire de la grande Inscription du Palais de Khorsabad, Paris, 1865; Histoire des Empires de Chaldée et d'Assyrie, Paris, 1865; Les Inscriptions de Dour-Sarkayan (Khorsabad), Paris, 1870.

Norris. Memoirs on the Scythic Version of the Behistun Inscription, London, 1853; Assyrian and Babylonian Weights, London; Assyrian Dictionary, vol. i. 1868, vol. ii. 1870, vol. iii. 1872.

Fox Talbot. Various papers in the Journal of

Sacred Literature, Journal of Royal Asiatic Society, and Journal of Biblical Archæology.

Lenormant. Essai sur un Monument Mathématique Chaldéen, Paris, 1868; Lettres Assyriologiques, Paris, 1871; La Magie chez les Chaldéens, Paris, 1874; Les premières Civilisations, Paris, 1874; Manuel d'histoire ancienne de l'Orient, Paris, 1869; Choix de textes Cunéiformes inédites, Paris, 1873.

Menant. Les Briques de Babylon, Paris, 1859; Sur les Inscriptions Assyriennes du Musée Britannique, 1862-3; Inscriptions de Hammourabi, Paris, 1863; Exposé des Éléments de la Grammaire Assyrienne, Paris, 1868; Le Syllabaire Assyrien, Paris, 1869-73; Leçons d'Epigraphie Assyrienne, Paris, 1873.

Sayce. On Akkadian Grammar, Journal of Philology, 1870; Assyrian Grammar, London, 1872; articles in Transactions of Society of Biblical Archæology.

Schrader. In Zeitschrift d. d. Morgenl. Gesellsch., 1869; Die assyrisch-babylonischen Keilinschriften, Leipzig, 1872; Die Keilinschriften und das alte Testament, Giessen, 1872.

Brandis. Ueber d. histor. Gewinn aus d. Entziffer. der assyr. Inschriften, Berlin, 1856.

De Saulcy. Recherches sur l'Écriture Cunéiforme Assyrienne, Paris, 1849.

Rawlinson (George). The Five Great Monarchies of the ancient Eastern World, second edition, London, 1871; Herodotus, second edition, London.

Chapter II.

DISCOVERIES FROM 1866 TO 1872.

Date of Jehu.—Annals of Assurbanipal.—Eclipse, B.C. 763.—Pekah.—Hoshea.—Azariah.—Early Elamite conquest.—Religious calendar.—Sabbaths.—Early Babylonian history.—Chaldean account of the deluge.—Offer of the "Daily Telegraph."

VERYONE has some bent or inclination which, if fostered by favourable circumstances, will colour the rest of life. My own taste has always been for Oriental studies, and from my youth I have taken a great interest in Eastern explorations and discoveries, particularly in the great work in which Layard and Rawlinson were engaged.

For some years I did little or nothing, but in 1866, seeing the unsatisfactory state of our knowledge of those parts of Assyrian history which bore upon the history of the Bible, I felt anxious to do something towards settling a few of the questions involved. I saw at the time that the key of some of the principal difficulties in the case lay in the annals of Tiglath Pileser, and I wrote to Sir Henry Rawlinson to ask him if the casts and fragments of the inscriptions of this reign were available for reference and examination. Sir Henry Rawlinson, with whom I had corresponded before, took a generous interest in any investigations likely to throw light on the studies in which he held so distinguished a place, and he at once accorded me permission to examine the large store of paper casts in his work-room at the British Museum.

This work I found one of considerable difficulty, as the casts were most of them very fragmentary, and I was quite inexperienced, and had little time at my disposal.

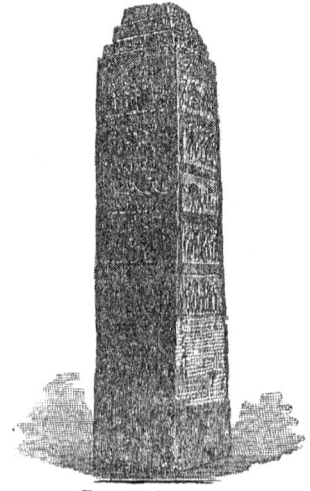

BLACK OBELISK.
Discovered by Layard at Nimroud.

In this my first examination of original texts, I did not obtain much of consequence belonging to the period I was in search of; but I lighted on a curious inscription of Shalmaneser II., which formed my first discovery in Assyrian. On a remarkable obelisk of black stone, discovered by Layard in the centre of the mound of Nimroud, there are five lines of sculpture, representing the tribute received by the Assyrian monarch from different countries; and attached to the second one is an inscription which was deciphered independently by Sir Henry Rawlinson and the late Dr. Hincks, and which reads, " Tribute of Jehu, son of Omri (*here follow the names of the articles*), I received." It was recognized that this was the Jehu of the Bible, but the date of the transaction could not be determined from the inscription. The new text which I had found gave a longer and more perfect account of the war against Hazael king of Syria, and related that it was in the eighteenth year of Shalmaneser when he received the tribute from Jehu.

A short account of this text I published in the "Athenæum," 1866, and being encouraged to proceed in my researches by Sir Henry Rawlinson and Dr. Birch, the keeper of the Oriental department of the British Museum, I next set to work on the cylinders containing the history of Assurbanipal, the Sardanapalus of the Greeks. The annals of this monarch were then in considerable confusion, through the mutilated condition of the records; but by comparing the various copies, I soon obtained a fair text of the earlier part of these inscriptions, and Sir Henry Rawlinson proposed that I should be engaged by the trustees of the British Museum to assist him in the work of preparing a new volume of "Cuneiform Inscriptions." Thus, in the beginning of 1867, I entered into official life, and regularly prosecuted the study of the cuneiform texts. I owed my first step to Sir Henry Rawlinson, whose assistance has been to me of the greatest value throughout my work.

My next discovery related to the tablet printed in "Cuneiform Inscriptions," vol. ii. p. 52, and there called a tablet of distribution of officers. This tablet I found to be a canon of Assyrian history, and ascertained that the eclipse mentioned in it corresponded with the one in " L'Art de vérifier les dates," for 15th June, B.C. 763. On pointing out my evidence to Sir Henry Rawlinson, he remembered a historical fragment which corresponded with this tablet, and by fitting it into the tablet he completed and proved the discovery.

I now again took up the examination of the annals of Tiglath Pileser, and had the good fortune to find several new fragments of the history of this period, and discovered notices of Azariah king of Judah, Pekah king of Israel, and Hoshea king of Israel.

In the same year, I found some new portions of the Assyrian canon, one with the name of the Shalmaneser who, according to the Second Book of Kings, attacked Hoshea king of Israel. In 1868, continuing my investigations, I discovered several accounts of an early conquest of Babylonia by the Elamites. This conquest is stated to have happened 1635 years before Assurbanipal's conquest of Elam, or B.C. 2280, which is the earliest date yet found in the inscriptions.

In the year 1869, I discovered among other things a curious religious calendar of the Assyrians, in which every month is divided into four weeks, and the seventh days, or "Sabbaths," are marked out as days on which no work should be undertaken.

During 1870, I was engaged in preparing for publication my large work on the history of Assurbanipal, in which I gave the cuneiform texts, transcriptions, and translations of the historical documents of this important reign. The work, which was very expensive, on account of the cuneiform type, was published in 1871, at the cost of Mr. J. W. Bosanquet and Mr. H. Fox Talbot.

My next discoveries were in the field of early Babylonian history, and these were published in the first volume of the " Transactions of the Society of Biblical Archæology."

In 1872, I had the good fortune to make a far more interesting discovery, namely, that of the tablets containing the Chaldean account of the deluge. The first fragment I discovered contained about half of the account: it was the largest single fragment of these legends.

As soon as I recognized this, I began a search among the fragments of the Assyrian library to find the remainder of the story.

This library was first discovered by Mr. Layard, who sent home many boxes full of fragments of terra-cotta tablets, and after the close of Mr. Layard's work, Mr. Hormuzd Rassam and Mr. Loftus recovered much more of this collection. The fragments of clay tablets were of all sizes, from half an inch to a foot long, and were thickly coated with dirt, so that they had to be cleaned before anything could be seen on the surface. Whenever I found anything of interest, it was my practice to examine the most likely parts of this collection, and pick out all the fragments that would join, or throw light on the new subject. My search for fragments of the

Deluge story was soon rewarded by some good finds, and I then ascertained that this tablet, of which I obtained three copies, was the eleventh in a series of tablets giving the history of an unknown hero, named Izdubar; and I subsequently ascertained that this series contained in all twelve tablets. These tablets were full of remarkable interest, and a notice of them being published, they at once attracted a considerable amount of attention, both in England and abroad. I arranged to give the public, as soon as possible, a translation and account of these fragments in a lecture before the Biblical Archæological Society, and this was delivered on the 3rd of December, 1872. My latest discoveries and completer accounts of these tablets will be given in my present work.

In consequence of the wide interest taken at the time in these discoveries, the proprietors of the "Daily Telegraph" newspaper came forward and offered to advance a sum of one thousand guineas for fresh researches at Nineveh, in order to recover more of these interesting inscriptions, the terms of agreement being that I should conduct the expedition, and should supply the "Telegraph" from time to time with accounts of my journeys and discoveries in the East in return.

Chapter III.

FROM LONDON TO MOSUL.

Paris. — Marseilles. — Mediterranean. — Palermo. — Etna.— Syra.—Smyrna.—Alexandretta.—Beilan.—Hotels.—Pass of Beilan.—Afrin.—Robber.—Aleppo.—Turkish holiday.—Euphrates. —Tcharmelek.—Orfa.—American missions.—Christians in Turkey. — Varenshaher. — River Khabour. — Nisibin. — Rising of Shammer Arabs.—Lofuk.—Abdul Kareem.—Tellibel.—Djezireh. River Tigris.—Khabour.—Zaccho.—Mule driver.—Nineveh.

THE offer of the proprietors of the "Daily Telegraph" being accepted by the trustees of the British Museum, I received leave of absence for six months and directions to proceed to the East and open excavations for the recovery of further cuneiform inscriptions. It would have been better to have waited until the next autumn before starting, but I desired that there should be no disappointment to the proprietors of the "Daily Telegraph," who had generously offered to pay the expenses, and who naturally wished some letters in return while the subject was fresh in the public mind, so I resolved to start at once, and after receiving much advice and assistance from my friend Mr. Edwin Arnold, himself an old Eastern traveller, I got off from London on the evening of the 20th of January, 1873, and crossed the Channel during the night. As the weather was stormy, I paid the usual tribute to Neptune; but reached the French coast in good condition for breakfast. On my way I fell in with an active partizan of the fallen empire, going back to France to try to work a change in political affairs there. This gentleman lightened my journey and amused me very much by his endeavours to whitewash the late French government, and to persuade me to read some recent passages in history through his spectacles.

I rested the next night in Paris, and on the morning of the 22nd went to view the Assyrian collection at the Louvre, some notice of which I sent to the " Telegraph."

It is impossible in a short notice to give a correct description of this admirable collection, which, although not of great extent, contains several valuable antiquities, the larger part of which were discovered by M. Botta at Khorsabad, and principally belong to the reign of Sargon, the monarch mentioned by Isaiah.

Among the remarkable objects in the Louvre there is a bronze statuette of the time of Kudur-mabuk, an early Elamite king, and a series of metal tablets inscribed with the records of Sargon, which were buried in the foundations of his city in the mound of

Khorsabad. After a hasty glance at these and numerous other treasures, I departed in the evening for Marseilles, where I arrived on the afternoon of the 23rd, and at midday on the 24th of January I left Marseilles for the East.

The whole of this part of my journey was new to me, and consequently had a double interest; but it has been passed over by many travellers and often described before, so I can dismiss it with a short notice. I took passage on one of the steamers of the Messageries Maritimes company, named the " Said."

Passing out of the harbour of Marseilles, I got a good view of the fortifications built for the defence of this port, and looking from an unprofessional point of view, it seemed to me that if they ever came into use some of the fine houses near the sea would be in very exposed positions; but it is always difficult to accommodate fortifications to a large and flourishing city.

There is a desolate, weather-worn appearance about the south coast of France, and an apparent absence of good sites for seaports and harbours; rugged rocks appear everywhere, and although in many places romantic, they appear to be of the same character all along the shore. Passing along the straits which divide Corsica from Sardinia, some fine scenery presents itself, beautiful rocks, bays, promontories, and islands are seen in succession, and among other places, Caprera, the island home of Garibaldi, comes into view. The coast, however, still presents the same desolate appearance, and very few boats are seen.

The captain of the "Said," M. Girard, was a capital companion on the voyage, and paid the greatest attention to his passengers. I was much indebted to him throughout the journey; he had read of my recent Assyrian discoveries, and whenever we came to any place likely to interest me, he took me on shore to examine it.

On the morning of the 26th we came in sight of Sicily, and entered the bay of Palermo. The weather was now fine, and the appearance of the island beautiful. The city of Palermo is built round the bay, and it is backed by fine sloping mountains, which seemed covered by verdure even at this time of the year. The appearance of the city from the sea is charming, and the bay appears well sheltered, and affords excellent anchorage. Palermo seems to enjoy a fair amount of prosperity; there was at this time in the bay a good show of foreign shipping, including some British vessels. I went on shore with Captain Girard, and we made our way up the principal street. There are many noble old mansions, and much on every side to remind one of days gone by. We passed into the cathedral, a fine building evidently the work of different ages, and in it we saw the tombs of the old kings of Sicily. Some of these monuments are very fine, and the interior of the building altogether seemed fitted for the gorgeous ceremonials of the Italian worship.

Service was then going on in the cathedral, but the point that seemed most painful to English eyes was the confessional, which was carried out during the service and in the church. Over the principal entrance of the building stood a portrait of Victor Emmanuel. This astonished me very much, on account of the hatred of the Catholic clergy to him.

Passing out of the cathedral, we went to view a Roman villa which had been excavated and cleared for inspection, being protected all round by an iron rail. The solid thick walls, the mosaic pavements, courtyard, and various rooms and offices, formed a curious picture of the style of this great nation now passed away. Considerable interest appears to be taken in archæology at Palermo, and other remains have been discovered in the same neighbourhood. Palermo has prospered very much since the formation of the kingdom of Italy, but there still remains round it the curse of brigandage. Passing out of Palermo in the evening, we steamed towards the straits dividing Italy from Sicily. Just before dawn the next morning the captain sent to wake me, and I went on deck to enjoy the lovely view of sunrise over Etna. Night still hung over the landscape, and the lights of Reggio on the Italian shore, and Messina on the Sicilian coast, fringed the sea on either side like rows of stars. Soon after, the first rays of the morning sun tinted the top of Etna with a fiery pink, and the mountain stood out like a giant, towering above all the surrounding hills, clothed in a mantle of snow, with a few light, fleecy clouds playing about its summit. Gradually the glow of light crept down the side of Etna, while a dark leaden hue spread over the rest of the scene; then as the light descended, and peak after peak caught the rays, new effects of light and shade were given, ever varying, but always beautiful. The morning dispersed the clouds, and put an end to these pleasing views; but there continued to be ample interest in watching the southern shore of Italy, with its romantic and beautiful scenery.

Our course now lay towards the Greek archipelago, and on the 28th we passed the bay of Navarino, the scene of the disastrous defeat of the Turkish fleet. A little later we passed a bold rock, jutting out into the sea with steep and lofty sides, having half-way up from the sea a solitary cell, in which resides a hermit who cultivates a patch of sloping ground round his dwelling, but principally subsists on the alms of strangers. Just past his hermitage are seen on a ledge of the rock the remains of a considerable monastery, the ruined arches of which seem almost like fantastic portions of the rocks which back them. The feelings which prompted men to build on these rugged rocks, and to inhabit such lonely and inaccessible spots, must have been in marked contrast to the spirit of intercourse and activity now so universal.

Next morning, 29th, we came in sight of Syra, and anchored in front of the town. Syra is the principal port of the Greek archipelago, and is a thriving and important place. It has a large and increasing trade, and appeared to be much frequented by Austrian vessels. The town presents a beautiful appearance from the sea, being situated on the side of a hill facing the harbour, the houses rising one above another until they nearly crown the eminence.

Many of the buildings are of marble, and look very fine in the distance, while it is a common custom to paint a light tint over the faces of the houses, so that these add to the general effect.

The main portion of the town is inhabited by Greeks, who profess the faith of the Eastern church, but some of the people are Catholics, and such is the feeling between the two that they have to inhabit different portions of the town, the Catholic quarter lying higher up the hill with a zone of neutral territory to separate it from the Greek town. Even this division does not prevent strife, and the intermediate space is sometimes the scene of conflicts between adherents of the two faiths.

I went on shore with the captain, landing at the base of the rocks to the left of the town. On approaching the shore I found that the appearance of fertility observed from the vessel was deceptive; the rocks round Syra having a green colour, while the ground is as barren and stony as it can well be. The captain tried some shooting, but only bagged one bird about as large as a sparrow. We now abandoned the field and passed through the tanners' quarter, the place of a thriving industry, the appearance of which was very curious; from there we went to the office of the Messageries company, and afterwards visited the theatre and cathedral. The appearance of the public buildings is not so fine on close inspection, as the stone with which they are built is left too rough.

The Greeks of Syra, and in fact of most other places, are large, strongly-made people, but they have not the symmetry of form and classical features of the Greeks of antiquity; they are active and enterprising, and are taking the lead all over the East.

In the afternoon we left Syra, and next morning anchored in front of the town of Smyrna. I had now arrived in the Turkish dominions, and Smyrna was the first town I saw in Asia.

On reaching the deck in the morning I was surrounded by a number of Greeks, touts for the different hotels; these men pressed their services upon me, offering to show me everything, from the temple of Diana to the bazaars of Smyrna. I declined their aid, and with some little difficulty got rid of them, but I was followed by one gentleman who thought me rather green; he informed me that the others were all cheats, advised me not to have anything to do with them, and wound up by hoping I would go ashore in his boat. I thanked him for his information, and told him that when I wanted to go on shore I could find a boat, and so I sent off the last of my persecutors. Later in the day I went on shore with the captain, and we no sooner touched the land than we were followed by two men who wanted to show us over the town; one of these, an old Jew, followed us all the time, and did all he could to induce us to make purchases at the various shops. We passed along the principal streets and through the bazaars; all the thoroughfares were very narrow, and crowded with various animals and people carrying packages: it was difficult to pick our way among these crowds, which distracted our attention from the shops and goods. All sorts of things were exposed for sale, including antiquities, arms, uniforms, and Eastern dresses. Here and there were Eastern refreshment houses, where natives were cooking dirty-looking messes; one of these dishes appeared to me particularly repulsive, it consisted of small portions of meat and intestines of kids strung on skewers like cat's meat, and roasted before a charcoal fire. This dainty appeared in particular request, and the sellers were calling aloud to the passers-by not to miss the opportunity of trying it, as it was then in perfection. In the market-place we saw a number of natives getting up a fight between some turkeys and a cock, and they seemed to enjoy it immensely. Next day we went to Caravan Street, the spot from which all the caravans start for the interior of Asia. This road was in a worse state than any of the others, and if possible more crowded; it was nothing but one long mud-pudding, through which continually passed strings of camels in each direction, every caravan being led by a donkey, which carried the personal effects of the owner. Smyrna itself is a town of very mixed appearance, half European and half Asiatic; the inhabitants do not appear to be very favourable specimens; a well-known Oriental traveller has described the place as containing the rag-tag of Europe and the bob-tail of Asia. The commerce of the city is considerable, but the water grows shallower every year, and the port is gradually silting up.

At Smyrna we had several new passengers bound for the same port as myself, Alexandretta. We also took on board a number of Asiatics going on pilgrimage; they travelled fourth class, living on the deck at the fore part of the vessel: they were exceedingly devout and equally filthy, and from the time they took possession we avoided that part of the vessel.

On the 1st of February we arrived at Rhodes, and again landed to inspect the town. There are some curious old cannon in the fort, and many buildings worth visiting. Among other places we looked into one of the mosques; some of the faithful were devoutly engaged in worship within the building, and their shoes, which they had taken off according to Oriental custom, stood at the porch. I could not avoid the reflection that in our own highly-favoured country those boots would not have remained long at the door.

Next day we passed along the southern coast of Asia Minor, here called Caramania. This coast is bold and rocky in the extreme, and there did not appear to be either shelter or port over the whole distance. At one spot there stood the ruins of a large town, walls, houses, aqueducts, and other structures covered the whole space, and some parts seemed as if only abandoned yesterday; the whole scene, however, was utterly desolate, not a human being or sign of cultivation being visible.

On the 3rd we arrived at Mersina, a small port doing a great amount of trade, the goods being brought from the interior on camels. The appearance of Mersina is very unfavourable, and the town is unhealthy, there being always a great amount of fever. The port is not sheltered, and in rough weather landing is difficult. From Mersina we steamed to Alexandretta, the port to which I was bound; and bidding farewell to Captain Girard, I went on shore in company with Mr. Forbes, an English merchant, and we called on Mr. Franck, the British consul.

The consul and Madame Franck received us very kindly, and we stayed and lunched with them before starting. Mr. Franck at once assisted me to get a servant, and Mrs. Franck packed up some useful things for the road. I remained some hours at Alexandretta while preparations were made for the journey, and was able to examine the place.

Alexandretta is the finest port on the Syrian coast; the bay is well sheltered and the anchorage good; the place seems shut in by mountains, and on a broad spit of sand lying along the water at the foot of the mountains the town is built. The scenery round is beautiful, and the position is suitable for building a large port, but Alexandretta is only a small place, badly built and unhealthy. The commerce of the place is considerable, and all goods, to go overland to Aleppo or Baghdad, pass through here.

I landed at Alexandretta on the 4th of February, and the same day in the afternoon started for Mosul. After passing along the level ground for a little distance, we began to ascend the mountains, which looked so picturesque from Alexandretta. The road here is very fair for Turkey, and the scenery beautiful. As I was new to this travelling, it took us three hours to get from Alexandretta to the first station, Beilan. I was accompanied by two of my fellow-passengers in the "Said," Mr. Forbes and Mr Kerr. Mr. Forbes was on a pleasure trip into the interior, and Mr. Kerr was going to Aleppo on business. Arriving in the evening at Beilan, we looked for accommodation, and first turned to a new khan just building; only the skeleton of this place was up, and it did not appear sufficient for our purposes, so we went further on to the residence of one named Yakub, who kept what he was pleased to call the "hotel" of Beilan. This place consisted simply of rough wooden rooms and benches, with a strong suspicion of vermin. Mr. Forbes, an experienced traveller, declared he smelt bugs and fleas, not to mention other things, and mounting again, he rode back to the khan, choosing the insufficient shelter in preference to the small company.

Mr. Kerr and I resolved to stay and try it, and Mr. Forbes called on us a little later to dine. Our hotel had no windows, holes in the wall served that purpose, and the boards or logs of the floor were placed so wide apart that there seemed some danger of slipping down into the next apartment; a bench served as table, the guests brought their own cutlery, &c., and dispensed with tablecloths as a useless luxury. The single course consisted of a tough fowl that might have remembered the Assyrian empire. After our rich repast, Yakub, the proprietor, brought to us a book, in which his various visitors had written their experience of his place. Yakub, who could not read, thought that these entries were all praise, and begged us to add some notice of our satisfaction to the collection. We took the book and looked it through; it was full of the richest and most appropriate remarks about the "hotel:" one discoursed about the age of the fowls, another about the vermin; others gave cautions to the travellers who might come after; one advised his successors not to fall through the holes in the floor, as they would be astonished at the appearance of the apartment below, another wrote that the place was comfortable, and the holes in the floor "very convenient." After inserting some remarks in this book, Mr. Forbes left, and Mr. Kerr and myself commenced a battle with the fleas; ultimately our weariness got the better of us, and we fell asleep. I awoke in the night and found a heavy storm was raging, which bid fair to spoil our next day's travelling. Next day Mr. Forbes went on to Antioch, and Mr. Kerr and I rode through the Beilan pass. Beilan itself is romantically situated in the gorge of the pass, the houses being built up the mountains on each side. There are beautiful springs and streams of water, and the rocks in some places are covered with maiden-hair. The pass of Beilan is the only road from Alexandretta to the interior, and if a railway is ever constructed in this part of the world, this pass is the only place which will present any great engineering difficulty. The local traffic in the interior of Asiatic Turkey is, however, so small, that a railway could only pay the contractors, and it would take many years before any internal traffic could be developed. The storm which had happened in the night had made the pass slippery and difficult to travel over, and I was glad after riding through it to rest at the coffee station of Delebekir. This station is situated near where the pass opens on the plain of Antioch; on the right lies the lake of Antioch, a large sheet of water with swampy sides, which sometimes extends over a considerable part of the plain.

The resting place at Delebekir is a hut of the rudest description, and here we sat a few minutes to partake of Turkish coffee before going on the next stage of the journey. Our road now lay across an extensive plain, through which wanders the river Kara Su, a tributary of the Orontes, a broad, shallow, sluggish stream. The whole plain is wild and desolate, overgrown with rushes and wild plants, but capable of a high degree of cultivation. Across the swampy parts were ruined causeways and ancient bridges, all in a state of dilapidation very characteristic of Turkey. In the evening we came to Ain Bada. a station where the plain is broken by ranges of hills. Here we put up at the khan, and shared its accommodation with a number of native travellers going between Alexandretta and Aleppo. The khan was as usual a rough building of stones and mud thatched over to keep out the rain. The ground formed the floor, a slight depression in the middle made a place for a fire, and round the sides was a rough platform of boards to sleep upon. We sat on this platform, smoking and drinking coffee, and watching with amusement the native travellers. These gentlemen appeared to have been playing some game of chance and quarrelled over it ; they broke out into bad language and called each other cheats, the matter ending in a fight. The Arabs pulled and tugged each other all about the place, and presently laying hold of one of their number, pushed him by general consent out of the khan. We now had peace, and soon made ourselves comfortable for the night, and early in the morning started again on our way. The road from Ain Bada passes through a wild and more rugged country, intersected by sterile mountains, on which a few goats only find subsistence; it is broken about the middle by a plain really part of the plain of Antioch, through which here runs the river Afrin, also a tributary of the Orontes. At Afrin we rested to have our mid-day meal, and here we heard of the exploits of a famous robber who was at large in the district. This man had been one of the irregular soldiers in the Turkish army, but afterwards had abandoned the service and taken to the road. He had carried on his depredations for some years, and with all their efforts the authorities had failed to capture him. A reward was now offered for his capture, but had as yet produced no result. This man was guilty of no cruelty in his robberies, and through a little generosity to some of the villagers he secured himself friends and hiding-places when the agents of the government were after him. A little while before I arrived there, he had plundered the station of Afrin. Coming in the night with a band of followers, he hammered at the door and called out that they were travellers who had lost their way, and begged shelter until the morning. On the owner opening the door, he was seized and bound, while the robbers ransacked the place and carried off everything but an old clock. While we were at Afrin a party of Turkish irregulars arrived, and the officer in charge of the detachment immediately inquired my business in the country; but without waiting for an answer, he showed his penetration by saying, "Oh, I know, you are come to survey the country for a railroad." Leaving Afrin, we journeyed to Termanin, where we put up for the night. Here we lodged at a private house, and were more comfortable than we had yet been. I saw little of the place, but the country seemed to consist of rich plains, crossed and broken here and there by barren, stony mountains. On the morning of the 7th of February we started early from Termanin, and rode to Aleppo. The road was rough and hilly, and this part of the country lies a considerable height above the sea. Outside the city we were met by M. Costi, a friend of Mr. Kerr, and we put up at an apology for an hotel, called the "locanda." Aleppo is a fine city, and is said to have nearly half a million of inhabitants. It has a noble castle, and is surrounded by fortifications. All the best of the city is Saracenic in its architecture, and the castle and walls are now partly in ruins. The streets are narrow, and paved with small slippery stones; the houses are very fair for an Eastern town, and there are many public buildings.

In the evening, Mr. Kerr and I paid a visit to M. Costi, who lived in the Christian quarter of the town. It was late at night when we returned to the locanda, and, as there are no lights in the streets of these Eastern cities, we were escorted home by a man bearing a large Oriental lantern.

Next morning, I called on Mr. Skene, our consul at Aleppo. He received me in a most friendly manner, and offered me every assistance in his power.

I was afterwards continually indebted to his good offices while in the Turkish territory.

It was now the Turkish festival of Korban Bairam, and all business was suspended, so I could not move from Aleppo; and being obliged to stay, I wandered round the city to see the festival. Everybody was out, and all seemed enjoying themselves in a very childish fashion, grave, bearded men taking turns in swings like so many boys at a fair. On Sunday we rode out to see the public gardens, which are very good: they were established by a former pacha, but have been for some time neglected, as his successors, being pious Moslems, and consequently bigoted and ignorant, do not understand the use of such places.

On the 11th, I completed my arrangements, and started on the 12th of February for Mosul. A Swiss gentleman, travelling on business to the same place, asked leave to accompany my caravan, and we started together from Aleppo about midday, arriving in the evening at Tel Karamel, where we put up with the chief of the village. We were installed in a large building, divided by mud partitions into four or five parts, in one of which was a raised place, which was assigned to us. Into the rest of the building they brought our mules and all their own cattle. As soon as we were settled, a crowd of natives came in, and stood all round us, to observe our manners and customs; such was the curiosity of these people that they did not separate until they had seen us go to bed.

Next morning we rode to the village of Beglabeg,

and, on the 14th, from Beglabeg to Muzar. On the 15th of February, we started early in the morning, and after a ride of about three hours came in sight of the river Euphrates. As I looked on this noble stream, called in ancient days the Great River, thoughts of the mighty empires and powerful monarchs once ruling beside its waters passed through my mind. The river is worthy of its associations: it is a broad, powerful stream, grand even now in its neglected condition.

We arrived at the river opposite the town of Biradjik, and, crossing in one of the ferry-boats, made our way along the narrow, crooked streets to the khan. When I started from Aleppo, I intended to ride to Diarbekr, and take a raft from there to Mosul; I consequently engaged my caravan to go to Diarbekr. I now asked my mule-driver to go to Mosul, but he refused: he was a native of Baghdad, and wanted to go to that town, and Mosul was 200 miles nearer to his home than Diarbekr, so that it was to his advantage to go to Mosul; but he saw that I desired to change the route, and resolved to make as much money as possible out of the circumstances.

Finding I could do nothing with him, I took him to the court. The court house was like a fair Eastern dwelling. On reaching it, we were ushered through the door into an open court, surrounded by a balcony; and ascending to the balcony by a flight of steps, we were admitted into the police-court, or judgment hall. The method of proceeding here is very comfortable, and the officials were very polite. All sat round the room on cushions, as is the custom in the East, and coffee and cigarettes were passed round before entering upon business. After some little difficulty an agreement was made with the driver, and we prepared to start next morning. Biradjik, the town at which I was staying, is more substantially built than most Eastern towns; a light, soft stone, apparently half chalk, half limestone, serves for many of the structures. The town is situated on an uneven elevation of this stone, just at the edge of the Euphrates; it is a station of some importance, and possesses a large ruined castle, which is very curious. Biradjik is probably the Tul-barsip of the Assyrian inscriptions, which was added to the Assyrian empire B.C. 856.

On the 16th of February, I started from Biradjik, and travelled to Tcharmelek. Tcharmelek is a curious-looking village, and its dome-shaped dwellings strikingly resemble some of the pictures of villages in the Assyrian sculptures. On finding an apartment here, the natives crowded round us as they did at Tel Karamel. But there was a sound of rude music in the distance, which, they said, proceeded from a wedding company, so, after seeing us into bed, the natives turned off to see as much as they could of the bride and bridegroom. On the 17th, we rode to Orfa. The road from Tcharmelek to Orfa gradually becomes rougher and more rocky as you proceed, and in the latter part is artificial, being carried along the side of a mountain gorge. On emerging from this gorge, a wide fertile plain is seen extending for many miles, and almost entirely surrounded by mountains. Just by the gorge, Orfa is situated, partly built on the plain, and partly up the face of a hill. It is a very old town, with some relics of various ages: there are buildings of the Roman and Saracenic time, inscriptions in Greek, Pehlevi, and Arabic, and many curious tombs cut in the rock. I called on Pastor Hagub, of the American mission, and from him received a kind welcome. He gave me some details of the noble work now being accomplished by the American missionaries in these countries, and of the difficulties which they met with. People in England and America, who read every now and then in the papers that the Grand Vizier has issued an order for the protection of liberty of conscience, and conceding justice to the Christians, little know the useless character of such announcements. The grinding tyranny under which the Christians suffer, and the defiance of all solemn promises in places beyond the notice of the representatives of European powers, clearly show the nature of the Moslem rule. It is an astonishing fact that a Christian country like England upholds the Porte, and yet does not insist on justice being done to the Christians in Turkey. No end of promises are given, but anyone conversant with Turkey knows the distance between promise and performance. Probably it is not generally known in England and America that no Mahometan in Asia dare turn Christian. Until this state of affairs is altered, missions in Asiatic Turkey will not produce the fruit they ought.

After bidding farewell to Pastor Hagub, I made ready to leave Orfa on the 18th, but the weather was so stormy that it was some time before I could get off. A Turkish gentleman, who had come to Alexandretta in the same vessel as myself, had travelled up the country nearly at the same time, and was now at Orfa. He started on the 18th to go on further, but got wet through in the storm, and turned back. I tried to persuade him to start again with me, but he would not venture. I went off about midday, the storm having subsided. The road was in an awful condition through the rain, and resembled a mud-pudding; and we had not gone far before we came near a camel lying down in the path. Just before we reached it, the camel suddenly got up, and our animals taking fright started off; mine carried me half across a field, when I managed to pull it up. My Swiss companion was not so fortunate: he rode a mule, and this creature at once threw him. He dropped into the mud-pudding, and arose painted from head to foot. After this little misfortune, we managed to reach Adana without further adventure. Round Adana, and in the region beyond it, snow had been falling, and we could see the mountains in front covered with it. The house we put up in at Adana had one curiosity—its door was formed of an ancient threshing machine. This was a large frame of wood, in which were fixed hundreds of small worked flints, similar to those which are found in prehistoric deposits. The use of such an instrument shows the small amount of change produced by thousands of years in the East.

Leaving Adana we rode over part of the mountain range of Karajah Dagh, which was covered with snow and bitterly cold, and obtained a very indifferent shelter at Dashlook. The chief of Dashlook is much under the influence of his wife, who has more power than women usually possess in the East. This lady, who is a confirmed smoker, begged some tobacco from us, which I readily presented to her, as she was a hospitable hostess.

On the 20th we rode to Tel Gauran, or Telligori, where we had again a kind reception, and starting from there early in the morning, arrived in the middle of the day at Varenshaher. Varenshaher is a poor village situated in the midst of the ruins of a fine Roman town; it serves as a government station between Orfa and Nisibin. Here we changed our guides, and I then went on to an encampment which they called Engerlu. This part of the country is very curious; the soil is throughout a rich red earth, and the country is nearly level from the Karajah Dagh and Mardin mountains on the north, to the Hamma and Sinjar hills on the south; but all along the northern part the ground is covered by fragments of scored weatherbeaten rock, thicker near the mountains and gradually becoming less numerous further south; as a general rule, wherever a hill stands up in the plain the hill is covered with these boulders, even where there are few or none on the plain. The mountains north of this plain give rise to a considerable number of small streams, which unite lower down to form the river Khabour. On the 22nd we arrived at one of the principal branches of this river; we found it difficult to cross, as we had lost the road to the ford, and the whole country is so desolate that we found no one of whom to inquire. The banks of this stream were very beautiful; it had cut out a deep valley, passing through the top soil and a stratum of rock similar in appearance to the Mardin mountains; at the bottom of this cutting it was flowing then, a beautiful stream swollen by the winter rains. We contrived to descend this gully, and then forded the stream, and as we climbed up the face of the rocks on the other side we startled a pair of eagles which had made their nest in the rock.

Soon after we found again the road to Nisibin, and came in sight of the towers of Dinasar, which are visible for many miles. I endeavoured to reach the place, but at sunset found myself still many miles away. The evening was beautiful, and the setting sun threw splendid tints on to the Mardin mountains to the north; lovely colours which we seldom see off the painter's canvas played about these peaks, and I was so taken by the beautiful scene that I lingered to look at it until the sun went down. Darkness now setting in I lost my way, but was fortunately found by one of my guides, and after some difficulty we reached the village of Aburumcha. The inhabitants of this place were Christians, but they showed no hospitality, and at first refused to receive me. I could not, however, go on in the night, so I compelled them to give me a shelter, and in the morning started for Nisibin.

I tried hard to reach Nisibin, but the animals were too jaded, and I had to be content to put up at Kasr Serjan and start again for Nisibin on the 24th. Early in the day we arrived at this town. Nisibin was once a considerable place, but is now a poor town very little better than a village, it was a large Assyrian city, the seat of one of the governors, who took rank as an eponym, and there are extensive mounds and ruins attesting its former prosperity. I left Nisibin the same day, and travelled on to the Christian village of Kobuk. This village and many of the places round were plundered by the Arabs in the last Shammer war. The circumstances of this affair, as I heard them in the country, were as follows.

One great interest of the works of Layard consists in the splendid description he gives of the various Arab tribes he met during his travels. Layard relates how Sofuk, chief of the great tribe of Shammer, applied to the pacha of Baghdad for a body of Turkish troops to assist him in subduing some tribes who had thrown off their allegiance to him. The governor of Baghdad pretended to agree to this, and sent a detachment of soldiers; but when the Arab chief trusted himself to them, they murdered him and sent his head as a trophy to Baghdad. After this his son Ferhan became chief of the Shammer, and being of a pacific disposition, submitted to the Turkish government; but Ferhan had a brother, named Abdul Kareem, of more independent spirit, and great influence among the Arabs. The Turkish governors were anxious to break the power of the Shammer, and I was told that one of them tempted Abdul Kareem to a rising against the Turks. Abdul Kareem took the bait and broke out into rebellion, a considerable number of the tribes following his standard. The Turks had drafted into this region a considerable number of Circassian emigrants who had taken service in the Turkish irregular forces, and Abdul Kareem endeavoured to persuade them to revolt and join him; they, however, stood firm, and formed excellent auxiliaries to the Turkish army. The Arabs, under Abdul Kareem, spread themselves over the country and plundered as far as the Mardin mountains, but they were ultimately defeated in a battle by the Tigris, and many of them driven into the river. Abdul Kareem escaped from the slaughter and remained at large for a little time, but the Turks tempted one of his friends, the chief of the tribe of Mentaficc, and he invited Abdul Kareem to a banquet, at which the Turkish soldiers, being in ambush, captured the Shammer chief and sent him to Baghdad. Abdul Kareem was tried at Baghdad, but the court could not decide on his guilt in the matter, so he was ordered to be sent to Constantinople for his case to be judged;

but when he arrived at Mosul, the Turkish government sent orders to hang him without further trial, and the execution took place on the bridge of Mosul. It is of course necessary to keep under the Arab tribes, but every well-wisher to Turkey must desire that this should be accomplished without treachery and bad faith.

From Kobuk I travelled on the 25th to Tellibel; the whole road gave signs of cultivation and there were many villages, but the travelling was very tedious. At Tellibel our accommodation was bad; we received a little room in the interior of a house, with only one hole situated in the roof for ventilation and letting out the smoke. The place was very stuffy, and yet the natives crowded in to see us, and we were forced to clear them out of the room before we could do anything. In the night I was awakened by hearing somebody lashing about with a riding-whip; and calling out to ask what was the matter, my companion told me that a cat trying to descend from the hole in the roof had fallen on to him and woke him up; he took hold of his whip and laid about him, but as it was dark I think puss escaped.

Next morning we started for Djezireh over an undulating country crossed by deep ravines; the country gradually became more interesting as we neared the Tigris, and for a considerable part of the day we enjoyed a view of the Jebel Djudi range of mountains, which lay beyond Djezireh. These mountains were half covered with snow, and the contrast between the pure white of the snow and the black rock of the mountain range was remarkable. The whole of the country which we had traversed from the Euphrates was a vast table-land, and on gaining sight of the Tigris we saw that the stream ran at the bottom of an enormous valley or cutting worn out of this table-land by the action of the water. We descended by a precipitous path to the side of a smaller cutting, at the bottom of which flowed a tributary of the Tigris. The appearance of this cutting was curious. All the upper rocks, here and for a considerable distance along the Tigris, consist of a mixture of gravel stones and large pebbles cemented together like a pudding. The sides of the valleys were cut by the action of the water into steep upright faces, and in some places the cliffs were undermined. Enormous masses of the upper strata had become detached, and some had fallen into the valley below and into the rivers, others, catching on projecting ledges, stood as if ready to fall; in their fantastic shapes and curious positions they looked as if some giants had been there at play.

Crossing the tributary of the Tigris, I entered the town of Djezireh, situated on the right bank of the Tigris. When I was at Aleppo, I heard that there was a revolt at Djezireh, and that a Turkish force had been sent to quell it, which had been accomplished with considerable bloodshed. I gained no satisfactory information how far these statements were true, but I was advised by some timid people not to go to the town. Djezireh, when I reached it, was quiet enough; it was in possession of a large military force, and soldiers appeared everywhere. Djezireh is a miserable-looking town, its inhabitants are Kurds, and are a rough, savage-looking race; but the position of the town is very fine, and the scene on every side one of varied beauty. Rocks, streams, and mountains surround it, and in front flows the majestic Tigris, beyond which lies Jebel Djudi, with its dark, precipitous peaks. The town, however, lies too low, and is so shut in that it is not healthy.

At Djezireh, I saw a madman wandering about the streets perfectly naked, and we were here annoyed by some dancing boys, a race of professionals peculiar to Turkey. In the night, some of the Turkish soldiers turned our horses out of the stalls, and carried off some of the horse gear. My Swiss companion was unluckily the principal sufferer in this robbery; he had all along had great difficulty with his animal, which sometimes caused considerable fun by the pranks it played him, and now, having lost his stirrups, he was still worse off.

On the 27th we left Djezireh; but I had not got used to the native food, and was unwell in consequence, so when we reached Naharwan I halted my party and rested until the morning.

On the 28th we left Naharwan and rode along by the river Khabour. We first forded the Hazel, a tributary falling into the Khabour from the north, and then a little later we forded the Khabour. Both these streams are wide, powerful bodies of water, and are always forded with difficulty. After crossing the Khabour, we travelled along the south bank of the river until we reached Zaccho, a compact little town, well posted on an island in the middle of the Khabour, and connected with the south by a bridge across one arm of the river. There is a strong castle in Zaccho, once held by a Kurdish chief, of whose murder by a Turkish soldier Layard gives an account in his work. It was Friday when I arrived at Zaccho, and the Mahometan priest was calling out his prayers from the top of the minaret. I noticed then and at other times that, bitterly fanatical as the Mahometans are, their public and private prayers are a mockery, for which they have no real respect, although they seldom neglect them.

I saw that many of the women of Zaccho were bathing in the Khabour, and sitting in the sun on the bank to dry themselves, quite regardless of passers-by. Having made some purchases in Zaccho, I started after dinner to go through the Zaccho pass, a romantic passage across the mountain range of Jebel Abjad, and on reaching the southern side of the range, emerged on the wide plains of Assyria. That night I put up at Assi, a village just through the pass, and on the next morning went on to Tel Addas. My mule driver had been very troublesome all the way, and kept declaring that the animals were over-driven, especially one mule, which he said was worth "khamseen lira," or fifty pounds. On reaching Tel Addas, he declared they were being killed, and charged me to complete the cruel work by driving them at once to Mosul. I said certainly, if he wished it, and ordered my horse to be saddled again; but when he saw I was in earnest, he begged to stay there that night. He then quarrelled with his assistant, and with the villagers, and they took him outside, and gave him a sound thrashing. When undergoing this punishment, he kept calling out in most submissive tones to my people to come and help him; we thought, however, that the lesson would do him good.

Next day (2nd of March) I started before sunrise, and arrived about nine in the morning at the ruins of Nineveh. I cannot well describe the pleasure with which I came in sight of this memorable city, the object of so many of my thoughts and hopes. My satisfaction was all the greater as I thought that my journeys were over, and I had only to set to work in order to disinter the treasures I was seeking.

Chapter IV.

VISIT TO BABYLONIA.

Mosul.—The serai.—Turkish pacha.—French consul.—Inscription of Vul-nirari.—Raft.—Nimroud.—Kalah Shergat.—Rocks and cave.—Tekrit.—Baghdad.—Col. Herbert.—Babylon.—Babel.—Extent of walls.—Kasr.—Hanging gardens.—Birs Nimrud.—Seven stages of tower.—Ruin of Babylon.—Hymer.—Tel Ibrahim.—Cutha.—Arab encampment.—Road to Mosul.—Ervil.—The Zab.—The Ghazr.—Ferry.

ON arriving at the ruins of Nineveh, I resolved to examine them before going into Mosul; but I only went over the northern part, and had to leave the other portions for the afternoon and subsequent visits.

On the 3rd of March, I called at the serai, or government house, which lies outside the city of Mosul, towards the south. The serai is a square building of two storeys, built round a courtyard, one face overlooking the river Tigris. Here I paid my respects to the governor, Abdi Effendi, who had just arrived in Mosul. When staying in Aleppo, Mr. Skene, the British consul, had given me letters of introduction to Shibli Pacha, or Shimli Pacha, governor of Mosul; and, before writing, Mr. Skene carefully looked in the published lists, to see if the pacha was still at Mosul, as Eastern governors are continually changed. Shibli, however, was deposed before I reached Mosul, and Abdi Effendi appointed in his place. In illustration of the ruinous manner in which these countries are governed, I may mention that there have been nineteen pachas at Aleppo in the last seventeen years. When I called on the governor of Mosul, I asked for guides to accompany me to Kalah Shergat, as I wished to visit that site. Abdi Effendi at once stated that he had received orders from Baghdad not to allow anyone to inspect the sites and ruins in his district, and not to allow any collection of antiquities to be obtained. I told him that I knew I could not excavate without a firman, but I now only wished to see the sites, and he might send an agent with me to watch that I did not move anything. The pacha was, however, quite unreasonable about the matter, and declared that he must prevent me looking even at the mounds. I could not agree with this doctrine, and as we had no representative at Mosul, I called on the French consul, to ask his advice on the matter. The French consul had in his possession at this time a fine stone tablet from Kalah Shergat, which he showed me, and he asked me what the inscription was about. I examined it, and told him that it was a record of Vul-nirari I., king of Assyria, B.C. 1320, and as I desired to obtain all the Assyrian antiquities I could get, I arranged to purchase the stone of him.

On the next day I went over the water and examined the mounds of Nineveh again, and telegraphed to England to know if the firman was yet granted for excavating. As I obtained no satisfactory information I resolved to go to Baghdad, and the river Tigris being now in flood I directed a raft to be constructed to float down the river. The raft was composed of skins inflated with air and fastened to a frame of rough logs; on one part of this frame a rough shelter was raised and covered over with some matting; this shelter formed a sort of house in which we slept on the journey.

On the afternoon of the 7th I committed myself to this wretched craft and commenced to descend the river. As we floated down the Tigris from Mosul the gigantic mounds of Konyunjik and Nebbi Yunas, with the ruins of the wall of Nineveh, began to recede from our gaze; and we came in sight of the mound of Yaremjah, and later of the mounds of Hammum Ali, on the west of the Tigris. On arriving opposite the mound of Nimroud, the scene of Layard's first excavations, I stopped the raft and landed to examine the place. It was a long walk from the river to the mound, and after examining the trenches I turned to go back to the raft, but night came on, and I had considerable difficulty in reaching the place where it was moored. I resolved to stay the night there as the weather was stormy, and

I very soon found my house on the raft was almost useless, the rain coming down and penetrating the roof in various places, rendering us very uncomfortable

Next morning we started the raft, and soon heard the noise of the waters falling over the dyke of Nimrod. This obstruction in the river consists of an artificial dyke or causeway across the Tigris, which the natives ascribe to the giant hunter. Over this

VIEW OF NIMROUD.

obstruction the river fell roaring like a cataract, but as there was plenty of water in the stream we passed it easily. There are several of these obstructions in the river between Mosul and Tekrit.

After passing the dyke we saw many mounds on both sides of the river; among these were Tel Sharf by the Zab, Tel Nazir on the west bank, Ningoub and Tel Makook. Several of these mounds have been pierced, but no systematic excavations have been made. At night a storm came on and we were driven on shore. The raft house now proved utterly value less to keep out the rain, and the wind almost blew it down. Next morning we again started, but the storm continued, and we arrived at Kalah Shergat in a shower of rain. Although the mounds were very slippery from the rains, I went on shore and explored them under considerable difficulty, but as I did not expect to have another opportunity of visiting the site I took advantage of this, bad as it was. Kalah Shergat is an enormous site, embracing in the circuit of the walls over two miles and a-half, while all round this centre, mounds are scattered over the plains right away to the hills which back it. The ruins are rather triangular in shape, one face lying along the Tigris, and at the northern end rises a great pyramidal mound, the ruins of the ziggurrat or tower. Between this mound and the river Tigris the Turks have built a station for their soldiers, and every scrap of brick and stone that they could collect on the mounds, they have used in this structure. For this reason there is very little to be seen on the site. The mounds are mainly composed of clay and sun-dried bricks, and all the upper portions show numerous signs of later occupation.

I descended the northern face of the mounds and went to an encampment of the Shammer Arabs to enquire if they knew of any inscriptions, and they directed me to the Turkish station, where I saw the shaft of a column with a Pehlevi inscription.

Kalah Shergat marks the site of the city of Assur, a place of very great antiquity, which was the capital of Assyria as early as the nineteenth century before the Christian era. In the fourteenth century B.C. Nineveh began to take its place, and from that time Assur gradually declined, but the city continued to be a place of considerable importance and often a residence of the kings. About B.C. 828, jealous of the rise of Kalah, where Shalmaneser, king of Assyria, had fixed his court, the city of Assur revolted in favour of his son, Assur-dain-pal, but it was soon after captured by the royal army under Samsi-vul, a younger brother of the rebel prince, and from this time lost its importance, and is seldom afterwards mentioned. The town, however, continued to exist, and was occupied long after the Assyrian period.

Leaving Kalah Shergat, I again descended the river, and soon after came to an Assyrian fort on the same side of the Tigris. This structure is built of large stones and sun-dried bricks, it is now in very ruinous condition, and the Tigris is eating away the face next the stream. Some of the scenery along the river is beautiful, the rocks especially are very fine, one of them is crowned by the ruins of an old castle; in another place, where the cliffs tower up straight out of the stream, there is a cave in the rocks attached to which is a curious legend. It is said that a griffin or monster in the old times lived in this cave, and took human victims from the surrounding districts. The wild desolation of the spot, the romantic and inaccessible position of the cave, combine to make this a fitting place for such a legend.

Passing this place on my raft, I watched the Tigris roaring and foaming round the fallen masses of rock at the foot of the cave, and I could not help remarking the striking similarity of this story to one of the Izdubar legends. I believe that this is a modern version of this ancient story, and that the legend has been handed down in this country since the days of Izdubar.

The river was now rapidly rising, and its swelling, sweeping flood seemed almost the only thing of life in the whole picture, the cities which lined its banks are now most of them in ruins, their vast mounds the only witnesses of their former grandeur; the great races which once lived on its shores are replaced by a few wandering Arabs; the solitude of the scene, and the remembrance of the difference between the past and the present, have a depressing effect on the traveller, and he seems also exiled from all the life and activity of the world. Now and then, as the river pursued its swift and silent course, we were startled by a noise like thunder, and, turning to see the origin of the commotion, found that portions of the banks, undermined by the water, had fallen into the stream.

On the 10th of March we arrived at Tekrit, a miserable-looking town on the western bank of the Tigris. Here we changed our boatman and made a few new purchases for the journey, after which we again commenced the descent of the river. The character of the scenery now entirely changed; instead of the hills and rocks we had seen in the earlier part of our course the country became one dead level of alluvium, while the bare and desolate banks gave place to extensive plantations and groves of palm trees; the stillness of the desert was broken by the noise of Arab waterwheels, and signs of life and animation became more frequent as we proceeded, and at one place a number of Arab women swam from the shore to our raft to offer us some milk for sale.

Gliding past the town of Samarah, we saw the gilded dome of its mosque glittering in the evening sun, and next day reached within four hours of Baghdad. Now, however, a strong south wind sprang up, and our raft being unable to proceed, we moored it along the shore, and on the 12th of March, engaging some horses of an Arab, rode into Baghdad. Our road lay along the western bank of the Tigris, and for some distance consisted of a desolate wilderness; across this now swept a hot south wind, carrying with it blinding clouds of sand. On the right hand were visible the ruins of the walls of a gigantic Babylonian canal, and the lofty tower of Tel Nimroud at Akkerkoof. Nearer Baghdad the scene changed, and we passed gardens and groves of palms. Here the country was well cultivated and had a pleasing appearance; there stand near, a village and a Mahomedan religious edifice of some sanctity, and I saw what very much astonished me—a tramway working between the village and Baghdad. Entering the western suburb of Baghdad, I was just in time to cross the bridge of boats, which was being taken to pieces on account of the flood. I then made my way to a khan, and after some refreshment went to pay my respects to Colonel Herbert, our representative at Baghdad. Colonel Herbert was very kind, and at once offered me apartments in the Residency, with every assistance in his power towards fulfilling the object I had in view. I stayed with Colonel Herbert while at Baghdad, and took advantage of his kind offers. He assisted in the matter of the firman, procured me letters to the authorities, obtained for me guides and government orders, and gave me advice about the country.

Baghdad is a city of romantic associations, and in my mind was always associated with the stories of the "Arabian Nights." I think it often happens that such cities on inspection do not realize first expectations, but no complaint can be laid against Baghdad on this score. The city is large, and principally built on the eastern bank of the Tigris; there are many fine buildings and large bazaars, and outside the town there are miles of gardens and abundance of productions. From my window in the Residency I enjoyed a charming prospect; immediately in front was a plantation with orange trees, vines, and sweet-smelling plants, beyond this a splendid view of the river Tigris then in flood, and on the other side of the water a grove of palm trees with a primitive Arab machine for raising water from the river to irrigate the ground.

VISIT TO BABYLONIA.

On my mentioning to Colonel Herbert the difficulties I had met with at Mosul, he at once asked the pacha if he had issued orders to Mosul that no one should see the mounds, and the pacha declared that he had not. I cannot of course tell which was wrong, the pacha of Baghdad, or the one at Mosul; but I have since got used to the issue of orders and their denial or repudiation by Turkish officials.

As soon as I had settled my monetary affairs I set to work to obtain antiquities, and see as much as possible of the ruins in this region. On the 14th of March I purchased several inscriptions, including a number of dated tablets of the time of the Babylonian, Persian, and Parthian periods; and the same day I started to examine the ruins of Babylon, and rested the first night at Anazat.

Next day I reached Mahawil, and on the 16th of March left Mahawil for Babylon. The whole road was covered with vestiges of former civilization; mounds could be seen in various directions, and the country was intersected by the banks of numerous ancient canals.

The first ruin at Babylon which we came in sight of was the northern collection of mounds, called Babil, but sometimes known as the Mujelliba. I passed along the eastern side of this ruin, but could not reach it there, as a considerable canal lay between the road and the ruin, but I went further south and then turned up again to inspect it. This ruin is a square mound about 200 yards each way, the sides facing the cardinal points; it is steep and lofty, and in one place the south-east corner is said to reach a height of 140 feet. The surface is furrowed by numerous ravines, and there are traces of chambers, tunnels, and passages in various parts. No proper efforts have been made to examine the structure of this ruin, and in climbing through the old trenches and tunnels there is a sense of bewilderment and confusion which prevents an accurate survey of the indications of buildings. I descended into a cutting in the middle of the ruin, at the bottom of which lay a large block of stone; while there, part of the upper portion of this well fell in, showing the insecure condition of the place. This ruin I believe covers the remains of the temple of Bel and the great tower of Babylon; this mound is surrounded by a rampart which I think joined the northern corner of the wall of Babylon. Ancient authors have stated that Babylon was surrounded by a wall, represented by different authorities as from forty to sixty miles in circumference; this, however, I think a gross exaggeration, for which there is not the slightest ground either in the inscriptions or in the present remains. I saw remains of what appeared to be walls; these have been admirably surveyed by former travellers, and I believe indicate a wall about eight miles round, making Babylon nearly the same size as the sister capital, Nineveh. In shape the city appears to have been like a square with one corner cut off, and the corners of the walls of the city may be said roughly to front the cardinal points. At the north of the city stood the temple of Belus, now represented by the mound of Babil; about the middle of the city stood the royal palace and hanging gardens, both, I believe, represented by the mound of the Kasr. The Kasr is a vast mound irregular in height; its sides face the cardinal points; it is said to be in some places seventy feet above the plain, and is about 700 yards in length and breadth. All authorities agree that here was situated the palace of Nebuchadnezzar, but the hanging gardens have been placed in a different position by almost every writer. I have weighed the evidence and examined the site, and my own conclusion is that they were on the west side of the Kasr mound, between the palace and the river Euphrates. It is unfortunate that while whole volumes have been expended on dissertations and speculations on the size and buildings of Babylon, no satisfactory attempt has been made to ascertain the truth by excavation. The isolated pits and tunnels made here and there in the mounds are acknowledged to have had no effect on these questions, and the recovery of Babylon is yet to be accomplished.

On the mound of the Kasr there are still to be seen beautiful piers and buttresses of fine yellow bricks, but nothing has been done to trace the building to which they belong. Some writers make them part of the palace, but I think it more probable that they belong to the hanging gardens. In one of the hollows of the northern portion is seen the rough stone lion standing over the figure of a man, which has so often been referred to by travellers. Of the solitary tree once standing on the mound, by some supposed to be the last relic of the celebrated hanging gardens, only the trunk remains. Travellers and tourists have pulled it to pieces for the sake of having a fragment of the wood.

Passing south of the Kasr, I examined the mound of Amram, a large irregular elevation, by some supposed to cover a palace or temple; it appears, however, to be only an enormous rubbish heap, and probably only marks the spot where the old city was most thickly inhabited. Amram promises little or nothing to an explorer, the most important places to examine being the Babil and Kasr mounds, and the walls. From Amram I rode to the bridge of boats, and crossed to the western side of Hillah, where I took up my quarters at the khan.

On the 17th of March, I started from Hillah to the mound of Birs Nimrud, which lies to the south-west. We had scarcely left Hillah, when we saw this splendid pile; but a marsh now extended over a large part of the intervening country, and I had to travel several miles round its southern edge before I could reach the site. Birs Nimrud is one of the most imposing ruins in the country; its standing in the midst of a vast plain with nothing to break the view, makes the height of the ruins more impressive. The principal mound rises about 150 ft. above the plain; it is in the shape of a pyramid or cone, and at its top stands a solid mass of vitrified bricks. There is a splendid view of the country from the top, the surrounding towns and ruins being visible for many miles. Sir Henry Rawlinson, who examined this site, made out that it was a tower in seven stages: the lowest stage 272 ft. each way, and 26 ft. in height; the second stage was 230 ft. each way, and 26 ft. high; the third stage was 188 ft. in length and breadth, and 26 ft. high; and the fourth stage was 146 ft. each way, but only 15 ft. high. From receptacles in the corners of one of these stages, Sir Henry Rawlinson obtained inscribed cylinders, stating that the building was the temple of the seven planets, which had been partially built by a former king of Babylon, and, having fallen into decay, was restored and completed by Nebuchadnezzar. The Birs Nimrud is most probably the Tower of Babel of the Book of Genesis. Beside the large mound of the tower, there are other vast heaps of lesser elevation covering the ruins of the buildings and walls of the city of Borsippa, within which the temple of the seven planets stood. While I was at Birs Nimrud there came on a violent storm, which recommenced in the night. This weather seriously hindered my investigations.

On the 18th, I again examined the Kasr, and some of the smaller ruins of Babylon, and purchased some inscriptions from the mounds; but I closed my investigations with a feeling that the time I had spent here was far too short to make a proper examination of the ruins. Before parting with Babylon, I will give a short sketch of its history.

Babylon is said to have existed before the Flood, and in the Book of Genesis it is given as the site of the tower. The city is first mentioned in the inscriptions of Izdubar at the time when the Babylonian monarchy was being formed by the uniting of a number of little states. The great building, or rather block of buildings, at Babylon consisted of the temples of Merodach and Zirat-banit, and the accompanying ziggurrat or tower, called the house of the foundation of heaven and earth. When these buildings were first erected is lost in the obscurity of the past; they were restored by a king named Agu or Agu-kak-rimi at a very early period, and again by Hammurabi, who made Babylon the capital of the whole country somewhere in the sixteenth century B.C. Babylon was captured by the Assyrians under Tugulti-ninip B.C. 1271, and again by Tiglath Pileser B.C. 1110. In the ninth century B.C. it was considered a great sanctuary, and Shalmaneser, king of Assyria, came here to offer sacrifice to Bel B.C. 851. Babylon was taken by Tiglath Pileser II., king of Assyria, B.C. 731, who made himself king of the country, and performed a great festival to Bel B.C. 729-8. The city was captured B.C. 722 by Merodach Baladan, the Chaldean, who held it twelve years, until he was expelled by Sargon, who in turn ruled the city. On the death of Sargon the city passed through various evolutions, and was several times captured by the Assyrians, when at the close of the last war between Sennacherib and the Babylonians, B.C. 691, the Assyrian monarch captured the city again and destroyed it. Babylon was restored and rebuilt by Esarhaddon, the son of Sennacherib, and was once more besieged and captured by Assurbanipal, king of Assyria, B.C. 648. Again the city revolted and fell before the Assyrians B.C. 626, but now it was to enjoy a period of repose and prosperity.

Nabu-pal-uzur, the Nabopolassar of the Greeks, who commanded the army in this war, was appointed king of Babylon, B.C. 626, and at once commenced the restoration of the country. Some time later he sent and made an alliance with the Medes, and having revolted against Assyria took Nineveh in conjunction with the Medes, and at the close of his reign sent his son Nebuchadnezzar to conquer Syria. While the young prince was on this expedition, Nabopolassar died, and Nebuchadnezzar succeeded to his throne. He entirely rebuilt the city of Babylon, and made it the most magnificent city in the world. The tower and temple of Belus, the hanging gardens, the magnificent palace, and the walls of the city were all his work, and scarcely a ruin exists in the neighbourhood without bricks bearing his name.

A few years after the death of Nebuchadnezzar the Babylonian power declined, and Babylon itself was taken by the Medes and Persians under Cyrus B.C. 539.

After one or two fruitless attempts at revolt, the city finally settled down under the Persian dominion, and on the defeat of their power passed to Alexander the Great. From this time, whatever changes happened in Asia only brought a change of masters, and Babylon sank gradually until the city became a complete ruin. A little to the south rose the town of Hillah, built with the bricks found in the old capital. The natives have established a regular trade in these bricks for building purposes. A number of men are always engaged digging out the bricks from the ruins, while others convey them to the banks of the Euphrates. There they are packed in rude boats, which float them down to Hillah; and on being landed they are loaded on donkeys and taken to any place where building is in progress. Every day when at Hillah I used to see this work going on as it had gone on for centuries, Babylon thus slowly disappearing, without an effort being made to ascertain the dimensions and buildings of the city, or recover what remains of its monuments. The northern portion of the wall, outside the Babil mound, is the place where the work of destruction is now most actively going on, and this in some places has totally disappeared.

On the 19th of March I left Hillah, and rode out into the desert to see the ruins of Hymer. Here was a tower in stages similar to that at Birs Nimrud, but of much smaller dimensions. Some excavations had been made with no result, the place, as usual, not having been investigated on any scientific plan. One of our party found here a fragment of alabaster, with a cuneiform inscription. From this ruin I rode to an enormous site, named Tel Ibrahim, the principal mound at which is three-quarters of a mile long. It is in a crescent form, with a smaller mound lying in the hollow. I saw walls and masses of brickwork protruding from heaps of rubbish in various places. Sir Henry Rawlinson had identified the mounds of Tel Ibrahim as the site of Cutha, the great seat of the worship of Nergal.

Leaving Tel Ibrahim, I crossed a trackless desert, covered with numerous ruins, and intersected by the dry beds of ancient canals; it is now a waterless waste, with a few dry plants and flocks of locusts. As we proceeded, the mirage raised on the horizon deceptive appearances of gigantic ruins and great rivers, which vanished as we approached, and the sun went down before we reached any shelter. After sunset the lights of various Arab encampments were seen in the distance, and riding up to one of these, I asked a shelter for the night. This the Arabs refused, but they sent on two men to guide us to another encampment. Here also they refused my party shelter, so we lay down in the open beside the encampment. We purchased a kid of the Arabs, and made a supper, and, the night being cold, we got up a good fire; but in the morning I was astonished to find that my pillow, and the waterproof with which I had covered my bed were quite wet with the dew.

Unable to get water to wash, or breakfast, I started on the 20th before sunrise, and we found our way with considerable difficulty. We passed an Arab tribe migrating for pasture—a curious sight, camels, horses, and sheep, men and women, with all their furniture and effects, on the move. About midday we reached a station, and obtained some refreshment, and rode in the afternoon to Baghdad. I now examined some interesting inscriptions belonging to Michael Minas, the British vice-consul at Baghdad, which he has since presented to Sir Henry Rawlinson.

On the 22nd, I had an interesting visit to the Indian prince resident at Baghdad. He is a most hospitable and excellent man, well known in these parts for his kindness and generosity. Soon after this I heard that the firman was granted, and having my powers, I at once made preparations for starting, as I wished to reach Mosul and commence excavations as soon as possible. I had some difficulty in procuring animals for the journey, but ultimately made arrangements to go by post horses, and started in the afternoon, after bidding farewell to my hospitable friends at Baghdad. I left this part of the country with great regret, as I was far more desirous of excavating here than in Assyria. Babylonia is the older and richer country, and is a field not worked nearly so much as Assyria.

I left Baghdad on the 27th of March, at three o'clock in the afternoon, and rode to the first station,

VISIT TO BABYLONIA.

Gededa. Here there was no change of horses, so I went on at once to Naharwan, the next stage. This portion of the journey was travelled in the night, and under considerable difficulties. I rode a very good horse, but the driver of the luggage had a vicious animal, which upset the caravan by kicking over the luggage horse, and breaking my largest box. I was forced to exchange animals with the driver before we could again proceed, and my new horse gave me a most uncomfortable time, the result being that it was four o'clock in the morning before we reached Naharwan. Here, after a rest, I once more started, and rode to Delli Abas. On the 29th, I left Delli Abas, and rode in the morning to Kufre. After some refreshment at Kufre, I travelled in the afternoon to Karatapa. The people of the post-station at Karatapa tried to persuade me to stay the night there, as they said there was a flooded river between that place and the next station which was very difficult to pass. I declined to listen to them, and started about eight in the evening. The country across which I travelled here is in general a wide plain bounded on the east by mountain ranges, which are the sources of numerous rivers. These rivers take in general a southern or south-western direction, and cross the plain to fall into the Tigris. During the spring, the period of the year at which I was travelling, these streams are generally flooded by the melting snows of the mountains and the rains, and form serious obstacles in crossing the country. The Turkish

F

government has not bridged these waters, or constructed proper roads, and even at Baghdad, the capital of Turkish Arabia, there is only a bridge of boats.

On the night of the 29th, after leaving Karatapa, a heavy storm came on, and, as it was quite dark, I was astonished at our guides keeping the proper road. The echo of the thunder seemed to come from the mountains on our right, and roll across the vast plain with a desolate, empty sound, peculiar to these vast solitudes. The lightning vividly lit up the scene from time to time, showing us for the moment the features of the country, but only to deepen by contrast the darkness which followed.

About one o'clock in the morning we heard the roaring of the flood, and soon reached the river we had been told of. After riding some little distance along the bank, we came to a place where the river spreads out like a fan, and is divided by three islands into four channels, each as wide as a good-sized river. Here we crossed the stream, and then made our way to Kormata, where we lay down in the courtyard of the post-house until the morning. On the 30th, I had a bad headache, and only rode a single stage to Taou. The weather was very unfavourable, and the road in a bad state. On the 31st of March, I left Taou, and rode to Kerkook, intending to go on to Altun Kupri; but, after starting from Kerkook, I was driven back by the weather. A furious storm came on, and being soon wet through, we turned back, and waited until the morning. There is a considerable mound at Kerkook, and I was offered an inscription of Nebuchadnezzar found here. On the 1st of April I started for Altun Kupri, and soon reached it. Here there was again difficulty from the water. The river of the lower or lesser Zab, which passes here, is divided into two streams by an island, on which stands the town of Altun Kupri. There is a steep bridge of one arch, which connects the town with the south. This we crossed, and then awaited the preparation of a raft to cross the other branch of the river. As soon as this was ready we got off, and started for Ervil. It is a long stage between Altun Kupri and Ervil, and we arrived at the latter place after dark. Ervil is the site of the Assyrian city of Arbela, and in the plains outside it was fought the great battle between Alexander and Darius. I had no time to examine the place, but I saw in passing that there were mounds rivalling in size those of the Assyrian capital. Over the principal mound a Turkish fortress is built, which would make it difficult to excavate here; but as Arbela was a great city, much may be expected here whenever it is explored.

On the 2nd of April I left Ervil to ride to the post-station of Zab, on the river of that name. The Zab, a rapid, strong stream, was much swollen by the rains, and again presented a difficulty as to crossing. It was a long time before we could get a raft, and the passage was difficult on account of the swiftness of the stream. Once over the water, I started for Mosul, and accomplished the distance in three hours and three-quarters. On the way I passed the swollen stream of the Ghazr, a tributary of the Zab. This water was so deep that my horses had to be led through the stream by naked Arabs, the river reaching nearly to the backs of the animals. Passing through the outskirts of Nineveh, I now once more came in sight of the mounds of that capital, and the town of Mosul. We rode through the ruins of the great gate of Nineveh, past the mound of Nebbi Yunas, and to the junction of the Khosr and Tigris, where the ferry boats were kept, for the flood of the Tigris was so great that the bridge of boats was removed. All the ferrymen had gone home, and after a vain attempt to get assistance we turned back, and went to the stone bridge which juts into the Tigris, but does not go right across the river. Here we fired a pistol, and did what we could to awaken the watchman, but it was three hours before we got a boat to ferry us over the river.

Chapter V

EXCAVATIONS AT NIMROUD.

Toma Shishman.—The mound.—Tower.—Palaces.—History.
—Temple of Nebo.—South-west Palace.—Model of hand.—Southeast palace.—Painted wall.—Winged figures.—Graves.—House building.—Arab entertainment.—Close excavations.

ON the 3rd of April I resolved to commence excavations on the mound of Nimroud, and the same day I was visited by Toma Shishman, or Toma the Fat, who had been superintendent of the workmen under Mr. Layard. Toma was well worthy of the epithet attached to his name, being very fat and short-winded; he did not look at all a serviceable superintendent, but he boasted grand things about his knowledge of the mound and its contents. He had seen where everything came from, and was prepared to find tablets, inscriptions, or sculptures, in fact, whatever I liked. Toma said I could not find anything, he was sure, without his assistance, and he was rather astonished when I showed him some inscriptions. I got rid of him by telling him I would engage him as soon as I commenced at Kouyunjik, but at present I intended working at Nimroud. Toma returned to the charge next day, and visited me every day until I left for Nimroud.

On the 4th I called on the pacha to present my letters and orders and acquaint him with my plans; he now took a different turn and professed great friendship, offering me every assistance in his power. The preparation of tools and material for the work occupied some days, and in the meantime I rode over to Nimroud on the night of the 5th of April, and next day inspected the mound. The mounds of Nimroud represent the Assyrian city of Calah; they consist of an oblong enclosure formed by the walls of the city, and a mound in the south-west corner which covered the palaces and temples. The palace mound is the principal ruin, and to this I directed my attention; its length is about six hundred yards from north to south, and it is about four hundred yards in breadth from west to east. At the north-west corner of the mound stands a lofty cone 140 ft. in height; this covers the ruins of the great ziggurrat or tower of Calah, which was excavated by Mr. Layard and found to be square at the base, faced with hewn stone for a height of 20 ft., and 167 ft. 6 in. each way. The northern and western faces show rude piers and some ornamentation. Entering a tunnel in the eastern face of the cone, I made my way through a succession of galleries in the base of the building, but these are now in a dangerous condition from the fall of portions of the roofs. Excepting for these galleries the whole structure appears to have been solid, the body built of sun-dried bricks, cased at the bottom with stone, and above with burnt bricks. South of the pyramid lies a ravine, and crossing this we arrive at the north-west palace, one of the most complete and perfect Assyrian buildings known. This palace is about 350 ft. in length and breadth, and consists of a central court 120 ft. by 90 ft., surrounded by a number of halls and chambers, the principal entrance being on the north. The trenches excavated here by Mr. Layard are still partially open, and the gigantic winged human-headed bulls and lions at the entrances, the mythological scenes and processions, figures of the king and attendants, may be seen in their places; and many of the chambers can be traced. South of this ruin are some trenches with a few fragments representing what Mr. Layard calls the upper chambers, and east of this lie the ruins of the centre palace, also in a very dilapidated condition. Nothing can now be traced of the plan of these structures.

Crossing another ravine, which forms the principal ascent to the mound from the west, we come to the south-west palace, a building unfinished; the sculptures found in it belonging to earlier palaces, and having been transported here to be recarved for the new one. Some of the sculptures were placed with their face to the wall, and others upside down. Many of these sculptures can be seen, especially at the southern part of the building, and evidently come from the north-west and centre palaces.

East of the south-west palace, across another ravine, are the ruins of the south-east palace, an inferior building to the others, few of the walls being faced with stone, and none of them sculptured. Passing northward from the south-east palace, we come to the remains of the temple of Nebo, at the entrance of which stand two colossal statues of the deity. Next, to the north of this are the ruins of the causeway leading up from the city on to the mound, and past this is a space with no building, which was probably laid out in gardens; outside this space, towards the city, stood a wall which shut in the palaces from the gaze of the people. North of this space we come to two temples, one of which lays towards the east ornamented at the entrance by two lions, one now in the British Museum, the other remaining in its place. The other temple joins the south-east corner of the tower, and its entrance is guarded by two winged human-headed lions.

The Assyrian city of Calah, now represented by the mounds of Nimroud, is said to have been founded by Nimrod, but of this original city nothing is known. A city was at a later period built on the spot by Shalmaneser I., king of Assyria, B.C. 1300, but this afterwards fell into decay, and was destroyed during the subsequent troubles which came on the Assyrian empire. Assur-nazir-pal, who ascended the Assyrian

EXCAVATIONS AT NIMROUD.

throne B.C. 885, resolved to rebuild the city; and bringing numbers of captives taken during his wars, he set them to work to rebuild Calah, and then settled them there to inhabit it. The north-west palace and the temples near the tower were the work of this king, and from these came most of the fine Nimroud sculptures in the British Museum. Shalmaneser II., king of Assyria, succeeded his father Assur-nazir-pal B.C. 860. He built the centre palace and the base at least of the south-east palace. Vulnirari III., his grandson, B.C. 812, built the upper chambers and the temple of Nebo; and Tiglath Pileser II., B.C. 745, rebuilt the centre palace. Sargon, king of Assyria, B.C. 722, restored the north-west palace, and his grandson, Esarhaddon, B.C. 681, built the south-west palace. Lastly, the grandson of Esarhaddon, Assur-ebil-ili, the last king of Assyria, rebuilt the temple of Nebo just before the destruction of the Assyrian empire. Thus the city of Calah possessed buildings of all the best periods of Assyrian history, and during a considerable part of the time it was the rival of the city of Nineveh.

My first excavations at Nimroud were undertaken on a small scale, as I was awaiting the receipt of some money, and I commenced at the temple of Nebo. Here I discovered some inscriptions, but they were most of them duplicates of texts already known, belonging to Shalmaneser II., B.C. 860, and Assurebil-ili, B.C. 620. Excepting the stone basement of the temple and a few chambers round it, the whole was in a ruinous condition. After the city had declined, this part of the mound appears to have been used as a granary. An excavation had been made on the eastern face, and a large tunnel burrowed through the walls and chambers on this side. This tunnel I found packed with grain, black and rotten from age. In the central part excavations had been made for tombs, and these had also destroyed considerable portions of the temple. This part of the mound had evidently been founded by Shalmaneser II., B.C. 860, but the temple was mainly the work of his grandson, Vul-nirari III., B.C. 812. The front and more prominent parts of the building were of large squared blocks of stone at bottom and sun-dried bricks above. On each side of the entrance stood a colossal figure of Nebo with crossed arms, in an attitude of meditation. Inside the building were found during the former excavations four smaller figures of the god with inscriptions round the dress stating that they were erected by the governor of Calah in honour of the king Vul-nirari (B.C. 812) and his wife, the queen Sammuramat (Semiramis). Here was also found a monolith of the Assyrian king Samsi-vul, B.C. 825, which properly belonged to the temple of Ninip. My principal purpose in excavating on this spot was to obtain some additional fragments of the reign of Tiglath Pileser II., B.C. 745, and in one of the eastern chambers, just beside a fallen wall of kiln-burnt bricks, I came on the upper portion of a tablet of this monarch. I immediately searched the neighbourhood to find any other portion that might be there, but there was no other fragment of the inscription near. When passing along a tunnel cut through the main wall of the temple by some former excavator, a terra-cotta model of a hand which had once been embedded in the upper part of the wall fell from the roof of the tunnel, and I subsequently found here a second of these objects. Some fragments of winged figures and inscriptions also turned up, but nothing of great interest except the Tiglath Pileser inscription.

I excavated on the northern portion of the south-west palace principally to verify fragmentary texts already known; having uncovered these I took paper impressions and copies, but undertook no other work in this direction. Many of the inscriptions in the south-west palace have suffered very much since the excavations of Mr. Layard.

At the conical mound marking the site of the ziggurrat or tower, I resolved to search for the foundation cylinders; but when I came to examine the structure, I had very little hope of finding them. During the former excavations at Nimroud, unsuccessful efforts had been made to find these cylinders, and great tunnels had been driven into the solid brickwork at each corner in search of them. I tried all these places again, and with equal want of success. Incidentally, from the remains on the southern face exposed during these operations, I came to the conclusion that there was a flight of steps on that side leading up to the tower. Most of my trenches in the tower were, however, fruitless, only solid masses of sun-dried brick being met with. I selected the north-west corner for a more systematic effort, and had some machinery constructed for lowering men and material. I then sank a well inside the stone facing of the tower, and nearly reached the base of the structure, but no cylinder was found. Under these circumstances, I am compelled to suppose that the cylinders were higher up in the tower, and were lost at the time the casing of burnt bricks fell from the building. The stone basement of the tower reaches to a height of 20 ft., but about the line of the stonework it was faced with fine kiln-burnt bricks. Most of this brick facing has fallen, and subsequent inhabitants of these regions have used them in various later structures.

While I was working at Nimroud one of the men said that the rain had exposed the corner of a slab by the north-west palace, and I sent a party of workmen to investigate the spot; but the slab was only plain. In clearing the ground by the slab, the ruin of a brick wall was exposed. This wall was partly broken down, and in clearing away the rubbish there appeared a model of a fist planted upright in the wall, embedded in mortar between the bricks. On the fingers of the fist was an inscription of Assur-nazir-pal, king of Assyria, B.C. 885.

In the south-east palace I instituted systematic excavations, and discovered several chambers. On examining this part of the mound, I saw a considerable tunnel in the south face, commencing on the sloping part of the mound. This tunnel appeared to go along the middle of a chamber, the floor having been cut through and appearing in a line on each side of the tunnel. Further on, the tunnel reached the wall at the end of the chamber, and the face of this had been cleared for some little distance; then, descending below the foundation of this wall, the tunnel ran for some distance into the base of the mound. I commenced on the two sides of this cutting, and cleared away to the level of the pavement, soon coming to the wall on each side. The earth I cleared out of the chambers I threw down the old tunnel to fill that up. The southern wall of the chamber had fallen over into the plain, as it was here close to the edge of the platform, and the chamber commenced with two parallel walls running north and south. The right-hand wall, in a place near the edge where it was much broken down, showed three steps of an ascent which had gone apparently to some upper chambers. Further on, it showed two recesses, each ornamented on both sides with three square pilasters. The left hand showed an entrance into a second chamber, running east to west, and from this turned a third, going parallel with the first. Altogether in this place I opened six chambers, all of the same character; the entrances ornamented by clusters of square pilasters and recesses in the rooms in the same style. The walls were coloured in horizontal bands of red, green, and yellow on plaster; and where the lower parts of the chambers were panelled with small stone slabs, the plaster and colours were continued over these. In one of these rooms there appeared a brick receptacle let into the floor, and on lifting the brick which covered this, I found six terra-cotta winged figures, closely

packed in the receptacle. Each figure was full-faced, having a head like a lion, four wings, with one hand across the breast, holding a basket in the other, and clothed in a long dress to the feet. These figures were probably intended to preserve the building against the power of evil spirits. One of the chambers to the east of my first trench opened into a square apartment paved with slabs of stone, and walled round with the same material. This place, which was on the edge of the mound, appears to have been used for domestic offices. There was a circular hole in one of the pavement slabs, which opened into a drain, and I found that this and a second drain both passed along in an easterly direction, and traversed the south front of the palace to the south-east corner. Here the mound and the drains turned, forming a circular end, and from these the drains ran along the east face of the mound. At the circular corner (the south-east corner) of the mound, I found a fragment of the outer wall. This consisted of bricks enamelled and painted over with war scenes. The fragment I found has the figure of a warrior, and part of the wheel of a chariot. Over the scene was part of an inscription in painted characters, the word "warriors" still remaining. In the chambers little was found of the Assyrian period. I obtained some pottery, a plain bronze dish, part of a terra-cotta model, and numbers of large terra-cotta beads. The ornamentation of the south-east palace, and the nature of the few objects found in its chambers, led me to the conclusion that it was a private building for the wives and families of the kings. I had been quite uncertain as to the date, until, on opening the drains which went round the palace, I found the bricks were inscribed on the under side with a legend of Shalmaneser II., B.C. 860, who must have been the builder of this palace.

While excavating here, I ran several trenches

through the space between the south-east and south-west palaces; but the buildings here were totally destroyed. Fragments of elaborate carved pavements, wall plaster with paintings in the Egyptian style, portions of winged bulls and sculpture, were all that turned up, and I did not obtain any plan or idea of the buildings in this part.

In the centre of the mound I made some slight excavations; but my operations closed before anything of interest was discovered.

All the eastern and southern portions of the mound of Nimroud have been destroyed by being made a burial-place. The ruins had been excavated after the fall of the Assyrian empire, walls had been dug through, and chambers broken into, and the openings filled up with coffins. These coffins were various in shape, not two being alike. Most of them were so short, that the bodies had to be doubled up to get them in. The coffins were of terra-cotta, some of them ornamented and painted; but commoner graves of the same period only contained large jars or urns in which the remains were packed, the poorest being buried without any covering at all. Generally the coffins were covered with one or two stone slabs from the neighbouring palaces, and then closed up with large sun-dried bricks. These burials are of all ages; some I opened belonged to the period of the successor of Alexander the Great, in the third century B.C. From the tombs I obtained beads and ornaments, rings, bracelets, &c.

Figure of Warrior on Painted Brick
From S.E. Palace, Nimroud

EXCAVATIONS AT NIMROUD.

When I commenced excavations at Nimroud on the 9th of April, I lodged in the house of a man of influence among the Arabs here, named Udder. His wife was a woman of some intelligence for an Arab, and was continually blessing her husband with additions to his family. The young olive-branches lived about the place like so many pigs, any washing or attention being quite out of the question. Their mother, whose name was Tiha, remembers Mr. Layard very well. During the time this great explorer was in these parts Tiha was much younger, of course, and was then accounted one of the beauties of the place. The tribe to which these people belong is the Shematteh, and they inhabited in Layard's time the village of Nimroud, but since the excavations had ceased the village had declined and the people had abandoned it. In 1872 some of the people returned, and others were coming back when I was excavating. These families were patching up all the old huts and making the place available for their services.

I desired to have a house more to myself after a while, and therefore ordered the men to build me a place on the mound. First of all I traced on a spot chosen for the purpose the plan of my house, then the men appointed roved about over the mound and collected all sorts of fragments of old bricks and stones. I had to look sharp after them to prevent them from taking anything of consequence, and sometimes, after all my trouble, I found they had got hold of a valuable inscription or other antiquity and were about to wall it up in the house. With the fragments they gathered from the mound they joined a collection of sun-dried bricks brought from the old village of Nimroud. A donkey was regularly employed so many times a day transporting these materials, and after they were collected I laid the foundation of the walls by placing rows of bricks on the lines I had drawn. The builders then made some Arab mortar; and for this purpose they dug up and turned over a large square of ground. Next, donkey-loads of dung and skins full of water were brought and well mixed in this space, the workmen taking off their clothes and stirring up the pudding with their hands and feet. In building the walls the stones and bricks were laid in position and then well bedded in this mortar—all these operations being executed by hand. When the walls were high enough to serve as screens from my observation and the heat of the sun, the workmen would lie down behind them and smoke their pipes, and I sometimes caught the whole party so engaged. After the walls were finished preparations were made for roofing, and for this purpose the whole party went off on an excursion to the banks of the Zab, taking several donkeys with them, which they loaded with brushwood cut from the vicinity of the river. They were some days over this, and then made a fresh mud-pie to bind together the brushwood. This made a very good top, and it was levelled for walking on by spreading on the surface the usual mixture of dung and wet clay. An outside staircase to reach the roof, and some wooden doors which I had made in Mosul, completed the structure, which internally consisted of four rooms, and formed a very convenient residence for this country.

During my excavations at Nimroud I was sometimes annoyed by parties of the Jebour Arabs bent on forcing their services on me, or determined on plunder. In order to prevent the jealousy and disputes which sometimes arose I chose my workmen as far as possible from all the different tribes in the neighbourhood, from the Shematteh or people of Nimroud, the Jehaish or people of Naifa, a village just by the Tigris, the inhabitants of the village of Selamiyeh, and some of the Jebours.

On the 28th of April a party of Turkish military officers visited the mounds, and after I had shown them over the excavations we were escorted to the village of Nimroud by my workmen, who engaged in mock combats with sword, shield, and spear, for the amusement of my visitors. Later in the evening I went out with a guard of honour, and visited the doctors on their raft, which was moored by the bank of the river. After my return to the village the Arabs made up a musical entertainment opposite the door of the house where I was staying. The men of the village sat down in a circle, reserving the interior space for the performers. All the performers were men and boys, the women looking on from a distance. The entertainment began by one of the musicians starting a song, which was taken up by the others and accompanied by clapping of hands. The singing was succeeded by dancing in a slow Arabic fashion; it should, however, rather be described as capering about, for the great point appeared to be, to show as much action of the arms and legs as possible. After this followed some peculiar performances by two men, and then a dusky little Arab boy, quite naked, leaped into the ring and commenced springing about, all the bystanders attempting to strike him. He avoided these blows and leaped about the ring in all directions, to the great amusement of the assembled Arabs. Songs, dances, and performances succeeded each other after this until a late hour, when I retired from the meeting, and the Arabs broke up their party.

Toma Shishman, who had visited me at Mosul, being anxious for employment, got a passage on a raft passing down the Tigris and landed opposite Nimroud to call on me. I had already promised to employ him as soon as I opened excavations at Kouyunjik, and he feared I had forgotten this. One day, while I was engaged on the mound of Nimroud, he came to me and brought a petition written out for him in fair English by a Chaldean priest at Mosul. This petition set forth that he, Toma, had served Mr. Layard during the former excavations in the capacity of chief of the workmen, and since then he had been reduced in fortune and was now anxious to serve me in the same capacity. As I intended to work at Kouyunjik I engaged Toma from the 1st of May, and directed him to proceed to Mosul and get together a body of workmen to commence excavations at Kouyunjik.

The distance from Nimroud to Mosul is about twenty miles by road, and I had to provide for Toma an animal to ride upon. I found some difficulty in this, as Toma was fat, heavy, and unwieldy, and people did not care about his riding their donkeys so far. At last I succeeded in getting him an ass, and, setting him on it, packed him off to Mosul. The animal bore his weight for some time, but about the middle of the journey fell, making Toma kiss the ground. Toma declared himself much shaken, and on arriving at Mosul laid up, instead of engaging the men for me.

I stayed at Nimroud until the 4th of May, and then, after the workmen had finished, I started to ride during the night to Mosul. At this time the days were very hot and travelling by night was pleasant, and after an easy journey I reached the bridge of Mosul, to find, as before, neither bridge nor ferry for crossing to the town. I was so drowsy with my ride that I sat down on the stonework where the permanent bridge ends, and fell asleep while waiting for the ferry. In the morning I was ferried over to Mosul, and on the 8th of May I sent and closed the excavations at Nimroud.

Chapter VI.

EXCAVATIONS AT KOUYUNJIK.

Wall of Nineveh.—Northern gate.—The Khosr.—Great gate.—Nebbi Yunas.—Kouyunjik.—Palaces.—History.—Capture of Nineveh.—Library.—Hammum Ali.—North palace, Kouyunjik.—Law tablet.—Deluge fragment.—Discoveries.—Khorsabad.—Orders to close.—Syllabary.—Visit to Nimroud.

HEN I arrived at Mosul I was astonished to find Toma had done nothing, and I set to work to get men and prepare for the excavation.

Toma's excuse was that the joss (donkey) on which he rode from Nimroud had shaken him so much in the fall that he had been ill ever since; but when he saw that I engaged men without his intervention he began to fear I might exclude him from the work, and he soon collected a body of men, and when I came to the mound on the 7th of May I found Toma bringing his workmen to the spot.

The ruins opposite the town of Mosul, which mark the site of Nineveh, will be best understood by the aid of the accompanying plan.

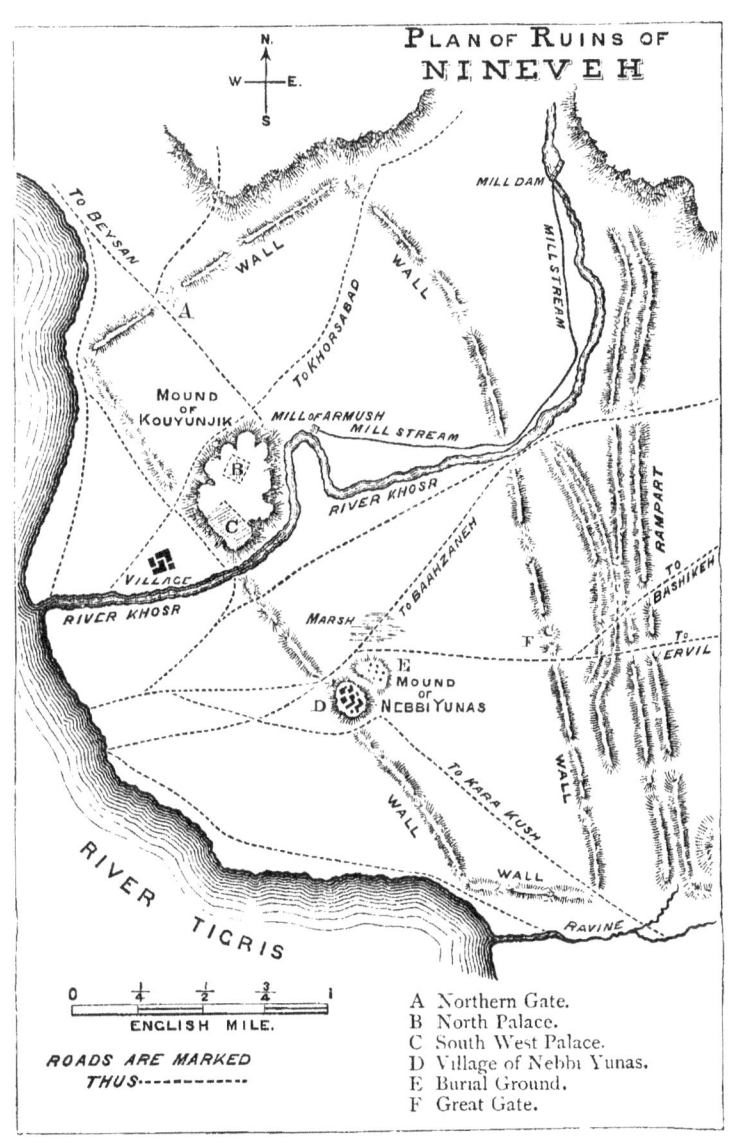

PLAN OF THE SITE OF NINEVEH

The ruins of Nineveh are situated on the eastern bank of the Tigris; they consist now of a large enclosure covered with low mounds surrounded by the ruins of a magnificent wall, about eight miles in circuit, and broken on the western side by two great artificial mounds, Kouyunjik or Tel Armush, and Nebbi Yunas. Through the middle of the city flows the stream of the Khosr, entering through the eastern wall and passing out through the western wall by the southern corner of the mound of Kouyunjik.

The mounds of the wall of Nineveh are said to be in some places even now nearly 50 ft. high, while the breadth of the *débris* at the foot is from 100 ft. to 200 ft.

Diodorus states that the walls of Nineveh were 100 ft. high, which was probably not beyond the truth; but, as the upper part of the wall is everywhere destroyed, it is impossible to prove the matter at present. The breadth of the wall was probably 50 ft.—excavation, however, might determine this with certainty.

The western face of the wall of Nineveh is over two and a half miles long; it faces towards the town of Mosul and the river Tigris. At the northern and southern corners the river closely approaches the wall, but between the two points the Tigris bends out to the west, making a bow-shaped flat of land about a mile broad between the wall and the river. On the western side, with their outer border in a line with the wall, lie the two palace mounds called Kouyunjik and Nebbi Yunas, to be described later.

Where the western wall at its northern corner abuts on the Tigris it is joined by the northern wall, which is about a mile and one-third long. There is a considerable mound in one part of this wall, which marks the site of a tower and of the great northern gate of Nineveh. The entrance, which was excavated by Mr. Layard, is adorned by colossal winged bulls and mythological figures, and paved with large slabs of limestone; it appears to have been under the centre of the tower, which had a depth from front to back of 130 ft. The northern wall is continued from the north-eastern corner by the eastern wall, which is three and a-quarter miles long. Nearly half way along this side the wall is broken by the stream of the Khosr, which, coming from the east, passes right through the site of Nineveh and runs into the Tigris. Where the stream of the Khosr breaks through the wall the floods have destroyed a portion of the defences; enough remains, however, to show that the lower part of the wall in this part is built of large blocks of stone, probably to resist the water; and in the river itself, in a line with the wall, stand fragmentary blocks of solid masonry, which Captain Jones, who made the best survey of the ruins, considers to be remains of a dam to turn the Khosr into the ditch. I am rather inclined to think that they are part of a bridge over which the wall was carried.

EXCAVATIONS AT KOUYUNJIK.

South of the Khosr, where the road to Ervil and Baghdad passes through the eastern wall, stands a double mound, marking the site of the Great Gate of Nineveh, the scene of so many triumphal entries and pageants of the Assyrian kings.

As this was the grandest gate in the wall of Nineveh, it would be an important spot to excavate. Outside the eastern wall Nineveh was shielded by four walls and three moats, making this side of the fortification exceptionally strong. The eastern and western walls are connected at their southern extremities by the south wall, which is the shortest and least important of the defences of Nineveh, measuring little more than half a mile in length.

The two palace mounds, called Kouyunjik and Nebbi Yunas, are situated on the western side of the city, and at one time joined the wall. Nebbi Yunas is a triangular-shaped mound, crowned by a village and burying-ground. It is called Nebbi Yunas from the supposed tomb of Jonah, over which a mosque is erected.

Excavations were made here by Mr. Layard, and afterwards by the Turkish government. The works showed the existence of palaces here, the first built by Vul-nirari, B.C. 812, the next by Sennacherib, B.C. 705, who, after finishing his great palace on the Kouyunjik mound, built a new one here late in his reign. From this building came the fine memorial cylinder, with the account of the expedition against Hezekiah, king of Judah. The third palace at Nebbi

Yunas was built by Esarhaddon, son of Sennacherib, B.C. 681, and from here came three memorial cylinders, containing the history of this reign. North of Nebbi Yunas, just above the stream of the Khosr, lies the largest mound, on the site of Nineveh, Kouyunjik. The eastern and southern faces of the mound, from the north-east to the south-west corner, are bounded by the stream of the Khosr, which has been artificially diverted to flow round it. The mound at one time was surrounded by a casing of large squared stones, and some former excavator had cleared a considerable space of this facing at the northern part of the mound. The Turks have since built a bridge part of the way across the Tigris, and for this purpose they pulled down and carried away the exposed facing wall of Kouyunjik, and the basement wall of the palace of Assurbanipal.

The northern part of the Kouyunjik mound is occupied by the palace of Assurbanipal, called the North Palace, and the south-western part by the palace of Sennacherib. Between the two palaces, and on the eastern part of the mound, there exists a wide space of ground, on which no Assyrian building has been discovered. According to the Assyrian inscriptions, there were at least four temples in this space—two temples to Ishtar, the goddess of Nineveh, a temple to Nebo and Merodach, and a ziggurat or temple tower.

Nineveh was founded by Nimrod, king of Baby-

Ionia, and during the dominion of his successors there stood here a temple to "Ishtar, daughter of the god Hea." In the nineteenth century B.C. we find Assyria constituted into a monarchy, under rulers whose capital was at the city of Assur (Kalah Shergat), and one of these, named Samsi-vul, restored the old temple of Ishtar at Nineveh. After this, for some centuries, we hear nothing of Nineveh, until the reign of Assur-ubalid, B.C. 1400, who restored again the temple of Ishtar. From this time, the city gradually rose, until B.C. 1300, when Shalmaneser, king of Assyria, repaired the temple of Ishtar, now again in ruinous condition, and built a palace at Nineveh, making the city the seat of government. His son, Tugulti-ninip, B.C. 1271, made some additions to the temple of Ishtar; and this structure was again restored by Assur-dan, king of Assyria, B.C. 1200. Mutaggil-nusku, his son, B.C. 1170, rebuilt the palace; and the next monarch, Assur-risilim, B.C. 1150, rebuilt both the palace and temple. Tiglath Pileser, his son, B.C. 1120, continued his father's buildings here; and the next king, Assur-bel-kala, B.C. 1100, made a public fountain, in the shape of a female figure. His brother, Samsi-vul III., B.C. 1080, again built the temple of Ishtar. Assur-nazir-pal, who reigned B.C. 885, rebuilt both the temple and palace with great splendour, and his example was followed by his son, Shalmaneser II., B.C. 860; but towards the close of this monarch's reign, the Ninevites were dissatisfied with the transfer of the government to Calah (Nimroud), and Nineveh revolted in favour of his son, Assur-dain-pal. This attempt at revolution was suppressed by Samsi-vul, brother of the revolting prince, and in B.C. 825, Samsi-vul IV. succeeded to the crown. He also adorned the temple of Ishtar, and his son, Vul-nirari III., B.C. 812, built a new temple to Nebo and Merodach. Hitherto all the public buildings had been on the platform of Kouyunjik, but Vul-nirari founded a new palace on the mound of Nebbi Yunas. The next monarch who embellished Nineveh was Tiglath Pileser II., B.C. 745, who built a palace by the bend of the river Khosr. After the death of Tiglath Pileser, Nineveh was neglected in favour of a new royal city, built by Sargon, B.C. 722, at Dur-sargina (Khorsabad); but the temples were kept in repair, and Sargon restored the sanctuary of Nebo and Merodach. In the year B.C. 705, Sennacherib came to the throne, and he at once set to work to restore the glory of the great capital of Assyria. The old palace of Nineveh, the work of so many monarchs, had again fallen into decay, and he entirely removed it. Then turning the course of the river Khosr, which had undermined the mound, he forced it to flow more to the south; and he increased both the height and extent of the mound. On the south-west part he now built a magnificent palace, which in extent exceeds all other Assyrian palaces yet found. On the northern part of the mound he built a palace for his son, and on the mound of Nebbi Yunas a second palace for himself. The great walls of the city were also the work of this monarch. After the death of Sennacherib, his son, Esarhaddon, B.C. 681, built a second palace on the Nebbi Yunas mound, and a temple to Shamas. His son and successor, Assurbanipal, B.C. 668, restored the various palaces and temples built by his father and grandfather, and constructed a beautiful palace on the northern part of the Kouyunjik mound, on the site of one formerly built by Sennacherib. Nineveh was now in the height of its glory, but these vast works had been raised in great part by slave labour, and the captives taken in war toiled in building her walls and palaces. The city saw triumph after triumph, until in the time of Assurbani-pal it ruled over an empire stretching from Egypt and Lydia on the west to Media and Persia on the east.

The end was, however, swiftly coming, and Nabopolassar, the Assyrian general who left the city at the command of his monarch to subdue a revolt in Babylonia, was destined soon to return the conqueror of Nineveh itself. A coalition of Necho, king of Egypt, Cyaxares, king of Media, and Nabopolassar, king of Babylon, was formed against Assyria, and the Medes and Babylonians, after defeating the Assyrian forces, laid siege to Nineveh. The lofty walls of the city long resisted their efforts, but after two years there happened a great overflow of the Tigris which swept away part of the wall of the city. Through the breach the besiegers entered on the subsiding of the flood, and captured the city. The last king of

Assyria, finding his city was taken, made a pile of all his valuables in the palace, and setting fire to it perished himself in the flames. The city was now plundered and at once destroyed; it did not gradually decay like Babylon, but from the time of its capture it ceased to have any political importance, and its site became almost forgotten.

On the 7th of May I commenced work at Kouyunjik on the library space of the south-west palace, the building raised by Sennacherib, and on the 9th of May I started some trenches at the south-eastern corner of the north palace built by Assurbanipal. There was nothing of interest in the trenches at first, as all the sculptures had been discovered by former excavators, and my object was the recovery of inscribed terra-cotta tablets. On the 10th of May I resolved to visit the site of Hammum Ali, and started out in the evening after paying the men. Hammum Ali is a site on the right or western bank of the Tigris, about sixteen miles below Mosul. The place is said to be a summer resort for the people of Mosul, and is noted for the medicinal properties of some bitumen springs. Passing through the southern gate of Mosul, the way lay for some few miles along a low good road; we then turned along a rugged rocky path which was very tiring to travel over, and at the end of this descended again into a plain in which stands Hammum Ali. War was at the time raging among the Arab tribes on the west of the Tigris. The great tribe of the Aneiza, which occupies the desert between Aleppo and the Tigris, had been moving as usual for plunder, and one branch or detachment had attacked a tribe named Abu Mohammed. The detachment of the Aneiza was defeated, and the Abu Mohammed, following up their success, put to death with great cruelty every one of the opposite party they met. In revenge the Aneiza were moving towards the Tigris, attacking the various tribes in that direction, and a few days before my visit to Hammum Ali, they had a brush in that neighbourhood with a division of the Shammer Arabs, and had plundered them of all their flocks and herds. The various wandering tribes on the west of the Tigris were now flying across the river to escape the Aneiza, and we met on the way to Hammum Ali numbers of the fugitives carrying all their goods and driving their cattle before them.

It was night when I arrived at Hammum Ali, but I contrived to get some refreshment, and afterwards spread my blanket on the ground and fell asleep. Early in the morning I rose, and having procured some breakfast went out to visit the mounds. There are several artificial elevations here, giving indications of the existence at one time of a considerable city, the principal mound appearing to be the ruin of a ziggurat or tower. A tunnel had been opened in this by the French excavators, but nothing of consequence had been found, the interior consisting of sun-dried bricks with layers of large stones. After inspecting the mounds I examined the village, and the bitumen springs or wells. A roofed bath-house is built over these, and the famous water is in a bath or pool, with a stage all round it for the convenience of the bathers. People of both sexes bathe in the pool, the water of which is of an inky colour, with lumps of bitumen floating about in it. The interior of the building round the pool has been used as a convenience, and is in a state of indescribable filthiness.

Turning from this I rode through the low ground by the side of the Tigris, and then along the face of the cliffs overhanging the water, and soon arrived at Mosul, from which I crossed over to Kouyunjik to see the progress of the excavations. My trenches in the palace of Sennacherib proceeded slowly and produced little result, the ground being so cut up by former excavations that it was difficult to secure good results without more extensive operations than my time or means would allow; inscriptions, the great object of my work, were however found, and served as compensation for the labour.

In the north palace the results were more definite. Here was a large pit made by former excavators from which had come many tablets; this pit had been used since the close of the last excavations for a quarry, and stones for the building of the Mosul bridge had been regularly extracted from it. The bottom of the pit was now full of massive fragments of stone from the basement wall of the palace jammed in between heaps of small fragments of stone, cement, bricks, and clay, all in utter confusion. On removing some of these stones with a crowbar, and digging in the rubbish behind them, there appeared half of a curious tablet copied from a Babylonian original, giving warnings to kings and judges of the evils which would follow the neglect of justice in the country. On continuing the trench some distance further, the other half of this tablet was discovered, it having evidently been broken before it came among the rubbish.

On the 14th of May my friend, Mr. Charles Kerr, whom I had left at Aleppo, visited me at Mosul, and as I rode into the khan where I was staying, I met him. After mutual congratulations I sat down to examine the store of fragments of cuneiform inscriptions from the day's digging, taking out and brushing off the earth from the fragments to read their contents. On cleaning one of them I found to my surprise and gratification that it contained the greater portion of seventeen lines of inscription belonging to the first column of the Chaldean account of the Deluge, and fitting into the only place where there was a serious blank in the story. When I had first published the account of this tablet I had conjectured that there were about fifteen lines wanting in this part of the story, and now with this portion I was enabled to make it nearly complete.

After communicating to my friend the contents of the fragment I copied it, and a few days later telegraphed the circumstance to the proprietors of the "Daily Telegraph." Mr. Kerr desired to see the mound at Nimroud, but, as the results from Kouyunjik were so important, I could not leave the site to go with him, so I sent my dragoman to show him the place, remaining myself to superintend the Kouyunjik excavations.

The palace of Sennacherib also steadily produced its tribute of objects, including a small tablet of Esarhaddon, king of Assyria, some new fragments of one of the historical cylinders of Assurbanipal, and a curious fragment of the history of Sargon, king of Assyria, relating to his expedition against Ashdod, which is mentioned in the twentieth chapter of the Book of Isaiah. On the same fragment was also part of the list of Median chiefs who paid tribute to Sargon. Part of an inscribed cylinder of Sennacherib, and half of an amulet in onyx with the name and titles of this monarch, subsequently turned up, and numerous impressions in clay of seals, with implements of bronze, iron, and glass. There was part of a crystal throne, a most magnificent article of furniture, in too mutilated condition to copy, but as far as it is preserved closely resembling in shape the bronze one discovered by Mr. Layard at Nimroud.

On the evening of Saturday, the 17th of May, after paying the workmen, I started to examine the mounds of Khorsabad. I crossed the Tigris, and passed through the ruins of Nineveh, by the side of the Khosr river, and went over the country to the mound of Kalata. From the lateness of the hour, I was unable to inspect Kalata, and put up in a village near that mound. Rising early next morning, I went to the mound of Kalata, a large, conical, artificial elevation, which had been tapped by former explorers. The only thing that could be seen of any account was a chamber in the side of the mound, which appeared to me like a tomb. The vault had been recently rifled of its contents, and I was told several antiquities had been found there. From Kalata I went to Barimeh, a well-built village near the foot of the mountains of Jebel Maklub, and, passing through a beautiful country, rode to Khorsabad. A fine stream, a tributary of the Khosr, flows from Barimeh to Khorsabad. In one place there is a pretty waterfall, and signs of cultivation and fertility are visible in every direction. The neighbouring mountains and streams, the fields and flowers, combine to make this district a contrast to the vast brown plains of most of Assyria, and fully justify the choice of Sargon, who fixed on the site of Khorsabad to build his capital.

The ruins of Khorsabad represent the old Assyrian city of Dur-sargina, and consist of a town and palace mound. The wall of the town is nearly square, rather over a mile each way, the angles of the square facing the cardinal points. On the south-west face of the wall there is the fortified enclosure of a citadel, and on the north-west face, along which runs the stream from Barimeh, stands the palace platform, somewhat in form of the letter T, the base of the letter being turned to the north-west, nearest to the stream. This part of the mound near the water is the highest, and covers the remains of the palace and a temple. The excavations here by M. Botta have been made in a systematic manner, and have laid bare a considerable portion of the palace, some of which can still be seen; but most of it has been covered again, to preserve it. I spent some time in inspecting these ruins, and then returned to Mosul.

I have said I telegraphed to the proprietors of the "Daily Telegraph" my success in finding the missing portion of the deluge tablet. This they published in the paper on the 21st of May, 1873; but from some error unknown to me, the telegram as published differs materially from the one I sent. In particular, in the published copy occurs the words "as the season is closing," which led to the inference that I considered that the proper season for excavating was coming to an end. My own feeling was the contrary of this, and I did not send this. I was at the time waiting instructions, and hoped that as good results were being obtained, the excavations would be continued. The proprietors of the "Daily Telegraph," however, considered that the discovery of the missing fragment of the deluge text accomplished the object they had in view, and they declined to prosecute the excavations further, retaining, however, an interest in the work, and desiring to see it carried on by the nation. I was disappointed myself at this, as my excavations were so recently commenced; but I felt

I could not object to this opinion, and therefore prepared to finish my excavations and return. I continued the Kouyunjik excavations until I had completed my preparations for returning to England, and in the north palace, near the place where I found the tablet with warnings to kings, I disinterred a fragment of a curious syllabary, divided into four perpendicular columns. In the first column was given the phonetic values of the cuneiform characters, and the characters themselves were written in the second column, the third column contained the names and meanings of the signs, while the fourth column gave the words and ideas which it represented.

I searched all round for other fragments of this remarkable tablet, pushing my trench further through the mass of stones and rubbish, the remains of the fallen basement wall of the palace. Large blocks of stone, with carving and inscriptions, fragments of ornamental pavement, painted bricks, and decorations, were scattered in all directions, showing how complete was the ruin of this portion of the palace. Fixed between these fragments were found, from time to time, fragments of terra-cotta tablets; and one day a workman struck with his pick an overlying mass of mortar, revealing the edge of a tablet, which was jammed between two blocks of stone. We at once cleared away the rubbish, and then, bringing a crowbar to bear, lifted the upper stone block, and extracted the fragment of tablet, which proved to be part of the syllabary, and joined the fragment already found. The greater part of the rest of this tablet was found at a considerable distance in a branch trench to the right. It was adhering to the roof of the trench, and easily detached, leaving the impression of all the characters in the roof.

Two other portions of the sixth tablet of the deluge series also came from this part. They relate to the conquest of the winged bull, and will be given with the other portions of the Izdubar series.

On my left in this excavation stood a mass of solid rubbish, which had been undermined during the former excavations; and a crack having started between this and the mound at the back of it, it stood as if ready to fall into the trench. For some time the workmen were afraid to touch it; but I expected some fragments there, so I directed them to attack it from the top, and was rewarded by several parts of tablets. A second trench on the right yielded a good text, being a variant account of the conquest of Babylonia by the Elamites, B.C. 2280. Most of the fragments from this part were obtained with considerable difficulty, on account of the masses of stone which had to be removed to get at the inscriptions.

In the northern part of Sennacherib's palace I made some excavations, and discovered chambers similar to those in the south-east palace at Nimroud. Here no inscriptions rewarded me; but in the part of the temple area near this I discovered a new fragment of the cylinder of Bel-zakir-iskun, king of Assyria, B.C. 626. Further to the south-east in this part of the mound I discovered brick inscriptions of Shalmaneser, B.C. 1300, and his son, Tugulti-ninip, B.C. 1271, both of whom made restorations and additions to the temple of Ishtar. Here was a later wall, in constructing which some fine sculptures of the age of Assur-nazir-pal, B.C. 885, had been cut up and destroyed.

Such were my principal discoveries at Kouyunjik, and I closed the excavations there on the 9th of June. While I stayed at Mosul I made many friends among the Catholic missionaries and the merchants in the town, and in company with some of them I paid a farewell visit to Nimroud on the 4th and 5th of June. On the 8th of June, as I was about to leave the country, I gave a farewell dinner to my friends, and next day we took leave of each other, I starting for Europe with my treasures.

Chapter VII.

FROM MOSUL TO ENGLAND.

Backsheesh.—Mill stream.—Jebel Abjad.—Power of rivers.—Deluge mountains.—Stories.—M. Costi and Mr. Kerr.—Desert Arabs.—Nisibin.—Wounded Arab.—Orfa.—Abraham's pool.—Castle. — Biradjik. — Aleppo.—Turkish custom-house.—Deceit.—Alexandretta.—Antiquities seized.—Their release.

ON the 9th of June, when preparing to start, I had to meet those innumerable applications for backsheesh, that is, presents, which are so disagreeable in the East. Everyone, whether he had done me any service or not, equally felt justified in asking for money, and it seemed as if half the town were coming for presents. I kept one of my boxes open until six o'clock in the evening to receive the last discovered antiquities, and, my caravan being in readiness at the khan, I at once started for England. Several of my friends went across the Tigris with me, and on the beach of the eastern bank, between Nineveh and Mosul, I bid farewell to them and rode on to Tel Adas. Passing the gloomy shadows of the ruins of

Nineveh, I rode along by night to the next station, and reached Tel Adas about a quarter to three on the morning of the 10th of June. I stayed at Tel Adas until the afternoon, and about a quarter to five started again. The road here was beautiful by night, and in one place we came to a fine stream and mill. The road here gradually ascended from the south until it reached a high ridge almost like an embankment; then it descended by a steep path to the bank of the stream. Turning on one side of this, we travelled to the east a little distance up the stream until we found a place where we could ford it; then, turning to the left, we passed along the other bank, and had to ford some more water before reaching the straight road. Our way now lay through an undulating country, with low swelling hills and ridges of red earth. I passed Semil and went on to Gershene, where I stopped until the afternoon of the 11th of June. About a quarter past four in the afternoon of the 11th I started from Gershene, intending to go round the western end of the range of mountains named Jebel Abjad, but my guide turned out to be unacquainted with the road. We travelled along the plain for some distance, and about sunset, taking a wrong turn to the right, got entangled in the mountains. We rode about in the dark in the vain attempt to find the way, or to cross into the plains north of the mountains. The moon now rose, brightly shining over the scene and seeming to light up the upper parts of the mountains; but the shadows of the higher peaks, some of them 2,500 feet above the sea, fell over the glens and ravines through which we tried to force our way, rendering the light uncertain and deceiving.

The scenery by day would have been very romantic, and it was rendered in some respects more so by the uncertain light in which we were travelling. Towering rocks, precipices, caverns, and waterfalls seen in succession, sometimes half shrouded in shadow, sometimes in the pale light of the moon, made far more impression on the imagination than they would have done in the day. After some hours of wandering we got across the mountains, and then tried to reach the banks of the Khabour. The river Khabour and its affluent, the Hazel, here run in a direction from east to west in the plain, which is bounded on the north by the Jebel Djudi, or Mountains of the Ark, and on the south by the Jebel Abjad, across which we had just passed. The dark rugged forms of the Jebel Djudi could be seen standing out in the distance, and towards this range we directed our steps. On reaching the plain of the Khabour we rode through a vast field of wild plants, the smell from which was most fragrant, but they grew so thick and high that they almost covered us on horseback; and, fearing to lose ourselves in this jungle, we turned back and skirted the mountain until we came near a village, and entering this, tired with my night's wandering, I threw myself on a heap of corn and slept until sunrise. At dawn I obtained a guide from the village and went down to the Khabour, the crossing of which was a work of some difficulty. I passed over it where it is divided into several streams, and, passing some rocky heights, descended into a wide level plain, originally the bed of the Tigris, when in this part of its course it flowed more to the east. Vast water-worn cliffs and rocks stood on either side, some worn into shapes resembling the old ruins which lower down now line the river. In all this country the one natural phenomenon that impressed me most was the power of running water. The enormous cuttings, valleys, and river beds, and the power and swiftness of the rivers are very marked, and it is evident that in former times the strength of these waters was very much greater. Riding up out of this hollow we came to a beautiful scene; there was a ruined station on a rocky height, many trees and numerous wild flowers, conspicuous among which was the bright Oleander. Here was a waterfall, which now, supplied with abundant water, was, I think, the prettiest I had ever seen. Directly after, I passed among masses of recent pebbly rocks along a ledge overhanging the Tigris. Here the river seems undermining the eastern bank, and vast fragments of rock torn from the cliffs lay in the stream below.

Passing down from the rocks to the sands, I rode along the bank to the bridge of boats at Djezireh, and crossed into the town about half-past nine on the morning of the 12th of June. I soon found the residences of my old friends, M. Costi and Mr. Kerr, and, receiving a hearty welcome from them, put up at their house. When I lost myself on the Jebel Abjad I also lost sight of my luggage and antiquities, and now I waited at Djezireh until they arrived. Almost my only amusement was to sit on the top of M. Costi's house and watch the evolutions of a detachment of Turkish soldiers then encamped on the pebbly beach between Djezireh and the Tigris. On the other side of the Tigris, past some gently sloping hills, stood the Jebel Djudi, or Deluge Mountains. In these mountains they have found coal and bitumen, which may account for the tradition of the ark being localized here. In the valley at the foot of Jebel Djudi there is a village where, according to the popular tradition, Noah lived after the deluge and planted his vineyard. When I was in the East mining operations were going on at the Jebel Djudi, and many absurd stories were in circulation among the people. One of these reports was to the effect that a miner at work on Jebel Djudi had suddenly come on an ancient door buried in the earth, and that they had telegraphed to Constantinople before venturing to open it. In the East, in times of trouble and expected attack, it is customary to bury treasures, and the people are always dreaming of such hoards. Next day, the 13th of June, my luggage arrived safely, and at six in the evening I started on the road to Nisibin.

M. Costi made up an entertainment at parting,

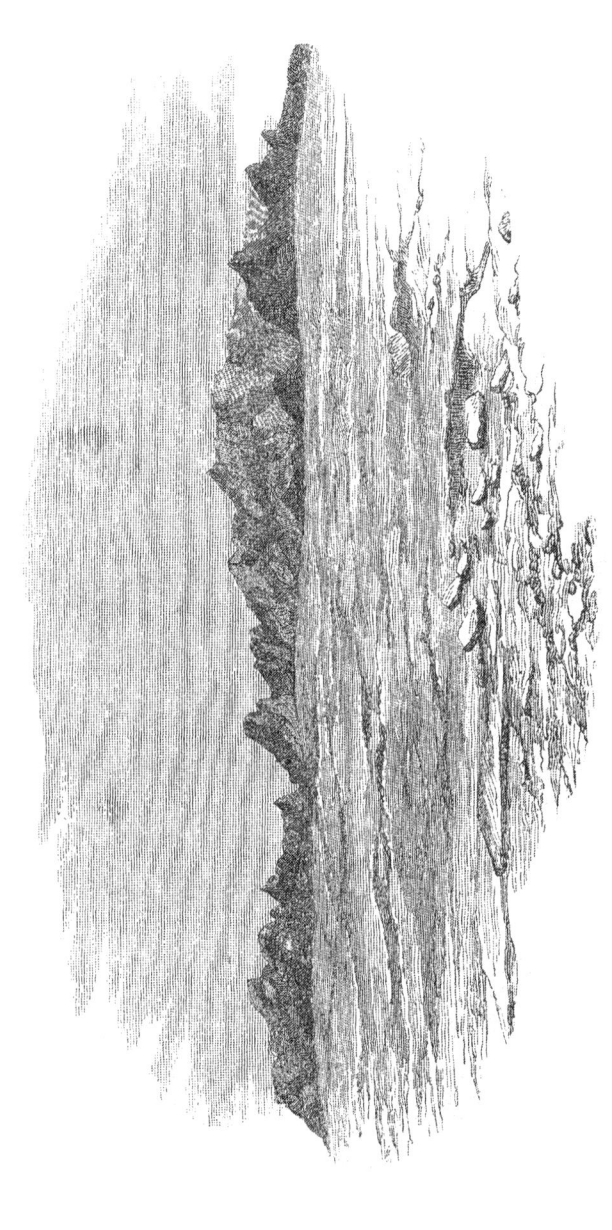

The Jebel Djudi or Deluge Mountains.

consisting of a lamb stuffed and roasted whole, and we found an old garden under the shadow of some ruins where we partook of it, and I then got off on my journey. We wound up the mountain road which ascends the side of the gorge in which Djezireh is situated; through the trees we saw the stream, looking charming in the evening light, and then passing out of sight of this, we rode along undulating plains, strewn here and there with glacial boulders, and arrived at Tellibel, where we had stayed on the journey out. Leaving Tellibel, I rode to Deruneh, a miserable village, where we changed guides. I stayed the day at Deruneh and started in the evening of the 14th of June for Nisibin. The road here at this time of the year is excellent, and the riding by night enjoyable. Along the southern horizon I saw the reflection of numerous fires; the people of the villages having reaped their fields, were burning everything in their neighbourhood, that the desert Arabs might find no forage. The hand of the wandering Arab is to-day, as ever, against every man's hand, and their hand against his. During these nightly rides I enjoyed magnificent views of the heavens; Venus rose each morning like a lamp, and all the stars had a brilliancy with which people in northern climes are not familiar.

It was daylight before I reached Nisibin, and I found the town presenting a much more pleasing appearance than on my former visit. The spring had produced a verdure in the surrounding scenery which made a good contrast to its winter appearance. At Nisibin I saw, in passing, the mounds of the old Assyrian city and the columns of a classical temple. On the evening of the 15th of June I left Nisibin, but my horse falling lame I stopped in the middle of the night, and did not start again until five o'clock in the morning; even then my progress was slow, and it was two o'clock in the afternoon before I reached Dinasar. At Dinasar there are large mounds and ruins of minarets and other buildings, attesting the former existence on this spot of a large city.

At half-past three in the morning of the 17th I left Dinasar for Varenshaher, but, taking a wrong turn, travelled too much to the north on a much longer road, near the Mardin mountains; the result was I fell in with a region covered with worn glacial boulders,—these stones were black in colour, weatherbeaten, and pitted all over with holes, like so many great cinders. Riding over these was very fatiguing, and at six in the evening I gave up hope of reaching Varenshaher, and rested in some tents which fortunately stood near at hand. Next morning I started at half-past five and toiled again over this cinder bed, not reaching Varenshaher until midday. Here, while waiting for my luggage, the Turkish officer in charge invited me to take some refreshment, and while we sat together a man was brought in who had been attacked by one of the Circassian zabtis, or irregular troops. His clothes were cut through and covered with blood, and there were six long sword-cuts on his back, which presented a sickening spectacle, resembling a piece of hacked meat.

The Turkish officer sent orders to search for the man accused of this attack, and afterwards sat down to judge some smaller cases. Two men then came forward, and disputed about the ownership of a sheepskin, and made as much bother about it as if it had been a thousand pounds. After hearing the learned arguments in this case, I prepared to leave Varenshaher, and bade farewell to the Turkish official.

Varenshaher stands in the midst of the ruins of an extensive city; there are remains of fine fortifications, columns of buildings, arches and vaults, all of the same black stone which is so thickly spread over this region. I started from here at a quarter to four in the afternoon, and reached Tel Gauran in two hours. The chief of Tel Gauran received me kindly, remembering me from my former visit. While at Tel Gauran I saw a wandering Mahomedan holy man, or dervish; he was very dirty, very lazy, and very devout, and only interrupted his prayers to light his pipe or search for the vermin that annoyed him. Many of these wandering holy men are to be seen at this time of the year, and coming just after the harvest they are able to get better gifts from the faithful.

At a quarter to six in the morning of the 19th of June I started from Tel Gauran, and arrived at ten o'clock at a good village named Mizar. The chief of

Mizar was a stranger to me, but a hospitable man, who gave me a good reception. From Mizar I started in the afternoon and rode to Dashlook, where I met again the old lady who seemed to rule this village; she was the sister of the chief of Mizar, and had married the chief of Dashlook; in her house again I was well received. I made her a present of a pipe and some tobacco, as the old lady is an inveterate smoker. At Dashlook also there was a holy man, who complained that with all his sanctity he was neglected for me. I did not stay the night at Dashlook, but passed on in the evening to Yedok, and at six o'clock in the morning started from there for Orfa. Our road lay along by dry white rocks which reflected the glare of the sun and made the heat oppressive.

When we reached Adana, I turned into a fruit-garden and bought some fruit while I enjoyed a rest, then started again, and came into the plain in which Orfa stands. This region is so shut in by mountains that the air seems still and oppressive, and on this day the sun appeared to give an intense heat here, which was difficult to bear; the air seemed luminous, and floated in waves before the eyes, while any little wind that arose appeared as if it came from an oven. Glad to escape this I hastened into Orfa, which I reached about half-past twelve in the day, and visited Pastor Hagub, whom I have formerly mentioned. I talked over my work and various discoveries with the pastor, and then went with him to see some of the curiosities of Orfa. We came first to a beautiful stream and pool as full of fish as it could be; this is the Pool of Abraham, the inhabitants believing that Orfa is the Ur of the Chaldees, the birthplace of the Father of the Faithful. The pool is consequently held sacred, and no one is allowed to catch the fish with which it abounds. Passing from here we entered a garden and partook of Turkish coffee, and then began to ascend a rocky height on which the castle is situated. The road lay on the left, and formed a steep winding ascent reaching to the top of the rock on which the castle stands, but I saw before reaching the summit that artificial means had been used to make the fortress more impregnable. A deep and wide cutting had been made behind the walls of the castle, completely isolating that portion of rock on which the fort was built. In various places in the face of the rock, excavations had been made for tombs, but all these appeared to have been rifled. From the top of the rock we gained a splendid view of the city, which lay stretched at our feet like a panorama. We had to pass right round to the front of the castle to enter, and when inside found ourselves in the midst of ruins of all ages. I copied a stone covered with a Greek inscription, and further on came to two Corinthian columns standing in a heap of ruins. On the shaft of one was a Pehlevi inscription, and below it an inscription in Arabic. On the outside wall of the castle was another Arabic inscription.

Leaving the old city of Orfa about six o'clock in the evening of the 21st of June, I travelled along the rough, stony road leading to the Euphrates, and rested in the night at a village about one hour east of Tcharmelek.

Early the next morning I started for Tcharmelek, and arrived there about seven o'clock. Then, leaving Tcharmelek in the evening, I travelled towards Biradjik. Some of my people becoming sleepy on the way, and no village being near, we all wrapped ourselves in our blankets, and lay down on the top of a well. Before morning we had started again, and arrived about eight o'clock at Biradjik.

Biradjik, like most other towns on the route, seemed much improved in appearance by the change of season; the numerous small streams looked very refreshing, and the fruit-gardens were in excellent order. The whole town, in fact, had a superior look, so much of it being built of stone, different from the squalid mud huts so common in the East.

On the 24th I crossed the Euphrates by the ferry, and rode to Okusolderan, taking a different and better road than that I travelled on before; and next day I journeyed to Tel Karamel. In this part of the way I got into a rugged valley, between two lines of hills—a wretched road, full of stones and impediments. Turning to the right, out of this, I crossed to Tel Karamel, and found my caravan, which had come by a better road. On the 26th I rode from Tel Karamel to Aleppo, over a chalky region, and, entering the city, put up again at the locanda. I was now involved in a difficulty with the Turkish authorities, as the custom-house officials refused to let the antiquities pass. I was deprived of the assistance of Mr. Skene, the English consul, as he was away on a holiday; but I showed my firman, to prove my right to the antiquities, and the customs officers said, if I would unpack all the antiquities, and show the things to them at the custom-house, they would give me a letter to the port to pass the things. I accordingly opened all my boxes, and, having new boxes made there, repacked the antiquities. The Turkish officers laughed at the appearance of the old fragments of inscriptions, and called them rubbish, making fun at the idea of taking care of such things. They gave me the letter to the port of Alexandretta; but although the things were worthless in their eyes, they could not resist the temptation to play me false, and I found later, on presenting my letter, that it was an order to seize my boxes. On the 1st of July, in the evening, I left Aleppo, having engaged a caravan to Alexandretta. This journey was no pleasure, as I rode a wretched beast, which had a fixed idea that the true road always lay to the left of where I wanted him to go. He had a queer, pump-handle motion, and was inclined to drop on his knees on the slightest occasion. My first station past Aleppo was Elkod, and, leaving there on the 2nd of July, I rode to Afrin, where I dined under the cool shade of the trees. In the afternoon I went on to Ain Bada, where I put up for the night, and next morning started across the plains of Antioch. Most of the streams here were now dry, and the plain was in good condition for travelling. At Delebekir I left the plain, and began to ascend the pass of Beilan. For some distance I saw on the left the lake of Antioch, until, turning at the spot where the Aleppo and Antioch roads meet, on the way to Beilan, I lost sight of the lake, and passed along the right of a deep defile in the mountains to Beilan. At Beilan I put

View of Bay of Alexandretta from Beilan.

up at the new khan, which was just finished, and is excellent in accommodation and position. From here I once again caught a glimpse of the sea through a gorge between the mountains, and saw the vessel riding at anchor which was to take me home. At Beilan I met a number of engineers sent out by the Porte to survey the line of the proposed Euphrates Valley railway; but their presence here was a standing joke. Nobody believed the Turks would ever make the proposed line; and it was said that Turkey was seeking a loan in the European market, and as soon as that matter was concluded the engineers would be recalled, and signs of activity again cease. Before I returned to the East, it did happen curiously enough that these engineers were withdrawn; and I do not think anything has come of this survey, any more than of others which have preceded it.

On the 4th of July I left Beilan, and rode down the rocky path leading to Alexandretta, then along the spit of sand into the city. Here I called on Mr. Franck, the British consul, who was delighted to see me, and hear of my success. He went with me to the custom-house to present the letter for passing the antiquities; but when the letter was opened, it was found to contain an order to stop them, the Turkish officials having made me the bearer of a letter directed against myself. Mr. Franck, as British consul, now assisted me in every way. We showed the firman of the Sultan, but it was cunningly pointed out that even this was given with a flaw in it. We reminded the officials that the boxes were the property of the British Government, and took other steps, but all was of no avail, and the customs authorities ended by seizing the antiquities.

Such was the conduct of the Turkish officers to the agent of a nation which had been foremost in upholding Turkey. Deprived of the antiquities I had gained with so much toil, I at once took passage for England, where I arrived on the 19th of July. The antiquities were afterwards released at the request of the British ambassador at Constantinople, and were shipped by Mr. Franck for England, where they arrived safely, and were deposited in the British Museum.

Chapter VIII.

SECOND JOURNEY TO MOSUL.

Release of antiquities.—New discoveries.—Syrian robber.—Severe winter.—Tcharmelek.—Calah.—Dinasar.—Turkish conscription.—Abdul Kareem.—Irregular soldiers.—Nisibin.—Entertainment.—Dancing boy.—Derunah.—Post travelling.

AFTER the Turkish government had released the collection of antiquities, and they had arrived in England, great interest was taken in the results of the expedition, and the trustees of the British Museum, seeing that other portions of the Museum cuneiform inscriptions existed at Kouyunjik, directed me to return to Mosul and excavate during the remainder of the period of the firman, this concession closing on the 9th or 10th of March, 1874, and the trustees set aside a sum of £1,000 for this work.

While I remained in England, between my first and second journey, I made some interesting discoveries, partly in the old collection, and partly in the new collection which I had just excavated.

Among these were the fragments of an official Babylonian chronology, and a valuable portion of the Assyrian canon, referring to the period of Shalmaneser, King of Assyria. These were published at a meeting of the Society of Biblical Archæology, and the same evening the decision of the trustees of the British Museum was announced.

Under the direction of the trustees of the British Museum I left London on the 25th of November, 1873, and, traversing the same route as before, arrived at Alexandretta on the 9th of December. Mr. and Madame Franck received me very kindly, and my arrangements were soon made for going up the country. On the same day I bid farewell to the consul and Madame Franck, little thinking that for one of us it was the last time. Soon afterwards, while Mr. Franck had gone to England on business, Madame Franck was taken suddenly ill and died. I journeyed on the 9th to Beilan and put up at the khan, but the place was much duller than on my former visit; all the engineers who had been surveying for the railway had been withdrawn, and there was only the usual caravan traffic. On the morning of the 10th I left Beilan and travelled through the pass to Delebekir, intending to go on from there to Afrin, but my horses were such poor animals that I gave up the attempt and turned into Ain Bada, putting up at the khan. Next day I went on to Injerlikoy, and on the 12th to Aleppo. Here I received a welcome from Mr. Skene, our consul, and Mrs. Skene insisted on making up a basket of good things for the road, to refresh me on my journey to Mosul; the thoughtful kindness of my friends was afterwards of excellent service to me in the wilderness. While I stayed at Aleppo I met a gentleman whom I had known at Mosul during my former visit. He told me that things had changed for the worse since I was there; suspicion was entertained as to my object, and the irregular soldiers who were in my employ had been closely questioned as to what I had discovered and taken to Europe. One of these irregular soldiers, named Dervishaher, had been faithful and trustworthy while with me before, and I wished him to come and meet me on the road, intending again to employ him; so I sent a telegram from Aleppo to Mosul to ask him to come to Nisibin to meet me.

The country round Aleppo was now free from the incursions of the robber whom I mentioned in the account of my former journey. A reward had been offered for his apprehension, and a friend of his, the keeper of the mill of Tel Karamal, resolved to betray him for the money. One night, a little before my second journey, Gurro, as the robber was named, called at the mill, and was hospitably received; but while sitting at supper, he was set upon, and after a desperate resistance, overpowered and carried to Aleppo, where he was in prison when I arrived.

On the 15th of December I left Aleppo, and met in my course very bad weather. I travelled to a village named Achtareen and there put up for the night, departing next morning for Zambour, which I made my next station. On the morning of the 17th I started from Zambour, when the weather suddenly becoming worse I was enveloped in a storm of rain and snow. I galloped along to get out of this and soon descended to the bank of sand on the right of the Euphrates, but had to wait there a long time before I could get a ferry-boat to take me across. This difficulty was, however, ultimately removed, and I was ferried over to Biradjik, glad enough to get shelter. Next morning the weather looked unpromising, but I was anxious to get on, and started for Tcharmelek. We had scarcely got disentangled from the rocks round Biradjik when the storm commenced and gradually increased in violence. If there had been a convenient village on the road I would have turned in to it, but there was nothing in the way of a station until I came to Tcharmelek, a distance of about thirty miles. The storm was so furious that I could not see Tcharmelek even when I was close to it, and the first intimation I had of my approach to the village was from smelling the smoke from the native fires. I think shelter was seldom more welcome than it was to me on reaching this village, as my animal was exhausted and would not have stood the weather much longer. Our host at Tcharmelek ushered us through a low door into one of the tall sugarloaf-shaped houses, and soon made up a good fire of camels' dung in the middle of the room, round which we sat warming and drying ourselves. Here we were forced to stay the next day, as, although the weather was better, our animals and goods were not yet fit to start again. On the 20th I got off again and reached Orfa, where I had some trouble with my mule driver, who did not want to go to Mosul. Ultimately, I agreed to let him off at Nisibin, and started for that town on the 22nd. The road from Orfa to Nisibin is long and severe in winter, and there are very few good stations on the way. I made my first stage at Adana, and moved on the 23rd to Zibini. Here a curious circumstance happened: we were sitting in a hut, crowded round a fire in the middle of the building, as it was very cold, when one of the company in the course of conversation mentioned that in that neighbourhood there was a holy tribe, the men of which could lick red-hot iron without it harming them. I do not take any notice of such statements myself; but one of my party, against my wish, challenged the villagers to produce a man of this tribe and try his powers. Directly afterwards a dark sinister-looking Arab entered the hut, and I saw at once that he was the magician. The villagers produced a sickle, which was laid on the fire and heated until red-hot, and then the Arab, taking it up by the handle, held the glowing mass in front of him and started a chant or incantation; this was taken up by all the bystanders, and while they were repeating it the man put out his tongue and appeared to lick the red-hot iron over and over again, producing a seething noise like that of heated metal in contact with water. Immediately after this exhibition all the natives round, who fully believed in this man's supernatural powers, clustered round him, kissing his hand and the hem of his garment. I gave the magician a small backsheesh, which he showed no thanks for, and he soon relieved us of his presence and disappeared in the darkness.

Next day I went on from Zibini to Varenshaher, where I changed my guards, and in the afternoon I started from Varenshaher to find a lodging in the wilderness. This appeared to be no easy task; but we fell in with a chief going towards Varensha, and, offering him a cigarette, got into conversation, and induced him to show us to his tents, where we put up for the night.

This encampment was called Calah. Its chief was a man of business. He set me down as a merchant at once, and told me that if I would leave him a sum of money he would purchase for me all the wool from the tribes round the neighbourhood, and we might do a profitable business. I excused myself for the present from this venture, and next morning left the chief, who still harped on this string. One of the Arabs went a short way with us from the encampment to show the road, and after a good day's travel, I stopped at Dinasar on the evening of Christmas Day. At Dinasar I stayed at the same house I put up at during my former visit to this part. The reception room for travellers at Dinasar is on the upper floor of the house, and is reached from the courtyard by a flight of stone steps; the room is oblong in shape, one end being occupied by the chimney, the other by the door, while there is a raised platform on each side for the mats and carpets of guests.

On this occasion, I found one side of the room occupied by a Turkish officer, who had come on recruiting business, and I took possession of the other. After greeting each other, I had time, while waiting for tea, to examine my companion. He was dressed in the inevitable blue uniform, and buttons ornamented with the device of the crescent and star. Over his legs he wore a capacious pair of boots reaching to his thighs, and he had a long sword, which trailed on the ground. Otherwise he seemed rather sparely provided, but being a soldier he made himself at home wherever he went. The mission of this officer was in connection with the conscription, which is rigorously carried out in this part of the world. The Turkish government keeps up a force in Asia which seems excessive in a time of peace, and the conscription by which the army is recruited falls heavily on the Mahomedan population. The young men, the strength of the Mahomedan villages, are drained away into the army, and the wealth and population of the country, instead of increasing, in some places decline. There is, however, less reason to regret this as the army is recruited entirely from the Mohamedans, and their decay gives some hope for civilization.

The officer whom I met at Dinasar in pursuit of his mission, summoned to his presence the chief of Dinasar and the head man of the neighbouring village, and they attended, looking not particularly delighted with his business. Proceedings commenced by the officer drawing a large roll of papers from his pocket; and the learning of the military official appearing rather slender, he was assisted in deciphering the documents by an intelligent young soldier in attendance on him. After reading out the government orders to the chiefs, the Turkish officer made them a speech, reminding them of the result of disobedience, and calling their attention to the fate of Abdul Kareem. No blush appeared on the face of the Turk as he alluded to the death of the unfortunate chief, which he appeared to think was justly deserved. I invited the officer to take tea with me, and when my cooking apparatus, travelling bed, and other useful things were exhibited, his men broke out into exclamations of astonishment; but the Turk himself said he was well acquainted with such things, in fact, he had some precisely like them, only he had left them at Constantinople. Next morning I rose early to ride to Nisibin, and the Turkish officer happened to mount at the same time. He appeared to desire my company on the road, and deceived me by saying that the road he was going on was a nearer way to Nisibin, his direction being towards the Mardin mountains. I, however, had no idea of staying with him, and, putting spurs to my horse, was soon out of sight. A shower of hail now coming on, I turned into a village by the road for shelter, and was told the deception he had practised on me. Leaving a message with the villagers to turn back my caravan, I led my party across the fields, and regained the Nisibin road. The road to Nisibin from Dinasar is good; but the weather was a great obstacle, a strong east wind blew all day, and, being in our faces, hindered the animals a great deal, while the sharp storms of hail from time to time, driven in our faces by the wind, cut like pins and needles. At Amudia, about six hours from Dinasar, I put up for a rest and dinner, and after dinner, resolving to ride at once to Nisibin, directed the zabti, or irregular soldier who accompanied me, to bring on the saddle-bags afterwards, as there was no danger or need for his attendance on the road.

These irregular soldiers commonly attend Europeans travelling in the East in the capacity of guides and guards, and are very useful to the traveller. The men are supposed to be paid a monthly salary by the government for maintaining themselves and their horses, and they are appointed two suits of clothes a year. I suppose the necessary sums for these objects regularly appear in the estimates; but, from some unknown reason, very often the clothes and pay never reach the soldiers. I have known some men who had received no money or clothes for fourteen months. The appearance and condition of these men are sometimes most miserable: scarcely two are dressed alike, and scarcely two armed alike; some have gun and pistols, some only a sword or spear. The most remarkable points about them are their boots and shoes; all of course have something on their feet, but very often the two boots are not a pair, and sometimes they had one boot and one slipper. They are in every sense of the word " irregulars." In the section of country from Varenshaher to Derunah, most of these zabtis or zaptiya are Circassians, numbers of whom are colonists in Asiatic Turkey. These Circassians are called by the natives Chetchen; they are brave, fanatical, and inveterate thieves. When I informed my Chetchen that I would ride to Nisibin without him, the Arabs round also said there was no need of protection on the road; but a second Chetchen, who happened to be in the room, asserted that the road was sometimes dangerous. One of the Arabs at this answered, "Oh, no, there is no danger; and if there is any, then it is only from the Chetchen." This turned the laugh against the Chetchen, who are both hated and feared by the Arabs.

 I left Amudia with my dragoman, and we urged our horses to reach Nisibin. Coming in sight of a village built among the ruins of an ancient fort, about half way between Amudia and Nisibin, I did not stop to examine it, but rode past as quickly as possible, as the weather was becoming worse and worse. A storm of rain and hail was gathering. I was anxious for a good shelter, and therefore glad enough to see Nisibin, which I entered about four in the afternoon. I went to the khans, but they were in a wretched state with mud and rain. I tried the coffee-shop, but there was no accommodation, so I turned at last to the serai, and asked the governor to recommend me a lodging. The governor kindly gave me shelter in the serai, and the place proved tolerably comfortable. The room allotted to me was that in which official business was usually transacted, but it was similar in arrangement and appearance to the one at Dinasar. There was a good fire of logs at the upper end of the apartment, and altogether it was a welcome shelter from the storm, which now raged with pitiless fury. Coffee, after the Turkish fashion, was brought round, and soon afterwards my host invited me to dinner. While the repast was preparing, there entered a tall, powerful-looking man, and a youth, apparently about fourteen years old. The youth was evidently a dancing boy, one of a class peculiar to Turkey; and I saw that he and his companion had come to take part in a musical entertainment. Our dinner was a good one, served with the politeness and gravity of the East: it included various meats, fish, preserved grapes, beautiful honey, and wound up with pilaw or pilaff, a native dish of rice. After coffee had again been handed round, the guests began to drop in, and preparations were made for an evening's entertainment. Two musicians now entered, one having a tambourine, and the other an instrument called a kanun, resembling a dulcimer, the strings resting on two bridges. The performer sits with this instrument on his knee, and plays with both hands. The assembly included the rank and fashion of Nisibin. One officer present understood Russian; and a gentleman from the town who was present took occasion to inform me that he was a Christian. After the necessary tuning up, the tall man, who appeared to be the leader of the party, commenced the entertainment. He gave out a series of coarse jokes, and went through performances of a disgusting character, and when these had gone on for some time, one of the company presented him with a cigarette, which he eyed with some show of suspicion, and then proceeded to smoke: it was half filled with gunpowder, and exploded in his face, and he then pretended to be much injured. His performances produced roars of laughter among the audience, in which the gentleman who called himself Christian joined. Meanwhile the boy had retired and changed his clothes, returning to the room in a dress of faded finery, fringed all round, flounced, and coloured red and blue. Next followed tunes on the kanun, and songs in Turkish, Kurdish, and Arabic, in some of which the dancing boy joined. The youth then commenced dancing, and kept it up for a long time. His movements were rather odd than graceful: he swung about, waving his arms, and rattling some little brass bells attached to his fingers, jumped, capered, and rocked his head backwards and forwards on his neck, as if it was loose on its joint.

Music and dancing continued until a late hour, but the interest of the audience never flagged, and whether it was an obscene jest, a dreary song, or an idiotic twist of the head, it came all the same to the company. I was glad when the entertainment came to an end, and I was able to retire to my couch. Next day the storm raged as fiercely as ever, and I could not move from Nisibin, but on the 28th I resolved to start, in spite of the weather, and having sent on my luggage and animals early in the afternoon, only stayed to lunch with the governor before leaving. I had previously requested the governor to give me an escort across the desert, as I desired to go by the shorter road to Mosul, and he promised to do so, but said I must first go to Deruneh, and cross the country from there. He gave me a letter, which he said contained the requisite instructions to the governor of Deruneh, but on arriving afterwards at that place I found his instructions were to the reverse effect. This was the second time I had been treated in this way by a Turkish official. I engaged two zabtiya or irregular soldiers, directing that one should be sent forward with my luggage, while the other stayed behind to accompany me. Late in the afternoon I left Nisibin, and rode on to overtake my luggage, which I found not far off. It was raining heavily all the time, and I saw, on coming up with my caravan, that the authorities had sent out with them a guide who was ill with fever and scarcely able to sit on his horse. The man was wretchedly clad and wet through, presenting a spectacle which any one but a Turk would have pitied. I gave the poor fellow a present, and sent him back to Nisibin, after which, as the weather did not improve, I turned into the village of Arbat to rest for the night. At this place the people swept out a tolerable room for my party, but outside the houses the village was a wretched sight, and the natives were walking about with their naked feet in the mud, which was in some places a foot deep. Next morning, the 29th, I started for Derunch, but the travelling was a wretched job, partly from the state of the roads and partly from the fact that my caravan, which I had hired at Nisibin, consisted of poor animals quite unfit for my purpose. My efforts made little impression upon them, and it was night before I reached Deruneh. Deruneh is about midway between Nisibin and Djezereh and is principally a military and post station. I wandered all round the village in a vain attempt to find a shelter dry enough to put up in, but everything was in such a state with mud and dirt that I was forced to go to the governor and ask for apartments. The governor offered me a shelter, and as he was suffering from fever I presented him with some medicine. I delivered to him the letter from the governor of Nisibin, and he on reading it informed me that the order was not to send me by the short road to Mosul as I wished, but to send me on to Djezireh. I had now no help for it, as I did not know the desert road, so I had to be contented with going to Djezireh. Soon after I arrived at Derunch the post came in from Diarbekr, and as I doubted if my present animals would carry me to Mosul by the Djezireh road I engaged post horses for the journey. I desired if possible to go before the Tartar who carried the letters, and for that purpose started early on the morning of the 30th of December from Derunch; but the post horses are trained to run together, and those I engaged, finding their companions absent, would not do more than a walk. No amount of persuasion, in the shape of spurs and whip, had any effect on them until the Tartar came up with me just by Djezireh. He swung his great whip and gave a prolonged shout, and my animal joined his herd in a minute. I had no more trouble to make him go; he dashed through the small stream near Djezireh at a gallop, and landed me at the post-office in very little time. I now saw that it was best to go on with the Tartar, and told him I should like to accompany him, but he expressed a doubt if I could stand the fatigue, he and some others believing that post travelling was very rapid and tiring. I laughed at this, as it was evident from the little I had seen of post travelling that the Tartars did not exert themselves very much, and very seldom galloped until they came in sight of a town.

The same evening I left Djezireh with the Tartar, but took a slightly different road from the one I had travelled before. After passing the rocks near Djezireh we went to the village of Naharwan, outside which we waited while the guides were changed, then rode to the river Hazel, which we crossed, and went along the north bank of the river Khabour until we reached Zaccho, then fording the north branch of the Khabour entered Zaccho a little before daybreak. The night was cold and the journey without interest, as the darkness prevented any accurate observation of the country. Leaving Zaccho on the morning of the 31st, I went through the pass, where I had much difficulty, as my luggage did not sit well on the post horses, and in going up and down the mountain paths they upset it; this, however, was put right when we got into the plain, and we proceeded without further trouble to Semil. On the night of the 31st of December I rode from Semil to Mosul; during most of the time I was very drowsy, and slept on horseback, but I roused myself in the morning, when about half-past four I saw in the dim twilight the mounds of Nineveh; then putting spurs to our horses, we rode along by the walls of the old city, and with a shout of joy entered the town of Mosul about five in the morning of the 1st of January, 1874.

Chapter IX.

EXCAVATIONS AT KOUYUNJIK.

Ali Rahal.—Turkish governor.—Redif Pacha.—New policy.—Turkish demands.—Temples.—Curious pottery.—Early palace.—Roman bottle.—North palace.—Ruined entrance.—Perfect bilingual tablet.—Inscriptions of Shalmaneser I.—Palace of Sennacherib.—Entrance.—Library chamber.—Fork.—Historical cylinders.—Difficulties.—Close of work.

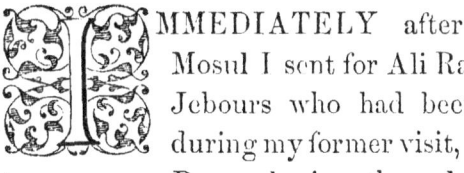IMMEDIATELY after my arrival at Mosul I sent for Ali Rahal, a chief of the Jebours who had been in my service during my former visit, and he soon came to see me. Remembering the salary and profit he had before, he demonstrated his joy at meeting me by falling on my neck, embracing me, and kissing my beard. I directed Ali to engage a number of men and proceed to Kouyunjik, and to dig over the earth on the spot where I was excavating last year. I then gave out the digging implements, and afterwards sat down to breakfast. Ali at once led a party to the mound and commenced work, bringing me soon after a fine fragment of a tablet and a bronze figure,

the firstfruits of the excavation. After breakfast I went to the serai to pay a complimentary visit to the governor, Abdi Effendi. Some officious person had already been to him and told him of my arrival, and when I entered he did not look very pleased at my visit.

Just before my return to England on my last expedition, the Turkish government, in pursuance of the ruinous plan of continually changing the governors, recalled the pacha of Baghdad and appointed in his place Redif Pacha. I was told that Redif Pacha understood French and was acquainted with something of European civilization, but instead of learning from the West I was informed that his policy at Baghdad was hostile to all foreigners. Before Redif Pacha was well settled in his government I left the East, but soon after I was gone he sent to Mosul, which is subordinate to Baghdad, to ask why the governor of that place had let me go, and what I had taken with me. The two irregular soldiers who had been with me during the former excavations were then called up before the court and questioned as to what I had discovered in the excavations, but they being ignorant men could give no satisfactory account, and application was then made to the French consulate. The French consul told the Turkish authorities that if they wished to know what I had found and removed they should have asked me while in the country, and that they were too late in moving in the matter then. Orders were afterwards sent from Baghdad to Mosul to impede me on my return, to place a guard upon me, and not to let me leave Mosul without giving up half the things I discovered to be sent to the Imperial Museum. I have stated that when at Aleppo I had sent to ask one of the irregular soldiers who attended me to meet me at Nisibin. On arriving at Nisibin I soon found he had not come, and when I reached Mosul I heard the reason. It appeared that on receiving my message, application was made through the French consul to allow the man to come and meet me, and the pacha answered that the soldier should be sent; but when the messenger's back was turned the Turk reversed the order, and said the man should not be permitted to leave the town. It is this line of conduct which makes it so difficult to deal with the Turks. When on my return to Mosul I visited the governor he told me part of the difficulty and declared that he should have to carry out his instructions, and he had therefore sent to stop my men from excavating until he saw me. I requested him to reverse this order to stop my men, which he did, and then we discussed the questions between the excavations and the Turkish orders. I declared that I was favourable to Turkey and should be very glad to see the Turkish government have a good museum, and to that end I should be glad to show them a number of good antiquities and assist them in getting others; but I said I could not part with half of my collection without spoiling it and doing them no good. I said I was sent to collect fragments to complete our inscriptions, many of which being imperfect were now useless, and I stated that if they took these fragments they would not get complete or satisfactory inscriptions, but they would prevent us from completing ours; and I asked them what would be the use if they had one half of an inscription at Constantinople while we had the other half in London? At this reasoning the Turks laughed; they said they did not understand antiquities, and if I pointed anything out I should point out worthless things to them and they must have half of the things I collected to make sure they had good ones. My visit ended without any satisfactory result, and from that time I was subject to perpetual annoyance. I was refused guards I could trust, the Turks saying that by kindness I had won the men to my interest; my movements were watched, a scribe as a spy was set over the works, and my superintendents were called up before the court and charged with concealing the antiquities.

I was informed that there were some in the town who ought to have known better, who fanned this ill-feeling, and told the pacha that I was only a newspaper correspondent and he might do as he liked with me. I must pass over the details of my disputes with the Turkish officials, and relate the progress of the excavations. My operations this time were confined entirely to the mound of Kouyunjik, as my difficulties with the Turkish officials rendered it unadvisable to attempt any other sites. In the large space extending over the middle and east of the mound where no building has been discovered I made some explorations and experimental trenches. On the eastern edge of the mound overhanging the stream of the Khosr were remains of sculptures and mounds which had yielded inscriptions stating that they came from the temple of Nebo and Merodach. This temple was built by Vul-nirari III. B.C. 812, and restored by Sargon B.C. 722. Here I excavated and found similar inscriptions, but I believe not in their original places.

Here I must remark that it should always be remembered that the site of Nineveh has been inhabited from the fall of the city until now, and care should be taken to ascertain, if possible, the original position of the inscriptions. I could gain from my short excavations here nothing satisfactory about the temple, but I found two inscribed bricks of Tiglath Pileser II., B.C. 745, which stated that they belonged to a palace of that monarch built at the bend of the Khosr, a description which applies precisely to the locality. These bricks, however, were not in their original position, and the building which stood here must have been raised after the Assyrian period. Broken fragments of sculpture from Assyrian buildings were found in various places, and among them a relief of a horseman and part of a gigantic winged man-headed bull. Here I also found part of a terra-cotta inscription of Sennacherib and some rude clay figures of idols. To the west of this position, and nearer the middle of the mound, I placed several trenches. In one place I found a small chamber like a shrine, solidly built of stones and cement, the walls plastered over and covered with a pattern of lines disposed in lozenges. The shape of the chamber was square, two corners being ornamented with square pilasters, and at one end was a large circular recess. In the chamber I found a bronze

BRONZE LAMP.

lamp with two spouts for wicks. I was not satisfied that this was really an Assyrian building, although it may possibly have been one. Very near the chamber, I found the capital of a large column but traced no building to which it could have belonged.

Near the entrance of the great palace of Sennacherib, and close to the spot where the former excavators found a broken obelisk, I discovered inscriptions of Shalmaneser I., king of Assyria, B.C. 1300, recording that he founded the palace of Nineveh; and mixed up with these were remains of inscriptions belonging to the same monarch, stating that he restored the temple of Ishtar. From the same spot came inscriptions of his son, Tugulti-ninip, the conqueror of Babylonia, relating that he also restored the temple of Ishtar; and inscriptions to the same purport of the monarchs Assurnazir-pal, B.C. 885, and Shalmaneser II., B.C. 860.

North of this spot I came on some very curious pottery ornamented with figures laid on the clay, the nature of which will best be shown by the accom-

POTTERY FROM KOUYUNJIK.

panying figure. Between the chambers in the centre of the mound and the eastern edge the trenches revealed fragments of a palace and temple. The remains of the temple were most of them found in a square chamber, seemingly of later date, built up of stones from the Assyrian buildings near it. All along the walls were placed small square slabs with inscriptions of Assurbanipal dedicated to the goddess of Nineveh, none of them in their original position. Near this chamber I found fragments of an obelisk in black stone built into a later wall and many fragments belonging to a palace which stood in this neighbourhood: among these was an inscription of Mutaggil-Nusku, king of Assyria, B.C. 1170, and several fragments from sculptured walls with representations of

PROCESSION OF WARRIORS.

processions of warriors. To the north of this spot near the southern corner of Assurbanipal's palace I found the head of a female divinity, the hair arranged in bunches of curls on each side, the face exhibiting the usual corpulent style of Assyrian female beauty. In the southern corner of the north palace I excavated again for tablets, but did not here obtain so many as I did in my first expedition, but among those I did find, were some of great importance. One of the first fragments which turned up here was the opening portion of a copy from an early Babylonian inscription, giving the names of six new Babylonian kings, and some curious details of early Babylonian history. Some time later I found here a new portion of the sixth tablet of the deluge series. Finding this deposit of tablets not yielding very freely I struck new trenches round it, but was rewarded by very few fragments. One of the new trenches, however, came upon some later remains, including a beautiful blue glass Roman bottle with heads on both sides; and another produced a large vase of the Sassanian period, with two or three coins. This vase, which was perfect, and one of the largest dis-

Roman Bottle.

covered, I presented to the Imperial Museum at Constantinople. Further search in the southern corner of this palace revealed a ruined entrance with the bases of two columns in the doorway; one of these I gave to the Turkish Museum, the other I brought to England. When excavating this entrance I discovered a beautiful bilingual tablet, perfect, lying on the pavement near the entrance of the palace.

In the south-west palace I excavated at the grand entrance to see if any records remained under the pavement, but there were none. This part of the pavement had been broken through, and anything under it had long ago been carried away. I placed some trenches in the grand hall and found a fragment of inscription, and further on in the palace I found several fragments. My principal excavation was, however, carried on over what Layard calls the library chamber of this palace. Layard, who discovered the library chamber, describes it as full of fragments of tablets, up to a foot or more from the floor. This chamber Layard cleared out and brought its treasures to England, but I was satisfied on examining the collection at the British Museum that not one half of the library had been brought home, and steadily adhered to the belief that the rest of the tablets must be in the palace of Sennacherib. In accordance with this idea I found nearly three thousand fragments of tablets in the chambers round Layard's library chamber, and from the positions of these fragments I am led to the opinion that the library was not originally in these chambers but in an upper storey of the palace, and that on the ruin of the building they fell into the chambers below. Some of the chambers in which I found inscribed tablets had no communication with each other, while fragments of the same tablets were in them; and looking at this fact, and the positions and distribution of the fragments, the hypothesis that the library was in the upper storey of the palace seems to me the most likely one.

Believing that the tablets were scattered over a wide area, I resolved to take a section of the palace round the region of the so-called library chamber,

AT KOUYUNJIK.

and clear away the top earth entirely, as the ground was so perforated by the old tunnels and trenches that further operations of this sort were impossible. Having to clear away the top earth my labour was very much heavier than that of the former excavators, and, necessarily, for some time my operations were slow and my results small, but on reaching the level of the palace I was amply rewarded by the discovery of numerous valuable antiquities. I commenced operations by drawing an oval line about 700 feet round as the boundary of my field of operations. This line passed over the centre of the south-east court of the palace, then turning west ran along north of the long gallery where Layard found the representations of the dragging along of the winged figures and building the mounds, then turning south it went along over the chambers at the west of the palace, and turning eastward ran along to the bottom of the south-east court. I placed my men along this line in companies, and directed them to first remove the hills of rubbish thrown upon the surface of the mound by the former excavators, carefully searching over the earth to recover any fragments of cuneiform inscriptions which might still remain in the rubbish. These hills of earth and fragments were considerable, and some time elapsed before we got rid of them. When these were cleared out of the way I commenced attacking the mound itself, clearing away layer after layer of the rubbish which had accumulated in ancient times over the palace. At first in removing this very little was found, and what did turn up consisted principally of modern objects—coins, pottery, and glass—but on going deeper we came to the Assyrian cuneiform tablets, rare and fragmentary at first, more plentiful as we descended to greater depths. In the south-eastern court I penetrated to the pavement, and in front of one of the entrances on the western side I discovered the lintel of a doorway; it was formed of a block of stone six feet long, and was sculptured along the face. In the centre was an ornamental cup or vase, with two handles; on each side of the vase stood a winged griffin or dragon, looking towards the centre, having a long neck and an ornament or collar round it just behind the head. Over the cup and the dragon was an ornament of honey-suckles. This curious lintel is the first Assyrian object of the kind which has been discovered, and I saw it lifted out of the excavation with much pleasure. In its fall from its elevated position it had broken in two, which rendered it easier for me to transport, but even then it required two donkeys to carry it.

TERRA-COTTA VASE.

In the long gallery, which contained scenes representing the moving of winged figures, I found a great number of tablets, mostly along the floor; they included syllabaries, bilingual lists, mythological and historical tablets. Among these tablets I discovered a beautiful bronze Assyrian fork, having two prongs joined by ornamental shoulder to shaft of spiral work, the shaft ending in the head of an ass. This is a beautiful and unique specimen of Assyrian work, and shows the advances the people had made in the refinements of life. South of this there were numerous tablets round Layard's old library chamber, and here I found part of a curious astrolabe, and fragments of the history of Sargon, king of Assyria, B.C. 722. In one place, below the level of the floor, I discovered a fine fragment of the history of Assurbanipal, containing new and curious matter relating to his Egyptian wars, and to the affairs of Gyges, king of Lydia. From this part of the palace I gained also the shoulder of a colossal statue, with an inscription of Assurbanipal. In another spot I obtained a bone spoon and a fragment of the tablet with the history of the seven evil

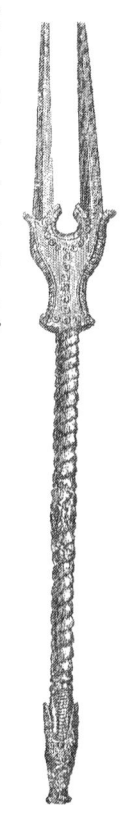

Bronze Fork.

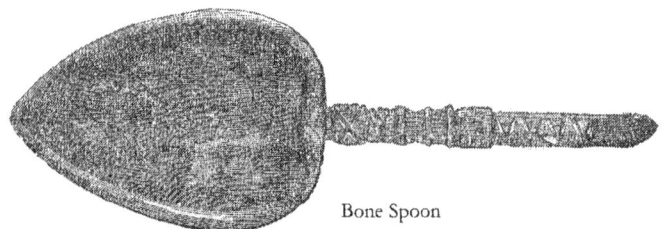

Bone Spoon.

spirits   Near this I discovered a bronze style, with

which I believe the cuneiform tablets were impressed. In another part of the excavation I found part of a monument with the representation of a fortification. In the western part of the palace, near the edge of the mound, I excavated and found remains of crystal and alabaster vases, and specimens of the royal seal. Two of these are very curious; one is a paste seal, the earliest example of its kind, and the other is a clay impression of the seal of Sargon king of Assyria.

DEAD BUFFALO IN WATER.

Near where the principal seals were discovered I found part of a sculpture with a good figure of a dead buffalo in a stream. Among these sculptures and inscriptions were numerous small objects, including beads, rings, stone seals, &c.

When I commenced the excavations in January I had only forty men, but I increased them every day until they numbered nearly 600, and when they were at work the mound presented an interesting appearance of bustle and activity. I was reluctant to engage so many men, as I could not exercise an efficient control over so large a number, but the short time I had for work compelled me to use every effort to realize as much as possible before the close of the firman. I have mentioned in the account of my journey the severe weather I met with on the road to Mosul. Similar weather continued while the excavations were on. Snow lay on the mountains in sight of Mosul, and on some days ice remained on the mound of Kouyunjik all day. Further up the country the snow was very deep, and in the gorges of the mountains attained a height of ten feet. The melting snows and heavy rains swelled the river Tigris, and the river overflowed large tracts of land on the east bank. During these inundations the bridge of boats was removed, and all traffic between the two sides of the river passed over in ferry boats. I had at one time to ferry all my men across the river for several days, at great expense and loss of time. At the beginning of February the excavations ceased entirely for several days, through the interference of the Turkish officials, and after I had recommenced a charge was brought against me that I had disturbed a Mahomedan tomb, and a Turkish officer was sent to examine the mound and report upon the subject. Directly I was cleared of this, I had a difficulty with the owners of the mound, who were encouraged by a third party to demand £250 compensation for my excavations. The agents of the British government had already paid in a lump sum for the ground, and they had no right to demand anything. I offered £10, which was ample compensation, or I would have rented the ground, but the owners declined these propositions, and carried the matter before the local court. Abdi Effendi, the governor of Mosul, then sent a commission to examine the mound, and report on the extent and nature of my excavations, with a view to fix an adequate sum for me to pay. The court and commission were prejudiced against me, but they were compelled to say I disturbed little ground, confining as I did my operations to the trenches already opened and paid for, but they said as I had offered £10 the court could not fix on a lower sum, and judged me to pay £12. I at once paid this money, telling them that I was not concerned about a pound more or less, but wished to be on good terms with them. After this I found out one of my chiefs, Ali Rahal, in dishonest practices, and dismissed him. He having a large following among the Jebour Arabs gave me afterwards some trouble, and to quiet matters I was obliged to again take him into my service. Just before the close of my excavations an accusation of blasphemy was brought against my dragoman, and as I saw that the governor listened to these stories, and that those around me took advantage of the hostility of the officials to cheat me, I closed the excavations on the 12th of March, and prepared to leave for England. Abdi Effendi, the governor of Mosul, refused, however, to let me go unless I gave him half the antiquities. I told him I could not comply with this, and I was kept at Mosul in consequence until the 4th of April. All this time the Turkish governor pretended to take an interest in preserving the various antiquities in the country, but this profession was only made to hinder me. The natives broke down one side of the northern gate in the wall of Nineveh, and the governor took no notice, although I called his attention to it. The ruin of this gateway is a great misfortune, as it was one of the most curious sights at Nineveh. After waiting nearly a month at Mosul, on the application of the British ambassador at Constantinople, the Porte granted satisfactory terms to settle the matter. I was to have six weeks' extension of time for excavations, and power to remove all discoveries excepting half of duplicates, which were to be given to the Imperial Museum at Constantinople. These terms, which I heard on the 1st of April, were very satisfactory, but they came so late that all my money was expended, and I was not able to recommence excavations. I therefore gave up to the Turkish officers the duplicate antiquities in my collection, and left Mosul on the 4th of April.

Before leaving the town, I pointed out to the Turkish officers who had charge of the collection I had given to the Porte, a number of fine sculptures and a colossal statue, which I recommended them to remove to Constantinople, but they said they would not pay for moving them; and I had even to give them a box to keep the smaller antiquities in which I had presented to them.

Chapter X.

RETURN FROM ASSYRIA.

Khan Baleos.—Mosul.—Departure.—Severe weather.—Stoppage.—Tel Adas.—Semil.—Discontent of soldiers.—Want of pay.—Durnak.—Crossing the Hazel.—Djezireh.—Circassian guides.—Their outrages.—Varenshaher.—Orfa.—Curiosities.—Biradjik.—Antiquities stopped.—Ride to Aleppo.—Difficulties with Pacha.—Release of boxes.—Embarkation.—Return.

HAVING gone so often over the same ground, I have only my troubles and difficulties to relate in this journey home. Having settled at last with the Turkish officials, and paid no end of backsheesh, in the afternoon of the 4th of April I left the khan Baleos, where I was staying, and went down to the Tigris. The khan Baleos is situated near the eastern corner of the town of Mosul, and is a very convenient place for travellers. Mosul itself is a large town surrounded by a wall and ditch, about four miles round. The city was an important one in the middle ages, but it is much decayed and the fortifications are in ruinous condition, the streets are as usual very narrow, dirty, and uneven, but there are some very good houses in the town. The severe winter weather had again flooded the Tigris at the time of my departure, and I had to cross my party over on ferry boats. No sooner had we reached the eastern shore than a storm came on, and after riding in it some time, finding it did not abate, we turned into the village of Kazekoi, and were obliged to stay there all next day as the weather did not improve. On the 6th of April I started from Kazekoi to reach Tel Adas, and my caravan proceeded all right at first, but a storm came on, and after riding through it for some time we reached a gully or rut in the road which passed across the whole country. The storm had filled this with water and it was utterly impossible to get the animals across, so I was obliged to turn and seek a village on the south side of it. We attempted to cross the country, but found the ground in such a state of bog that the mules sank over a foot in the earth, and sometimes got so fixed that they could not move. The storm continued furious, and I only got out of the difficulty by engaging some wandering Arabs to drag the animals out of the mud and help them along to the nearest village. This hamlet was called Kufru; it presented no attractions at any other time, but now in my need I was glad of any shelter and ready to put up with worse accommodation. After a night's rest we started on the morning of the 7th of April, our host, the chief of Kufru, going with me to show the way. The gully which we could not pass the day before was not so full of water now, and we forded it without danger. On this day I only made Tel Adas, as the animals were tired from the exertions of the previous day, and I wanted to dry my clothes before going further. To-day our lodging at Tel Adas presented an appearance like a laundry, all my clothes and other things being taken out of the boxes and arranged to dry. All these things being arranged, I started again on the 8th of April and rode to Semil. At Semil I found great discontent, as the zabtis, or irregular troops, declared that they had been paid no salary since the time when Abdi Effendi was appointed governor. Some of the men threw down their arms, and declared that they would serve no longer; but as I paid well for their services, I was easily able to change my guides, and went on from there to a place named Gulres. From Gulres I started on the 9th and went through the Zaccho Pass, then along to the east, ascending the south bank of the Khabour to an old high-crowned bridge, over which I crossed the river, then descended the north bank to a spot near its junction with the Hazel. Here, at a village named Durnak, I put up for the night. The chief of Durnak was a wretched-looking old specimen of humanity, whose appearance lent some colour to Mr. Darwin's theory, and he had a son as good-looking and well clothed as himself, but these people thought much of themselves because they were Mahomedans, and despised me as a Frangi, that is a Frank or Christian, and when the son did not immediately obey him, the father called out in anger, " Why don't you do it, are you a Mussulman or a Frangi?" The accommodation at Durnak was not first class, and I was glad to get away next morning to cross the Hazel. This stream was much swollen by the rains and too deep to ford, so we had to wait for a raft, which came in the course of the morning. This was the most rickety old concern I ever trusted myself upon, consisting of a few branches of trees laid on goat-skins; but I got over without any accident, and then went on towards Djezireh. Unable to reach Djezireh the same day, I turned to a village beside the Tigris and asked shelter, but this the people refused, and I passed on until I reached a swollen tributary of the Tigris, the name of which I do not know; I crossed this with difficulty, and ascended a steep hill to a village where I was again refused shelter. I started my caravan, and rode on again along a beautiful road with romantic rocks on one side and the valley of the Tigris on the other; ascending again a steep hill, I came to a village on the summit, and was enabled to stop. The place was not fit to sleep in, so I paid some Eastern gipsies to erect me a tent, and under that I slept. While here, a native band came to play before my tent, making a hideous noise; I told them I did not want them and that they should go away. These people answered that they must have their backsheesh whether they played or not, so I gave them some money to get rid of their noise.

On the 11th of April I left this village, which was named Kerook, and travelled to Djezireh. On reaching the shore opposite Djezireh I found the river Tigris flooded and the bridge of boats removed; I had consequently to wait for a ferry-boat to cross the river. At Djezireh I found a considerable change and great activity in the government offices; there was every sign of a new and efficient governor, and if this activity continues a better state of this part of the country may be expected. From Djezireh I rode to Sharabarazi and from there to Aznowa. In these districts the people were inhospitable and the accommodation bad, while the rains had rendered the roads so wretched that we had sometimes to drag the mules one by one through the mud and then wash them in the nearest stream. Slow progress was made, and on the 14th I only reached Nisibin, which I left next morning and travelled to Ibrahim.

My guides at this time were two Circassians, and on entering the village of Ibrahim the people said they would not receive them, and one old villager brought out his gun threatening to shoot the soldiers if they came into his house. After much bother I got another of the villagers to admit my party, and then, as we sat waiting for tea, the master of the house related some stories of the past exploits of the Chetchen or Circassians, which accounted for the aversion of the villagers to them. One of these stories was as follows. Some time previously two

Circassians called at the village and were entertained by my host, who after providing a supper for them offered them a bed for the night. The Circassians declined to stop through the night, and went on, as the villagers thought, to another hamlet; but they really only went to a ravine near, where they hid themselves until about midnight. In the middle of the night my host was awakened by the barking of the village dogs, and got up and went out with his son, each carrying a gun. They found the two Circassians had made an opening in their stable and were trying to get out a horse. The Circassians on being discovered fled and were fired after; but although shots were exchanged on both sides the darkness prevented anybody being hit. My Circassians admitted they were professional robbers, and listened with indifference to the complaints of my host; but when another native taunted one of the Circassians with having been driven from the house where they refused to admit me, the man roused and said to the native: "Beware, I roam these deserts like a wolf, and if I catch you outside the village I will murder you." And with these words of blood on his lips my Circassian turned to our host and asked the direction of Mecca, then, spreading his cloak on the ground, he looked towards the holy city and engaged in prayer as peacefully as if he did no violence. Such are the people I was forced to employ, and I was yet to hear more of their misdeeds.

Leaving Ibrahim I travelled along the desert towards Varenshaher, and got further to the south than in my former journey. On the evening of the 16th of April, after a long and tiring day's ride, I found refuge in some tents beside a small stream; the natives called the encampment Khazil, but the people shift about, and these names cannot be depended upon. From Khazil I rode on the 17th to Varenshaher, and on the way called at Calah, where I stayed on my journey out. The people here were glad to see me, and pressed me to stay; they told me they had been nearly ruined by the Circassians, some of whom had called and been well treated, after which, on leaving the tents, they had ridden off with the people's horses. My host at Calah had applied to the court, but could get no redress, as one of the principal officers was a Circassian and the judge or cadi had married a Circassian wife. The people of Calah said that having no redress they had resolved themselves to punish any stragglers of the Circassians who fell into their power, and they said if it had not been for my presence they would have seized my man. In the evening I reached Varenshaher, and intended to stay there, but found the place not very inviting. The governor had left Varenshaher on a visit to some neighbouring place, and the Chetchen or Circassians, although in the service of the Porte, had made up an expedition to plunder Varenshaher; the deputy whom the governor had left at Varenshaher was among the victims of this raid; one of the soldiers held him by the throat, while the others ransacked his place. When I saw him he appeared not to have recovered from his fright, and as he said the robbers were still prowling about I judged Varenshaher to be a bad place to stay in, and requested the deputy to give me a guide to Orfa, as my two Circassians now declared they would go no further. With the new guide provided by the deputy I started about eleven o'clock at night, but I had no sooner got outside Varenshaher than my guide and guard bolted, leaving me in the wilderness. I wandered on until, guided by the bark of some dogs, I found an Arab encampment, and here I got a shelter for the rest of the night. Next morning I resolved to travel without the government guards, and I got one of the Arabs to show me the road to Orfa, and he led me across the desert to a path which runs between Varenshaher and Raselain, a desolate road on which scarcely a tent appeared, and where there was very little traffic.

After a long day's ride I found some tents pitched beside a small stream, and rested there for the night; then starting again on the morning of the 19th of April, went along a fair road with ruins of old towns, and entered the range of mountains that girdles the plain of Orfa. On emerging into the plain I left my caravan and galloped across the flat, here about eighteen miles, to the city of Orfa. In Orfa I rested the next day, and called on the pacha, a polite and intelligent gentleman, who was always glad to see me. I was told that he was a bigoted

Mohamedan and strongly opposed to the Christians, but of course I saw nothing of this. He spoke to me of railways, canals, &c., and expressed the wish that some European company would make a canal from Orfa to the Euphrates, which would develop a considerable traffic. The pacha told me of a curiosity to be seen at Orfa, about which they relate a story worthy of the days of Herodotus. This curiosity consisted of two small figures, made of a peculiar shrub, partly trained and twisted, and partly cut into the form of a man and woman, very rudely done, and stained over to give them the appearance of having grown in that shape. The man who sold these articles declared that they grew in a field far away from there, and that anyone trying to draw one out of the ground would be killed by the noise they made, so the inhabitants, in order to obtain them, tied a dog by a string to each figure, and then went a long distance off. As soon as the dog pulled the string and drew the creature out of the ground the noise it made killed the dog, and the men coming up secured the curiosity. It is a sign of the intellectual state of this country that men who object to schools and Christian influence, believe such rubbish as this.

On the 21st I left Orfa and travelled to Dabun, and from there went on next day to Biradjik. At Biradjik the Euphrates was a difficulty; the flood of the river was enormous, and that day I could not cross. Next morning, after making my preparations and getting my things to the river, the custom-house people came down and declared that as my boxes contained antiquities they must seize them. I showed these gentlemen my firman giving me the right to the things; I showed them the order from Mosul, which stated that I had complied with all the demands of the Turkish government, and had the right to export the things; I showed them my government order for the road, directing all the functionaries to assist me on my journey with the antiquities: but it was all of no avail. I was dealing with Turkish officials, and they would not let the things pass. The utmost I could gain was that the boxes should be locked up under joint seals of the customs officer and myself. Now I resolved to cross the Euphrates with my dragoman and a guide and ride to Aleppo, a distance of thirty hours, to lay my complaint before our consul, Mr. Skene.

I started about half-past one in the afternoon, but the guide at once dropped behind and disappeared. Disregarding this, my dragoman and I rode on the rest of the day and all night, reaching Aleppo at six o'clock next morning. I at once laid my complaint of the illegal seizure before Mr. Skene, who promptly demanded that the pacha should send and order the officers at Biradjik to release the things, and Mr. Skene sent one of his own Cawasses to Biradjik with my man to see that the order was carried out. The pacha gave an order to release the things, but being a Turkish official he sent orders also that the Biradjik officials should send a soldier with them, and bring them to him at the serai or government house at Aleppo. When the things arrived at Aleppo I would not consent to their being taken to the serai, knowing that I had Mr. Skene to support me; and I sent the soldier to the serai without them, telling him they were the property of the British government and not of the pacha. The pacha did not make any further demand, as he knew he had no right in the matter, but he refused to let me leave Aleppo with the things, urging the ridiculous plea that my permission to export was signed by an officer lower in rank than himself, and therefore he could not recognize it. Mr. Skene, our consul, was obliged to telegraph to the British ambassador at Constantinople to ask the Porte to compel the pacha to let the boxes pass, and then, after the orders had come from Constantinople, the pacha declared he had not received them. On pressure from Mr. Skene he was afterwards forced to acknowledge the receipt of the orders; but even then our consul was obliged to demand that the letters from the pacha to his subordinates to permit the export of the antiquities should be open, that there might be no more tricks. Open letters were then given, which I presented at the port of Alexandretta, and exported the antiquities. During my forced detention at Aleppo I was often the guest of Mr. Skene, who so worthily represents British interests there. Mr. Skene has an extensive knowledge of Turkey, and great experience in dealing with the

Ottoman officials. Dr. Tomazini pointed out to me, during my stay here, some curious inscriptions built into the walls of old mosques and houses, and among these I found a new Hamath inscription. These texts are named after the city of Hamath, where they were first discovered. The characters in them are hieroglyphic, but quite distinct from the hieroglyphics of Egypt. At present very few specimens of these inscriptions are known; so that this one in Aleppo had some importance. No clue has yet been discovered to the reading of these texts. I visited also in Aleppo the Russian consul, a gentleman of considerable influence, who has a great taste for antiquities. I left Aleppo on the 14th of May, and arrived at Alexandretta on the 17th. Here Mr. Franck, the British consul, very kindly received me, and I stayed with him until the 23rd of May, when I embarked on a steamer for Alexandria, and on the 26th transferred myself from that to the Peninsular and Oriental Company's boat "Indus," on which I returned to England, arriving in London on the 9th of June.

Chapter XI.

THE IZDUBAR OR FLOOD SERIES OF LEGENDS.

Chaldean account of flood.—New portions.—Izdubar.—Probably Nimrod.—Antiquity of legends.—Conquests of Izdubar.—His illness.—Hasisadra.—The flood.—Erech.—Conquest of Monster.—Zaidu.—Heabani.—Humbaba.—Ishtar.—Divine bull.—Death of Heabani.—Izdubar's sorrow.—His journey.—The giants.—Hasisadra.—Account of deluge.—Building the ark.—The flood.—Mountains of Nizir.—The birds.—Translation of patriarch.—Cure of Izdubar.—His lament.—Ghost of Heabani.—Comparison with Bible and Berosus.—Remarks.

HESE legends, which I discovered in 1872, formed the subject of my lecture before the Society of Biblical Archæology on the 3rd of December, 1872, and attracted very great attention. On that occasion I principally translated the eleventh tablet in the series, which contains the Chaldean account of the deluge. About one-third of this tablet was then either mutilated or absent, and all the other tablets were in still worse condition. In my excavations at Kouyunjik I have recovered many new portions of these inscriptions, which number in all twelve tablets, and I now for the first time give an account of all the fragments.

There is still much required before the series will be complete, and I have as yet only identified six tablets out of the twelve, these are the 5th, 6th, 9th, 10th, 11th and 12th; I have found, however, a great number of fragments of the others which will serve to fill up and illustrate the legends. Independently of the fact that these tablets give the Chaldean account of the flood, they form one of the most remarkable series of inscriptions yet discovered. These tablets record primarily the adventures of an hero whose name I have provisionally called Izdubar. Izdubar is, however, nothing more than a makeshift name, and I am of opinion that this hero is the same as the Nimrod of the Bible.

The " Izdubar Legends " appear to me to have been composed during the early Babylonian empire, more than 2,000 years B.C. In primitive times, Babylonia was divided into several small states, and the rest of Western Asia was in a similar or worse condition.

So far as the fragments of the " Izdubar Legends " are preserved, they lead to the conclusion that Izdubar or Nimrod, a great hunter or giant, obtained the dominion of the district round Babylon, and afterwards drove out some tyrant who ruled over Erech, adding this region to his kingdom. Later, he sent and destroyed a monster which preyed on the surrounding lands; and a seer or astrologer named Heabani came to his court at Erech, becoming his close friend. Together Izdubar and Heabani destroy other wild animals, and conquer a chief named Humbaba, who ruled in a mountainous region full of pine-trees. Another chief named Belesu was next subdued, and then an animal called "the divine bull" was killed. Izdubar was now in the height of his power, and ruled over all the valley of the Euphrates and Tigris, from the Persian Gulf to the Armenian Mountains. Misfortunes now set in,—first Heabani was killed by a wild animal called a "tamabukku," the nature of which I have not ascertained; next Izdubar was struck with a disease, apparently, from the description, a kind of leprosy. Izdubar went on a wandering excursion to the sea-coast to be cured of his malady, and is supposed there to have met the deified hero who escaped the flood. In the new fragments I found at Kouyunjik, I discovered that this hero bore the name of *Hasisadra*, which is the origin of the Greek form of his name, Xisithrus. Hasisadra is supposed to have told Izdubar how to obtain his cure, and then the king returned to Erech, and again mourned over his friend Heabani. The legends close with a petition to the gods for Heabani, who, after his death, is in the lower region of the departed, or Hell. Hea, one of the gods, listens to this prayer, and releases Heabani, who then rises to heaven.

During the early Babylonian monarchy, from B.C. 2,500 to 1,500, there are constant allusions to these legends. The destruction of the lion, the divine bull, and other monsters, by Izdubar, are often depicted on the cylinders and engraved gems, and Izdubar in his boat is also on some specimens. The legend of the flood is alluded to in the inscriptions of the same epoch, and the "city of the ark" is mentioned in a geographical list, which is one of the oldest cuneiform inscriptions we possess. I have related how I heard, on the banks of the Tigris, what appeared to be one of the Izdubar legends, that of the animal dwelling in the cave; there appears to be another in the curious Arabic work called the "Stories of Nimrod," where we are told that Nimrod was by divine power struck with disease, from which he suffered torture, and ultimately died.

In my description of these legends I will first take up the unplaced fragments as they belong to the earlier tablets, and afterwards consider the more perfect portions of the story.

The legends of Izdubar open with the words: "The waters of the fountain he had seen, the hero, Izdubar." After this line it is not possible to place any of the fragments in position until we come to the fifth tablet, but there are many fragments which probably belong to this part, and first among these I am inclined to place the fragment numbered K 3200 in the museum collection.

This fragment is part of the third column of one of the tablets, and it gives a portion of the account of an ancient conquest of Erech, the city mentioned in Genesis x. 10. The following is rather a free than a literal translation.

1. his . . . . he left
2. his . . . . went down to the river

FLOOD SERIES OF LEGENDS. 169

3. in the river his ships were placed.
4. . . . . were . . . . and wept bitterly
5. . . . . placed, the city of Ganganna was powerless.
6. . . . . their . . . . she asses
7. . . . . their . . . . great.
8. Like animals the people feared,
9. like doves the slaves mourned.
10. The gods of Erech Subari
11. turned to flies and concealed themselves among the locusts?
12. The spirits of Erech Suburi
13. turned to Sikkim, and went out with *zabat* fishes.
14. For three years the city of Erech could not resist the enemy,
15. the great gates were thrown down and trampled upon,
16. the goddess Ishtar before her enemies could not lift her head.
17. Bel his mouth opened and spake
18. to Ishtar the queen a speech he made
19. " . . . . in the midst of Nipur my hands
20 . . . . my . . Babylon Bit-haduti
21. . . . . my . . I have given my hands."

This fragment relates an early conquest of Erech which is generally called in these legends Erech Suburi or Erech the "blessed." I conjecture that the lost portions of the tablet relate how Izdubar freed the city and obtained the government.

The next fragment is a considerable but obscure

portion of the story; it opens with a petition from Izdubar, who appears to have had a dream and desires to get a learned man named Heabani to come and explain it. Heabani is a sort of hermit, very learned and living a solitary life, and he appears to have been in the clutches of a dragon, which inhabited a cave or hole that it had dug out of the rock.

The legend is here mutilated, but it appears that someone begat or created a man named Zaidu or "the hunter," and he went to try to destroy the creature. Zaidu stopped three days in front of the den of the monster, but feared to encounter him, and turned back and told his father of his failure. His father in answer told him to go to Erech and lay the matter before Izdubar, which he did, telling him how he had climbed up to the den, but feared to attack the creature.

Izdubar directed Zaidu to go again to the place, and to take two females with him, that they might show themselves to the monster, and he might come forth and be killed. This was done according to the directions of Izdubar, and then one female tempted Heabani to come to Erech, in order to interpret the dream of Izdubar. Here the tablet reads—

a. He turned and sat at the feet of Harimtu.
b. Harimtu bent down her face,
c. and Harimtu spoke, and his ears heard,
d. and after this manner also she said to Heabani:
e. " Heabani like a god art thou,
f. Why do you associate with the reptiles in the desert?

FLOOD SERIES OF LEGENDS. 171

 g. I will take thee to the midst of Erech Suburi,
 h. to the temple of Elli-tardusi the seat of Anu and Ishtar,
  i. the place of Izdubar the mighty giant,
  j. and like a bull thou shalt rule over the chiefs."
 k. She spake to him and made her speech,
 l. The wisdom of his heart she turned, &c., &c.

After this Heabani goes to Erech to interpret the dream of Izdubar, and becomes the close companion and devoted servant of the monarch. Numerous fragments give parts of the exploits of Izdubar and Heabani; but it is only when the story reaches the fifth tablet that it becomes connected. At the commencement of the fifth tablet, one of the parties in the story is represented standing astonished at a splendid forest of pines, near the retreat of a person named Humbaba. Izdubar and Heabani are in conflict with Humbaba; and this tablet ends with the death of Humbaba, whose head is cut off. There is, however, not sufficient anywhere to make a literal translation.

The sixth tablet relates to matters between Izdubar and Ishtar, the goddess of Erech; who was the goddess of love and passion, both in man and animals. This fact accounts for some of the curious statements of the tablet. The following is a translation of the tablet:—

Column I.

1. . . . Belesu, he despised Belesu.
2. Like a bull his country he ascended after him.

3. He destroyed him and his memorial was hidden.

4. The country he wasted, setting up another crown.

5. Izdubar his crown put on (setting up another crown).

6. For the favour of Izdubar the princess Ishtar lifted her eyes,

7. "I will take thee Izdubar as husband,

8. thy oath to me shall be thy bond,

9. thou shalt be husband and I will be thy wife.

10. Thou shalt drive in a chariot of ukni stone and gold,

11. of which the body is gold and splendid its pole.

12. Thou shalt acquire days of great conquests,

13. to Bitani in the country where the pine trees grow.

14. May Bitani at thy entrance

15. to the river Euphrates kiss thy feet,

16. There shall be under thee kings, lords, and princes.

17. The tribute of the mountains and plains they shall bring to thee, taxes

18. they shall give thee, may thy herds and flocks bring forth twins,

19. . . . . . . mules be swift

20. . . . . . . in the chariot strong not weak

21. . . . . . . in the yoke. A rival may there not be.

The next portion of the legend is mutilated. It

records how Izdubar answered Ishtar. The remainder of Column I. (twenty-three lines) is too imperfect to translate; and then the legend proceeds as follows:—

Column II.

1. . . . his hand
2. to Dumuzi (Tammuz) thy injured husband
3. country after country is mourning his misfortune
4. Alalu bitru also thou didst love
5. thou didst strike him, and his wings thou breakest
6. He stood in the forest, and begged for his wings.

In the succeeding lines various amours of Ishtar are described. These I do not give, as their details are not suited for general reading. Izdubar concludes his speech by refusing to have anything to do with her. The legend then proceeds:—

36. Ishtar this heard, and
37. Ishtar was angry, and to heaven she ascended.
38. and Ishtar went to the presence of Anu her father,
39. to the presence of Anunit her mother she went, and said:
40. "Father Izdubar hates me, and

Column IV.

1. Izdubar despises my beauty,
2. my beauty and my charms."

There followed here a fragmentary dialogue between Ishtar and her father Anu, and she petitions her father to make a winged bull, to be the instrument of her vengeance against Izdubar.

The god Anu made the winged bull, and then commenced a contest between Izdubar and this animal. This contest is related on the mutilated fragments of the fourth column, and then on the fifth column and eighth line the legend is again perfect and reads:—

Column V.

8. And Ishtar ascended unto the wall of Erech Suburi,

9. destroyed the covering and uttered a curse:

10. "I curse Izdubar who dwells here, and the winged bull has slain."

11. Heabani heard the speech of Ishtar,

12. and he cut off the member of the winged bull and before her threw it;

13. "I answer it, I will take thee and as in this

14. I have heard thee,

15. the curse I will turn against thy side."

16. Ishtar gathered her maidens

17. Samhati and Harimati,

18. and over the member of the winged bull a mourning she made.

19. Izdubar called on the people . . . . .

20. all of them,

21. and the weight of his horns the young men took,

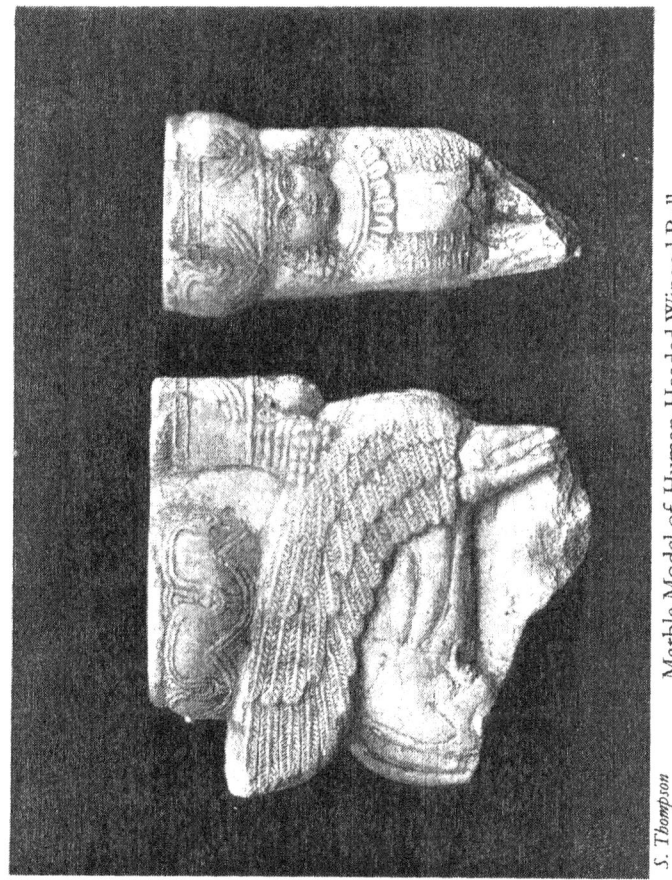

S. Thompson   Marble Model of Human-Headed Winged Bull

22. 30 manas of zamat stone within them,
23. the sharpness of the points was destroyed,
24. 6 gurs its mass together.
25. To the ark of his god Sarturda he dedicated it;
26. he took it in and worshipped at his fire;
27. in the river Euphrates they washed their hands,
28. and they took and went
29. round the city of Erech riding,
30. and the assembly of the chiefs of Erech marked it.
31. Izdubar to the inhabitants of Erech
32. .... a proclamation made.

Column VI.

1. " Anyone of ability among the chiefs,
2. Anyone noble among men,
3. Izdubar is able among the chiefs,
4. Izdubar is noble among men,
5. ..... placed hearing
6. ..... vicinity, not of the inhabitants
7. ..... him."

---

8. Izdubar in his palace made a rejoicing,
9. the chiefs reclining on couches at night,
10. Heabani lay down, slept, and a dream he dreamed.
11. Heabani spake and the dream he explained,
12. and said to Izdubar.

This is the close of the sixth tablet, and the seventh one opened with the dream of Heabani. Of the seventh tablet I have only recovered the first line which opens the speech of Heabani,—

"Seer why do the great gods take council?"

I am doubtful also if I have found any portion of the eighth tablet; but I have provisionally placed in it a fragment which I discovered in Sennacherib's palace at Kouyunjik, this fragment has, however, relations with the story of Humbaba.

The general tenor of the fragments enables me to say two things were related in the eighth tablet; one was the illness of Izdubar, which is related on the fragment here given, and the other was the death of Heabani, over whom Izdubar mourns bitterly.

The fragment of the illness of Izdubar reads:—

1. Izdubar in the . . . . . .
2. The goddess injurer of men upon him struck,
3. and in his limbs he died.
4. He spake, and said to his seer:
5. "Seer, thou dost not ask me why I am naked;
6. Thou dost not inquire of me why I am spoiled;
7. God will not depart; why do my limbs burn.
8. Seer, I saw a third dream;
9. And the dream which I saw entirely disappeared.
10. He invoked the god of the earth and desired death.
11. A thunder cloud came out of the darkness;
12. The lightning struck and kindled a fire;
13. and came out the shadow of death,
14. It disappeared the fire sank.

15. . . . . . . struck it and it turned to a palm tree.

16. . . . . . . and in the desert, thy lord was proceeding."

17. And Heabani the dream considered and said to Izdubar.

After this Heabani was struck down and killed, which added to the misfortune of Izdubar. Tambukku and Mikke are said to have killed Heabani; but who or what they were, the record is too mutilated to show, they appear to be the names of some wild animal. The ninth tablet commences the lamentation of Izdubar over his misfortunes, and his determination to go and seek Hasisadri or Xisithrus, a sage, who, according to the Babylonian traditions, had lived before the flood; and after that event had been translated, and now dwelt somewhere by the Persian Gulf.

The ninth tablet reads—

Column I.

1. Izdubar over Heabani his seer
2. bitterly lamented, and lay down on the ground.
3. I had no judgment like Heabani;
4. Weakness entered into my soul;
5. death I feared, and lay down on the ground.
6. For the advice of Hasisadra, son of Ubaratutu
7. The road I was taking, and joyfully I went
8. to the neighbourhood of the mountains I took at night.

9. a dream I saw, and I feared.

10. I bowed on my face, and to Sin (the moon god) I prayed;

11. and into the presence of the gods came my supplication;

12. and they sent peace unto me.

13. . . . . dream.

14. . . . . . Sin, erred in life.

15. . . . . to his hand.

The dream and message of the gods are lost, and there are no other fragments of the first column. The second commences with Izdubar in some fabulous region, whither he has wandered in search of Hasisadra. Here he sees some giants with their feet resting in hell, and their heads reaching heaven. These beings are supposed to guide and direct the sun at its rising and setting. This passage is as follows:—

Column II.

1. Of the country hearing him . . . . .
2. To the mountains of Mas in his course . . . . .
3. who each day guard the rising sun.
4. Their crown was at the lattice of heaven,
5. under hell their feet were placed.
6. The first man guarded the gate,
7. burning with terribleness, their appearance was like death,
8. the might of his fear shook the forests.
9. At the rising of the sun and the setting of the sun, they guarded the sun.

FLOOD SERIES OF LEGENDS. 179

10. Izdubar saw them, and fear and terror came into his face.
11. Summoning his resolution, he approached before them.
12. The first man of the third asked:
13. "Who comes to us with the limbs of a god on his body?"
14. To the first man, the third answered:
15. "His shape is divine, his work is human."
16. The first man of the hero asked:
17. . . . . . . of the gods the words he said
18. . . . . distant road
19. . . . . . . to my presence
20. . . . . . . crossing them is difficult.

These giants then discourse of the journey of Izdubar. And where the story is again legible, on the third column of the tablet, one of them is advising that Izdubar should go to Hasisadra, whom he calls his father; and he relates that he is immortal (established in the company of the gods), and has the knowledge of death and life.

COLUMN III.

3. to Hasisadra, my father . . . . . .
4. who is established in the company of the gods
5. death and life . . . . . .
6. The first man his mouth opened and spake,
7. and said to . . . . . .
8. "Is it not Izdubar . . . . . .
9. who to the country anyone comes . . . . . .

On the fourth column Izdubar prays to these giants; and the first one directs him the way to seek after Hasisadra. On the fifth column, this journey is related; the whole of it is much mutilated, and only some fragments can be made out. The stages are related in *Kaspu*, or lengths of from six to seven miles. The road is said to be shrouded in darkness, and there is no light along it. A fresh adventure is met with at every stage. In the ninth stage, there is a change, and he comes to splendid trees covered with jewels; and at the close of the journey (recorded on the sixth column) he arrives near the sea, at a place where there is a gate, and inside it a man named Siduri, and a woman named Sabitu. The tenth tablet commences with the transactions between Izdubar and Sabitu. Izdubar desires to pass through the gate, and Sabitu shuts it in his face. He then threatens to break it.

Column I.

9. To go on the distant path his face was set.
10. Sabitu afar off pondered,
11. spake within her heart, and a resolution made.
12. Within herself also she considered:
13. "What is this message
14. There is no one upright in . . . .
15. And Sabitu saw him and shut her place?
16. her gate she shut and shut her place?
17. And he, Izdubar, having ears heard her.
18. he struck his hands and made . . . .

19. Izdubar after this manner also said to Sabitu:
20. " Sabitu why dost thou shut thy place?
21. thy gate thou closest . . . .
22. I will strike the . . . .

In the rest of this column, which is lost, there is an account of the meeting of Izdubar and a boatman named Urhamsi. Urhamsi undertakes to navigate Izdubar to the region where Hasisadri dwells, and on the second column commences a discourse between Izdubar and Urhamsi. They then procure a ship and start for this region, they go along for fifteen days, and Urhamsi tells Izdubar about the waters of death, which he says will not cleanse his hands. This is related on the fourth column.

Column IV.

1. Urhamsi after this manner also said to Izdubar:
2. "The tablets Izdubar . . . .
3. the waters of death will not cleanse thy hands . . . . .
4. the second time, the third time, and the fourth time, Izdubar carried his breaches
5. the fifth, sixth, and seventh time, Izdubar carried his breaches.
6. the eighth, ninth, and tenth time, Izdubar carried his breaches
7. the eleventh, and twelfth time, Izdubar carried his breaches.
8. the twelfth time Izdubar ended his breaches
9. And he freed his body? to . . . .

10. Izdubar did violence . . . .
11. in his head affliction was ended ?
12. Hasisadra afar off pondered.
13. spake within his heart and a resolution made.
14. Within himself also he considered :
15. "Why to the shore does this ship not arrive ?
16. is not ended the voyage . . . .
17. the man is not come to me and . . . .
18. I wonder he is not . . . .
19. I wonder he is not . . . .
20. I wonder . . . .

These passages are mutilated, and it does not appear if the breaches of Izdubar were his sins or his illness, but it seems that his cure had now begun. We find from the passage in lines 12 to 20 that Hasisadra was expecting Izdubar and wondering why he had not arrived.

The next column introduces Izdubar talking to a female named Mua, and he tells Mua his feelings respecting Heabani and the history of their connection. The whole of this is too mutilated to translate with any certainty, but I give a conjectural translation to show the general meaning.

Column V.

1. Izdubar opened his mouth, and after this manner also said to Mua
2. . . . . my presence
3. . . . . did not rule
4. . . . . before me

FLOOD SERIES OF LEGENDS. 183

5. . . . . . . lay down in the desert
6. . . . . leopard in the desert
7. Heabani . . . . the same
8. a second there was not in the country.
9. We captured . . . . . Ninaru
10. we conquered Humbaba who in the forests of pine trees dwelt.
11. And again when . . . . . we slew the lions,
12. in the wilderness . . . . . became sick.
13. And he . . . . . was killed by the same,
14. he covered and . . . . . over him I mourn
15. like a lion . . . . . placed him in a tomb.

There are four other lines, and then comes the answer of Mua.

On the sixth column is related the meeting between Izdubar and Hasisadra. Izdubar has asked a question of Hasisadra, and the sage is answering him, where the legend becomes again clear.

Column VI.

1. I was angry . . . . .
2. Whenever a house was built, whenever a treasure was collected.
3. Whenever brothers fixed . . . . .
4. Whenever hatred is in . . . . .
5. Whenever the river makes a great flood.
6. Whenever reviling within the mouth . . . .
7. the face that bowed before Shamas
8. from of old was not . . . . .
9. Spoiling and death together exist

10. of death the image has not been seen.
11. The man or servant on approaching death,
12. the spirit of the great gods takes his hand.
13. The goddess Mamitu maker of fate, to them their fate brings,
14. She has fixed death and life;
15. of death the day is not known."

Izdubar appears to have been unsatisfied with the answer of Hasisadra, dealing as it did with the general question of life and death, and he desired to know how Hasisadra became immortal, he probably desiring a similar honour for himself. This introduces us to the eleventh tablet of the series, the most perfect and by far the most important of these legends. The tablet, of which I give a complete translation, opens with the second speech of Izdubar.

Column I.

1. Izdubar after this manner also said to Hasisadra afar off:
2. "I consider the matter,
3. why thou repeatest not to me from thee,
4. and thou repeatest not to me from thee,
5. thy ceasing my heart to make war
6. presses? of the, I come up after thee,
7. .... how thou hast done, and in the assembly of the gods alive thou art placed."

---

8. Hasisadra after this manner also said to Izdubar:
9. "Be revealed to thee Izdubar the concealed story,

FLOOD SERIES OF LEGENDS. 185

10. and the judgment of the gods be related to thee,

11. The city Surippak the city where thou standest not .... placed,

12. that city is ancient .... the gods within it

13. .... their servant, the great gods

14. .... the god Anu,

15. .... the god Bel,

16. ..... the god Ninip,

17. and the god ...... lord of Hades;

18. their will he revealed in the midst .... and

19. I his will was hearing and he spake to me:

20. " Surippakite son of Ubaratutu

21. .... make a ship after this .....

22. .... I destroy? the sinner and life ....

23. ... cause to go in? the seed of life all of it to the midst of the ship.

24. The ship which thou shalt make,

25. 600? cubits shall be the measure of its length, and

26. 60? cubits the amount of its breadth and its height.

27. ... into the deep launch it."

28. I perceived and said to Hea my lord:

29. " The ship making which thou commandest me,

30. when I shall have made,

31. young and old will deride me."

32. Hea opened his mouth and spake and said to me his servant:

33. .... thou shalt say unto them,

34. . . . . he has turned from me and
35. . . . . fixed over me
36. . . . . like caves . . . . .
37. . . . . . . above and below
38. . . . . closed the ship . . . .
39. . . . . the flood which I will send to you,
40. into it enter and the door of the ship turn.
41. Into the midst of it thy grain, thy furniture, and thy goods,
42. thy wealth, thy woman servants, thy female slaves, and the young men,
43. the beasts of the field, the animals of the field all, I will gather and
44. I will send to thee, and they shall be enclosed in thy door."

---

45. Adrahasis his mouth opened and spake, and
46. said to Hea his lord:
47. " Anyone the ship will not make . . . .
48. on the earth fixed . . . .
49. . . . . I may see also the ship . . . .
50. . . . . on the ground the ship . . . . .
51. the ship making which thou commandest me . . .
52. which in . . . . .

Column II.

1. strong . . . . .
2. on the fifth day . . . . it
3. in its circuit 14 measures . . . its frame.
4. 14 measures it measured . . . over it.

5. I placed its roof, it .... I enclosed it.

6. I rode in it on the sixth time; I examined its exterior on the seventh time;

7. its interior I examined on the eighth time.

8. Planks against the waters within it I placed.

9. I saw rents and the wanting parts I added.

10. 3 measures of bitumen I poured over the outside.

11. 3 measures of bitumen I poured over the inside.

12. 3 ... men carrying its baskets, they constructed boxes

13. I placed in the boxes the offering they sacrificed.

14. Two measures of boxes I had distributed to the boatmen.

15. To ..... were sacrificed oxen

16. .... dust and

17. .... wine in receptacle of goats

18. I collected like the waters of a river, also

19. food like the dust of the earth also

20. I collected in boxes with my hand I placed.

21. ...... Shamas .... material of the ship completed.

22. .... strong and

23. the reed oars of the ship I caused to bring above and below.

24. .... they went in two-thirds of it.

---

25. All I possessed the strength of it, all I possessed the strength of it silver,

26. all I possessed the strength of it gold,

27. all I possessed the strength of it the seed of life, the whole

28. I caused to go up into the ship; all my male servants and my female servants,

29. the beast of the field, the animal of the field, the sons of the people all of them, I caused to go up.

30. A flood Shamas made and

31. he spake saying in the night: "I will cause it to rain heavily,

32. enter to the midst of the ship and shut thy door."

33. A flood he raised and

34. he spake saying in the night: "I will cause it to rain (*or* it will rain) from heaven heavily."

35. In the day I celebrated his festival

36. the day of his appointment? fear I had.

37. I entered to the midst of the ship and shut my door.

38. To close the ship to Buzur-sadirabi the boatman

39. the palace I gave with its goods.

---

40. The raging of a storm in the morning

41. arose, from the horizon of heaven extending and wide.

42. Vul in the midst of it thundered, and

43. Nebo and Saru went in front,

44. the throne bearers went over mountains and plains,

45. the destroyer Nergal overturned,
46. Ninip went in front and cast down,
47. the spirits carried destruction,
48. in their glory they swept the earth;
49. of Vul the flood reached to heaven.
50. The bright earth to a waste was turned,

Column III.

1. the surface of the earth like . . . . . it swept,
2. it destroyed all life from the face of the earth . . .
3. the strong deluge over the people, reached to heaven.
4. Brother saw not his brother, it did not spare the people. In heaven
5. the gods feared the tempest and
6. sought refuge ; they ascended to the heaven of Anu.
7. The gods like dogs fixed in droves prostrate.
8. Spake Ishtar like a child,
9. uttered the great goddess her speech:
10. " All to corruption are turned and
11. then I in the presence of the gods prophesied evil.
12. As I prophesied in the presence of the gods evil,
13. to evil were devoted all my people and I prophesied
14. thus: " I have begotten my people and
15. like the young of the fishes they fill the sea."
16. The gods concerning the spirits were weeping with her,

17. the gods in seats seated in lamentation,
18. covered were their lips for the coming evil.
19. Six days and nights
20. passed, the wind, deluge, and storm, over-whelmed.
21. On the seventh day in its course was calmed the storm, and all the deluge
22. which had destroyed like an earthquake,
23. quieted. The sea he caused to dry, and the wind and deluge ended.
24. I perceived the sea making a tossing;
25. and the whole of mankind turned to corruption,
26. like reeds the corpses floated.
27. I opened the window, and the light broke over my face,
28. it passed. I sat down and wept,
29. over my face flowed my tears.
30. I perceived the shore at the boundary of the sea,
31. for twelve measures the land rose.
32. To the country of Nizir went the ship;
33. the mountain of Nizir stopped the ship, and to pass over it it was not able.
34. The first day, and the second day, the mountain of Nizir the same.
35. The third day, and the fourth day, the mountain of Nizir the same.
36. The fifth, and sixth, the mountain of Nizir the same.
37. On the seventh day in the course of it

38. I sent forth a dove and it left. The dove went and turned, and

39. a resting-place it did not find, and it returned.

40. I sent forth a swallow and it left. The swallow went and turned, and

41. a resting-place it did not find, and it returned.

42. I sent forth a raven and it left.

43. The raven went, and the corpses on the water it saw, and

44. it did eat, it swam, and wandered away, and did not return.

45. I sent the animals forth to the four winds, I poured out a libation,

46. I built an altar on the peak of the mountain,

47. by sevens herbs I cut,

48. at the bottom of them I placed reeds, pines, and simgar.

49. The gods collected at its burning, the gods collected at its good burning;

50. the gods like flies over the sacrifice gathered.

51. From of old also the great god in his course

52. The great brightness of Anu had created. When the glory

53. of those gods the charm round my neck would not repel;

COLUMN IV.

1. in those days I prayed for I could never repel them.

2. May the gods come to my altar,

3. may Bel not come to my altar,

4. for he did not consider and had made a deluge,

5. and my people he had consigned to the deep.

6. From of old also Bel in his course

7. saw the ship, and went Bel with anger filled to the gods and spirits:

8. " Let not anyone come out alive, let not a man be saved from the deep"

9. Ninip his mouth opened, and spake and said to the warrior Bel:

10. "Who then will be saved?" Hea the words understood

11. and Hea knew all things.

12. Hea his mouth opened and spake, and said to the warrior Bel:

13. " Thou prince of the gods warrior,

14. when thou art angry a deluge thou makest;

15. the doer of sin did his sin, the doer of evil did his evil.

16. May the exalted not be broken, may the captive not be delivered.

17. Instead of thee making a deluge, may lions increase and men be reduced;

18. instead of thee making a deluge, may leopards increase and men be reduced;

19. instead of thee making a deluge, may a famine happen and the country be destroyed;

20. instead of thee making a deluge, may pestilence increase and men be destroyed.

21. I did not peer into the judgment of the gods.

22. Adrahasis a dream they sent, and the judgment of the gods he heard.
23. When his judgment was accomplished, Bel went up to the midst of the ship.
24. He took my hand and raised me up,
25. he caused to raise and to bring my wife to my side;
26. he purified the country, he established in a covenant and took the people,
27. in the presence of Hasisadra and the people.
28. When Hasisadra, and his wife, and the people, to be like the gods were carried away;
29. then dwelt Hasisadra in a remote place at the mouth of the rivers.
30. They took me and in a remote place at the mouth of the rivers they seated me.
31. When to thee whom the gods have chosen also,
32. for the health which thou seekest and askest,
33. this do six days and seven nights,
34. like in a seat also in bonds bind him,
35. the way like a storm shall be laid upon him."
36. Hasisadra after this manner also said to his wife
37. "I announce that the chief who grasps at health
38. the way like a storm shall be laid upon him."
39. His wife after this manner also said to Hasisadra afar off.
40. "Purify him, and let the man be sent away;
41. the road that he came may he return in peace,
42. the great gate open and may he return to his country."

43. Hasisadra after this manner also said to his wife:
44. " The cry of a man alarms thee,
45. this do his *kurummat* place on his head."
46. And the day when he ascended the side of the ship,
47. she did, his *kurummat* she placed on his head.
48. And the day when he ascended the side of the ship,
49. first the *sabusat* of his *kurummat*,
50. second the *mussukat*, third the *radbat*, fourth she opened his zikaman,
51. fifth the cloak she placed, sixth the *bassat*,

Column V.

1. seventh in the opening she purified him and let the man go free.

2. Izdubar after this manner also said to Hasisadra afar off:
3. " In this way thou wast compassionate over me,
4. joyfully thou hast made me, and thou hast restored me."
5. Hasisadra after this manner also said to Izdubar.
6. . . . . thy *kurummit*,
7. . . . . separated thee,
8. . . . . thy *kurummat*,
9. second the *mussukat*, third the *radbat*,
10. fourth she opened the *zikaman*,
11. fifth the cloak she placed, sixth the *bassat*,

12. seventh in the opening I purified thee and let thee go free."

13. Izdubar after this manner also said to Hasisadra afar off:

14. . . . . Hasisadra to thee may we not come,

15. . . . . collected

16. . . . . dwelling in death,

17. . . . . his back? dies also."

---

18. Hasisadra after this manner also said to Urhamsi the boatman:

19. " Urhamsi , ... to thee we cross to preserve thee.

20. Who is beside the . . . . . of support;

21. the man whom thou comest before, disease has filled his body;

22. illness has destroyed the strength of his limbs.

23. carry him Urhamsi, to cleanse take him,

24. his disease in the water to beauty may it turn,

25. may he cast off his illness, and the sea carry it away, may health cover his skin,

26. may it restore the hair of his head,

27. hanging to cover the cloak of his body.

28. That he may go to his country, that he may take his road,

29. the hanging cloak may he not cast off, but alone may he leave."

30. Urhamsi carried him, to cleanse he took him,

31. his disease in the water to beauty turned,

32. he cast off his illness, and the sea carried it away, and health covered his skin,

33. he restored the hair of his head, hanging down to cover the cloak of his body.

34. That he might go to his country, that he might take his road,

35. the hanging cloak he did not cast off, but alone he left.

36. Izdubar and Urhamsi rode in the ship,

37. where they placed them they rode.

---

38. His wife after this manner also said to Hasisadra afar off:

39. "Izdubar goes away, he is satisfied, he performs

40. that which thou hast given him, and returns to his country."

41. And he carried away the breaches of Izdubar,

42. and the ship touched the shore.

43. Hasisadra after this manner also said to Izdubar:

44. "Izdubar thou goest away, thou art satisfied, thou performest

45. that which I have given thee, and thou returnest to thy country.

46. Be revealed to thee Izdubar the concealed story,

47. and the judgment of the gods be related to thee."

48. This account like bitumen . . . .

49. its renown like the sight of . . . .
50. when the account a hand shall take . . .
51. Izdubar, this in his hearing heard, and . . . .
52. he collected great stones . . . .

Column VI.

1. they dragged it and to . . . .
2. he carried the account . . . .
3. piled up the great stones . . . .
4. to his mule . . . .

5. Izdubar after this manner also said
6. to Urhamsi: "this account . . . .
7. If a man in his heart take . . . .
8. may they bring him to Erech Suburi
9. . . . . speech . . . .
10. I will give an account and turn to . . . ."
11. For 10 kaspu (70 miles) they journeyed the stage, for 20 kaspu (140 miles) they journeyed the stage
12. and Izdubar saw the well . . . .
13. For 13 kaspu (91 miles) to the midst of Erech Suburi.
14. noble of men . . . . .
15. in his return . . . . .
16. Izdubar approached . . . . .
17. and over his face coursed his tears, and he said to Urhamsi:
18. " At my misfortune in my turning,
19. at my misfortune is my heart troubled.

20. I have not done good to my own self;
21. and the lion of the earth does good.
22. Then for 20 kaspu (140 miles) . . . . .
23. . . . . . then I opened . . . . . the instrument
24. raised not its wall for . . . . I appointed"
25. And they left the ship by the shore, 20 kaspu (140 miles) they journeyed the stage.
26. For 30 kaspu (210 miles) they made the ascent, they came to the midst of Erech Suburi.

---

27. Izdubar after this manner also said to Urhamsi the boatman:
28. "Ascend Urhamsi over where the wall of Erech will go;
29. the cylinders are scattered, the bricks of its casing are not made,
30. and its foundation is not laid to thy height;
31. 1 measure the circuit of the city, 1 measure of plantations, 1 measure the boundary of the temple of Nantur the house of Ishtar,
32. 3 measures together the divisions of Erech . . ."

Comment on this remarkable story I must reserve for the close of the legends at the end of the twelfth tablet. The twelfth tablet opens with the words "Tamabukku in the house of the . . . . was left." There are then several lines entirely lost, and the narrative recommences half way down the first column with the lamentation of Izdubar over his dead companion, Heabani.

Column I.

1. Izdubar . . . . . .
2. " Where to . . . . .
3. to happiness thou . . . .
4. a seat . . . . .
5. like a dispersion . . . . .
6. The noble banquet thou dost not share,
7. to the assembly they do not call thee;
8. The bow from the ground thou dost not lift,
9. what the bow should strike surrounds thee;
10. The mace in thy hand thou dost not grasp,
11. the spoil defies thee;
12. Shoes on thy feet thou dost not wear,
13. the slain on the ground thou dost not stretch.
14. Thy wife whom thou lovest thou dost not kiss,
15. thy wife whom thou hatest thou dost not strike;
16. Thy child whom thou lovest thou dost not kiss,
17. thy child whom thou hatest thou dost not strike;
18. The arms of the earth have taken thee.
19. O darkness, O darkness, mother Ninazu, O darkness.
20. Her noble stature as his mantle covers him
21. her feet like a deep well enclose him."

There is a beautiful poetical feeling about this the earliest lamentation that has come down to us.

The story here again breaks off and where it again becomes legible on column ii. Izdubar is continuing his lamentation.

Column II.

1. " Thy wife whom thou hatest was struck;
2. Thy child whom thou lovest was kissed,
3. thy child whom thou hatest was struck;
4. The arms of the earth have taken thee.
5. O darkness, O darkness, mother Ninazu, O darkness
6. Her noble stature as his mantle covers him,
7. her feet like a deep well enclose him."
8. Then Heabani from the earth . . . . .
9. Simtar did not take him, Asakku did not take him, the earth took him.
10. The resting place of Nergal the unconquered did not take him, the earth took him.
11. In the place of the battle of heroes they did not strike him, the earth took him.
12. Then . . . . ni son of Ninsun for his servant Heabani wept;
13. to the house of Bel alone he went.
14. " Father Bel, Tambukku to the earth has struck me,
15. Mikke to the earth has struck me,

Column III.

1. Heabani who to fly . . . . .
2. Simtar did not take him . . . . .
3. the resting place of Nergal the unconquered did not take him . . .

4. In the place of the battle of heroes they did not . . . . .
   5. Father Bel the matter do not despise . . . .
   6. Father Sin, Tambukku . . . . .
   7. Mikke . . . . .
   8. Heabani who to fly . . . . .
   9. Simtar did not take him . . . . .
   10. the resting-place of Nergal . . . . .

This mutilated passage points to the idea that Heabani, who was killed, in vain tried to enter heaven. Simtar was the attendant of the god of Hades, and the other personages in this part of the story all have their appropriate offices. The spirit of Heabani does not rest under the earth, and attempts are made by petitioning Bel and Sin, to induce these gods to transfer him to heaven; but all is in vain.

After this in a small fragment of column iii. there is allusion to Zaidu and the female Samhat, who were mentioned in an earlier part of the story; and then when the legend reopens in column iii. application is made to the god Hea to bring Heabani up to heaven. The legend proceeds:—

   1. Simtaru . . . . .
   2. the resting-place of Nergal the unconquered . .
   3. In the place of the battle of heroes they did not . . . .
   4. Father Hea . . . . .
   5. To the noble warrior, Merodach . . . .
   6. " Noble warrior, Merodach . . . .
   7. the divider . . . . . .

8. the ghost . . . . . .

9. To his father . . . . . .

10. the noble warrior Merodach, son of Hea

11. the divider the earth opened, and

12. the ghost of Heabani like a prisoner from the earth arose

13. . . . . and thou explainest?

14. he pondered and repeated this.

Column IV.

1. Terrible seer, terrible seer,

2. may the earth cover what thou hast seen, terrible;

3. I will not tell, seer; I will not tell.

4. When the earth covers what I have seen, I will tell thee.

5. . . . . . thou sittest weeping,

6. . . . . . may you sit, may you weep,

7. . . . . . grow fat and thy heart rejoice.

In this obscure passage the ghost of Heabani appears to address the dead body of the seer. Further on, where the story is again legible, it reads—

1. " . . . . return me

2. from Hades the land of my knowledge;

3. From the house of the departed, the seat of the god Irkalla;

4. From the house within which is no exit;

5. From the road, the course of which never returns;

6. From the place within which they long for light;

7. The place where dust is their nourishment and their food mud.

8. Its chiefs also like birds are clothed with wings;

9. Light is never seen, in darkness they dwell.

10. To the place of seers which I will enter

11. . . . . . . treasured up a crown;

12. . . . . . . wearing crowns, who from days of old ruled the earth.

13. To whom the gods Anu and Bel have given renowned names.

14. A place where water is abundant, drawn from perennial springs.

15. To the place of seers which I will enter,

16. the place of chiefs and unconquered ones,

17. the place of bards and great men,

18. the place of interpreters of the wisdom of the great gods,

19. the place of the mighty, the dwelling of the god Ner."

The contrast here between the description of Hades or hell, and heaven, is striking and remarkable; and the whole passage shows the belief of the early Babylonians in an after life, and two states, one of sorrow and the other of bliss. From this point the legend is almost entirely lost, until the sixth column, which closes the series. The spirit or ghost of Heabani is still speaking here, relating his experience.

Column VI.

1. On a couch reclining and

2. pure water drinking.
3. He who in battle is slain, thou seest and I see;
4. His father and his mother carry his head,
5. and his wife over him weeps;
6. His friends on the ground are standing,
7. thou seest and I see.
8. His spoil on the ground is uncovered,
9. of the spoil account is not taken,
10. thou seest and I see.
11. The captives conquered come after; the food
12. which in the tents is placed is eaten.

---

13. The twelfth tablet of the legends of Izdubar.
14. Written like the ancient copy.

Thus, with a description of the burial of a warrior, ends these remarkable legends.

With respect to the age of these curious texts, they profess to belong to the era of Izdubar, and I am of opinion that they cannot have been composed long after his time. It is probable that the empire which he founded in the Euphrates valley fell to pieces at his death, and that this series of tablets was written in memory of his reign, during the period of confusion which followed. At any rate the allusions to this history during the early Babylonian period, prove that it already existed at that time. Izdubar, the hero of these legends, as I have already said, probably corresponds with the Biblical Nimrod. He is represented as a giant or mighty man, who, in the early days after the flood, destroyed wild animals, and conquered a number of petty kings, uniting their dominions into one monarchy, which stretched from the Persian Gulf on the south, to the land of Bitani or Bachtan, near Armenia, on the north. He is a representative of the beginning of empire, and a type of the great conquerors who succeeded him. Izdubar has a court, a seer or astrologer, and officers, like later sovereigns; and these tablets are of the utmost value, as showing the manners and customs and religious beliefs of his time. It appears that at that remote age the Babylonians had a tradition of a flood which was a divine punishment for the wickedness of the world; and of a holy man, who built an ark, and escaped the destruction; who was afterwards translated, and dwelt with the gods. They believed in hell, a place of torment under the earth, and heaven, a place of glory in the sky; and their description of the two has in several points a striking likeness to those in the Bible. They believed in a spirit or soul distinct from the body, which was not destroyed on the death of the mortal frame; and they represent this ghost as rising from the earth at the bidding of one of the gods, and winging its way to heaven.

This history of Izdubar appears to have formed a national poem to the Babylonians, similar in some respects to those of Homer among the Greeks. Izdubar himself was afterwards esteemed a deity, and at Nineveh I found part of a tablet with a prayer addressed to him.

The centre of the story of Izdubar is the city of Erech, now represented by the ruins of Warka, on the eastern bank of the Euphrates, between longitude 45° and 46° and latitude 31° and 32°. Here are extensive ruins of the ancient capital of Izdubar, surrounded by a wall nearly six miles in length. All round the city are vast burial-places, of such extent that they have led to the conjecture that the city was a holy place, like Kerbela and Nedjef in the present day.[1] Erech is one of the cities mentioned as the capitals of Nimrod in Genesis x. 10. In early times, according to an inscription which I recently discovered at Nineveh, it was called Unuk or Anak, the giant city, perhaps from its connection with the giant hunter Nimrod. Erech continued a great town down to the twenty-third century before the Christian era, when it was captured by Kudur-nanhundi, king of Elam, B.C. 2280, who carried off the famous image of Ishtar or Nana, which was in the temple there. After this the city passed through the same changes as the rest of Babylonia, and at a later period formed part of the empire of Assurbanipal. When the brother of Assurbanipal revolted against him, the city of Erech under its governor, Kudur, remained faithful to him, and Assurbanipal afterwards, when he captured Shushan, restored to the temple of Erech the image of Nana, which had been in Elam

---

[1] See Rawlinson's "Ancient Monarchies," second edition, vol. i. p. 85.

1,635 years. From Erech Assurbanipal appears to have transported to Assyria the legends of Izdubar, and these tablets were copied again in Assyria.

The principal incident in these legends, and the most important one in relation to the Bible, is the account of the flood. Izdubar is mourning for his seer Heabani, and deploring his inability to replace him, when he resolves to seek the advice of Hasisadra or Xisithrus, the sage who escaped the flood. The journey of Izdubar in search of Xisithrus is curious as showing that the Babylonians, although learned in some things, had no knowledge at this time of geography. They held the idea that at a little distance from them there were giants who controlled the rising and setting sun, and that the orb of day was looked after and sent on in its course by these beings, who had their feet in the lower regions of hell while their heads touched and probably upheld the heaven. Izdubar, after journeying through various fabulous regions, at last coming in sight of Hasisadra and his wife, asks the sage how he became immortal, and Hasisadra, after some general remarks about life and death, goes on to tell him the story of the deluge.

Having given a translation of this from the tablet, I will notice the account in the Bible and that which the Greeks have handed down from Berosus, with the view to a comparison with the cuneiform account.

The Biblical account of the deluge is contained in the sixth to the ninth chapters of Genesis; it is familiar to all and within reach of all, so I will only give the heads of it here.

According to the book of Genesis, as man multiplied on the earth, the whole race turned to evil, except the family of Noah. On account of the wickedness of man, the Lord determined to destroy the world by a flood, and gave command to Noah to build an ark, 300 cubits long, 50 cubits broad, and 30 cubits high. Into this ark Noah entered according to the command of the Lord, taking with him his family, and pairs of each animal. After seven days the flood commenced, in the 600th year of Noah, the seventeenth day of the second month, and after 150 days the ark rested upon the mountains of Ararat, on the seventeenth day of the seventh month. We are then told that after forty days Noah opened the window of the ark and sent forth a raven which did not return. He then sent forth a dove, which finding no rest for the sole of her foot, returned to him. Seven days after he sent forth the dove a second time, and she returned to him with an olive leaf in her mouth. Again after seven days he sent forth the dove, which returned to him no more. The flood was dried up in the 601st year, on the first day of the first month, and on the twenty-seventh day of the second month Noah removed from the ark, and afterwards built an altar and offered sacrifices.

The Chaldean account of the flood, as given by Berosus, is taken from "Cory's Ancient Fragments," pp. 26-9, as follows:—

FLOOD SERIES OF LEGENDS.

"After the death of Ardates, his son, Xisuthrus, reigned eighteen sari. In his time happened a great deluge, the history of which is thus described: The deity, Cronos, appeared to him in a vision, and warned him that upon the fifteenth day of the month Dæsius, there would be a flood, by which mankind would be destroyed. He therefore enjoined him to write a history of the beginning, procedure, and conclusion of all things; and to bury it in the City of the Sun at Sippara; and to build a vessel, and take with him into it his friends and relations; and to convey on board everything necessary to sustain life, together with all the different animals, both birds and quadrupeds, and trust himself fearlessly to the deep. Having asked the Deity whither he was to sail, he was answered, 'To the Gods;' upon which he offered up a prayer for the good of mankind. He then obeyed the divine admonition, and built a vessel five stadia in length, and two in breadth. Into this he put everything which he had prepared; and last of all conveyed into it his wife, his children, and his friends.

"After the flood had been upon the earth, and was in time abated, Xisuthrus sent out birds from the vessel, which not finding any food, nor any place whereupon they might rest their feet, returned to him again. After an interval of some days he sent them forth a second time, and they now returned with their feet tinged with mud. He made a trial a third time with these birds, but they returned to him no more: from whence he judged that the surface of the earth had appeared above the waters. He therefore made an opening in the vessel, and upon looking out found that it was stranded upon the side of some mountain, upon which he immediately quitted it with his wife, his daughter, and the pilot. Xisuthrus then paid his adoration to the earth, and having constructed an altar, offered sacrifices to the gods, and, with those who had come out of the vessel with him, disappeared.

"They who remained within, finding that their companions did not return, quitted the vessel with many lamentations, and called continually on the name of Xisuthrus. Him they saw no more; but they could distinguish his voice in the air, and could hear him admonish them to pay due regard to religion; and likewise informed them that it was on account of his piety that he was translated to live with the gods, that his wife, and daughter, and the pilot, had obtained the same honour. To this he added that they should return to Babylonia, and as it was ordained, search for the writings at Sippara, which they were to make known to all mankind; moreover, that the place wherein they then were, was the land of Armenia.

"The rest having heard these words, offered sacrifices to the gods, and taking a circuit, journeyed towards Babylonia.

"The vessel being thus stranded in Armenia, some part of it yet remains in the Corcyræan mountains."

In pages 33 and 34 of "Cory's Fragments" there is a second version, as follows:—

FLOOD SERIES OF LEGENDS. 211

"And then Sisithrus. To him the deity Cronos foretold that on the fifteenth day of the month Dæsius there would be a deluge of rain: and he commanded him to deposit all the writings whatever which were in his possession, in the City of the Sun at Sippara. Sisithrus, when he had complied with these commands, sailed immediately to Armenia, and was presently inspired by God. Upon the third day after the cessation of the rain Sisithrus sent out birds, by way of experiment, that he might judge whether the flood had subsided. But the birds passing over an unbounded sea, without finding any place of rest, returned again to Sisithrus. This he repeated with other birds. And when upon the third trial he succeeded, for the birds then returned with their feet stained with mud, the gods translated him from among men. With respect to the vessel, which yet remains in Armenia, it is a custom of the inhabitants to form bracelets and amulets of its wood."

These accounts of the flood are translated from the Greek historians, who copied them from the works of Berosus.

Berosus was a Chaldean priest who flourished in the third century before the Christian era, and who translated the records of Babylonia into the Greek language. As he was well acquainted with the history of his country, it is likely that his account would have striking features of resemblance to that in the inscriptions, and this is found to be the case. The traditions of several other nations give accounts of the flood, but none of them are so full and precise as the Biblical and Chaldean accounts; I have therefore omitted them, and confine my comparison to these three documents. The Bible, while it gives the account of the flood and the saving of Noah and his family, says nothing of the country he lived in, or the place where he built the ark. Now the cuneiform record supplies this information. It appears that after his wanderings, Izdubar comes to a city on the Persian gulf near the mouth of the Euphrates named Surippak, and this city Hasisadra tells him was the place where he himself had ruled and where he had built the ark. It is a curious fact that Surippak is called in another inscription " the ship city," or " the city of the ark," in allusion to this tradition, and the supposed maker of the flood was worshipped there as the " God of the deluge, Hea," Hea being god of the sea and the principal deity who brought the flood. These local names and traditions are a striking confirmation of the story of the deluge. It is also remarkable that Hammurabi, king of Babylonia, whose date cannot be later than the sixteenth century before the Christian era, conquered Surippak, and it is called in his inscription the " city of the ark," showing that the tradition was well known at that time, and in one earlier document the same name is given to the city. In this city before the flood it is related that there lived Ubaratutu, the Otiartes or Ardates of Berosus, and the Lamech of the Bible, and after him Adra-hasis or Hasis-adra, the Xisithrus of Berosus and the Noah of the Bible, a sage reverent and devout towards the gods. According to both the Bible and the cuneiform account the world was at this time very wicked, and the Deity resolved to destroy it as a punishment for its sin. In the Greek account from Berosus it is the god Cronos who warns Xisithrus of the coming deluge, and in the cuneiform version it is the Babylonian deity Hea, showing the identity of Hea with the Cronos of the Greeks. In the message of Hea to Hasisadra he tells him the size he is to make the ark, but the numbers are mutilated; I conjecturally read 600 cubits for the length of the vessel and 60 cubits for its breadth and height, but no dependence can be placed on these characters. The Bible, Genesis vi. 15, gives the length 300 cubits, the breadth 50 cubits, and the height 30 cubits. The account from Berosus gives five stadia in length and two in breadth. The inscription agrees with the Bible in giving the dimensions in cubits, but agrees with Berosus in giving two dimensions instead of three as in Genesis. The answer of Hasisadra to the Deity shows reluctance to build the vessel, which he fears will only bring him derision from old and young, and which he thinks is too great an undertaking. The Deity further encouraging him, he builds the vessel. The cuneiform tablet describes the building of the vessel, the details of which are not given in either the Bible or Berosus.

The vessel being prepared, details are given of the storing of the ship with food, and placing in it the treasures and animals: these matters are only slightly paralleled by the Biblical and Greek accounts. There is here a striking difference between the inscription and the Bible with regard to the nature of the ark; the inscription making the ark a regular ship, which is guided and navigated by boatmen, and it is launched into the sea, all the details of the story agreeing with the view that this is the tradition of a seafaring people, or at least of a people lying in the lowlands near the mouth of a great river such as the Euphrates. Floods here are frequent, and the people are familiar with these catastrophes, and the record describes the deluge with a precision and power in accordance with this position and the traditions of the country. The Biblical account on the other hand is apparently the account of an inland people, unacquainted with navigation; the ark is called a תבה, a chest or box, and not a ship, no guiding or navigation is mentioned, and there is no allusion to seamen.

In one point in the preparation already mentioned, there is an agreement between the Bible and the inscription; both represent that the ark was coated over inside and outside with bitumen. The Biblical account states that only Noah, his three sons, Shem, Ham, and Japhet, and their wives, eight persons in all, were saved in the vessel. On the other hand the cuneiform inscription represents Hasisadra as taking into the ark with himself, his wife, his servants, his young men or "sons of the people," and boatmen or seamen, in this agreeing with Berosus, who states that many were saved in the ark.

FLOOD SERIES OF LEGENDS. 215

In the description of the coming of the deluge there is a difference between the Bible and the inscription from the fact that the Bible gives the flood as the work of one God, while the cuneiform inscription states that a number of divinities were engaged in it. The description of the deluge itself is much fuller in the inscription than in the Bible or in the Greek text of Berosus, and the description is very vivid. As in the Bible, the text partly attributes the deluge to heavy rain. With respect to the duration of the flood, there appears to be a remarkable difference between the Bible and the inscription. In the Bible we read, Genesis vii. 11, 12: "In the six hundredth year of Noah's life, in the second month, the seventeenth day of the month, the same day were all the fountains of the great deep broken up, and the windows of heaven were opened. And the rain was upon the earth forty days and forty nights." And again in the 17th verse: "And the flood was forty days upon the earth." And in the 24th verse: "And the waters prevailed upon the earth an hundred and fifty days." Again in the eighth chapter and 3rd, 4th, and 5th verses: "And the waters returned from off the earth continually, and after the end of the hundred and fifty days the waters were abated. And the ark rested in the seventh month on the seventeenth day of the month upon the mountains of Ararat. And the waters decreased continually until the tenth month: in the tenth month on the first day of the month were the tops of the mountains seen."

And the 13th and 14th verses: "And it came to pass in the six hundredth and first year, in the first month, the first day of the month, the waters were dried up from off the earth: and Noah removed the covering of the ark, and looked and behold the face of the ground was dry. And in the second month, on the seven and twentieth day of the month, was the earth dry." Thus the dates are here given with great precision and clearness, and state that the deluge altogether lasted for one year and ten days. On the other hand the cuneiform text relates that the storm and flood prevailed only seven days, and that on the seventh day the storm ceased, then the ship was stranded for seven days on the mountains of Nizir, and on the seventh day Hasisadra sent forth the birds. Thus the cuneiform record only speaks of fourteen days for the flood, and even allowing that it did not end on the fourteenth day the time implied cannot be so long as the duration of the flood in the Biblical account. With respect to the mountain on which the ark rested there is again a curious difference. The cuneiform text states that the ark grounded on the mountains of Nizir, and the indications as to the place of Nizir fix it between the 35th and 36th parallels of latitude east of the river Tigris. The position of the mountains of Nizir is given in the inscriptions of Assurnazirpal king of Assyria.[1] The Assyrian monarch to reach Nizir started from Kalzu (modern

---

[1] "Cuneiform Inscriptions," vol. i. p. 20, lines 34 and 36.

Shamamek near Ervil) and crossed over the lower Zab near Altun Kupri. The mountains near there correspond to the described position of Nizir and probably represent the place mentioned in the cuneiform legend. The present tradition of the country places the mountain of the ark in the Jebel Djudi opposite Djezireh, far to the north of the Chaldean site, and the popular traditions of Western Europe place the mountain on the modern range of Ararat, still farther to the north. The more southern locality Nizir is most likely the spot of the oldest tradition, and the story has probably been subsequently attached to the other mountains as later peoples learnt the legend. The account of the sending forth of the birds shows some points of difference. In the book of Genesis it is stated that Noah sent forth a raven which did not return, and a dove, which finding no rest for its feet returned to him. Seven days after, he again sent out the dove, and the bird returned with an olive leaf in her mouth. After another seven days, he once more sent out the dove, which returned no more. The account of Berosus mentions the sending forth of the birds, but does not mention what kinds were tried. On the first trial the birds returned, and on the second trial they came back with mud on their feet, but on the third occasion they did not return. The cuneiform inscription gives first the trial of the dove which was first sent out, and finding no resting-place returned. Next that of the swallow, which returned in the same manner, and last that of the raven, which did not return. Not to pursue this parallel further, it will be perceived that when the Chaldean account is compared with the Biblical narrative, in their main features the two stories fairly agree; as to the wickedness of the antediluvian world, the divine anger and command to build the ark, its stocking with birds and beasts, the coming of the deluge, the rain and storm, the ark resting on a mountain, trial being made by birds sent out to see if the water had subsided, and the building of an altar after the flood. All these main facts occur in the same order in both narratives, but when we come to examine the details of these stages in the two accounts there appear numerous points of difference; as to the number of people who were saved, the duration of the deluge, the place where the ark rested, the order of sending out the birds, and other similar matters. The cuneiform inscription differs widely at its close from the Biblical account with respect to the fate of the patriarch who built the ark. The Bible says that Noah lived 350 years after the flood and then died, but the cuneiform tablet and Berosus both state that Xisithrus was translated to the company of the gods for his piety, a reward which, according to Genesis, was conferred on Enoch, the ancestor of Noah. Xisithrus being translated dwelt somewhere on the Persian Gulf near the mouth of the Euphrates, and here Izdubar sought and found him. The district of the Persian Gulf was counted as a sacred region by the early inhabitants of Babylonia, and in their fabulous account of the period before the flood, they represented certain composite creatures, half man and half fish, as rising out of the sea there, and coming to Babylonia to teach the primitive inhabitants of the country the arts of civilization.

In answer to the request of Izdubar Xisithrus is supposed to have related to him the history of the flood, and to have given directions for curing the monarch of his illness, which appears to have been a sort of leprosy or skin disease. On returning from this journey to seek Xisithrus, Izdubar indulges in some reflections on the waste of his former life, and the defencelessness of his great city Erech. After the account of the visit to Xisithrus, and the story of the flood, comes the twelfth and last tablet in the series, in some respects the most remarkable and important of the legends, for it clearly shows that the early Babylonians believed in the existence of the soul, of a future life, and of heaven and hell.

Heabani, the seer or astrologer of Izdubar, has been killed by a tambukku, a wild animal, and Izdubar utters a lamentation over him which is full of poetical feeling.

Next we are told that Heabani does not rest under the earth, and petitions are made to various deities to transfer him to heaven. These requests are not listened to until they reach Hea, who rules the infernal regions; when Hea directs a god, most probably his son Merodach, to release the soul of Heabani, and he performs this order. It appears from these passages that the Babylonians believed in a spirit or soul in man which they called a "*vadukku*," and the *vadukku* or ghost of Heabani on being called out of the earth makes a speech, apparently addressed to Heabani himself, indicating a notion of a dual nature in man. The abodes of the dead were supposed to consist of two regions, one in the sky, presided over by Anu the god of heaven and Bel the god of the earth, and the other beneath the world, presided over by Hea the god of the ocean and infernal regions. In the upper regions or heaven were the abodes of the blessed; there the departed wore crowns, they drank beautiful waters and consorted with the gods; but the notions of glory and honour at that day come out in the description of the inhabitants of this happy region, they are the kings and conquerors of the earth, the diviners and priests and great men, in fact, the strong and successful among mankind. On the other hand, the description of the infernal regions is most vivid and powerful, and is almost the same as that in the splendid inscription of the descent of Ishtar into Hades, where we read:—

1. " To Hades the land of my knowledge;
2. Ishtar daughter of Sin, her ear inclined;
3. Inclined the daughter of Sin, her ear;
4. To the house of the departed, the seat of the god Irkalla;
5. To the house from within which, is no exit;

6. To the road the course of which, never returns;
7. To the place within which, they long for light;
8. The place where dust is their nourishment, and their food mud;
9. Light is never seen, in darkness they dwell;
10. Its chiefs also like birds are clothed with wings;
11. Over the door and its bolts, is scattered dust."

This dark region where the inhabitants in their hunger devour filth and thirst for light is guarded by seven gates, and surrounded by the waters of death; it is the home of the weak and conquered ones, of wives who stray from their husbands, and men who abandon their wives, and disobedient children. These are represented as weeping in misery and corruption in their dark and eternal prison-house, "the place from which there is no return."

By the power of Hea, who here corresponds to Pluto, the lord of Hades, the ghost of Heabani was delivered from this hell, and, rising out of the earth, soars up to heaven. These religious ideas are remarkable on account of their close similarity to those of later religions and subsequent races, and their importance is increased by their antiquity, as at the latest they date more than 2,000 years before the Christian era. The heaven or region of the blessed was called *Samu*, and was divided into various sub-regions bearing different names, the highest being the "Heaven of *Anu*," the supreme celestial god. Hell, on the other hand, was generally called *matnude* or *aralli*, but has various other titles.

The legends of Izdubar close with the description, still by the *vadukku* or " ghost," of the burial of a warrior, which shows to some extent the customs of the time, a time when personal prowess and courage in battle were esteemed as the greatest glories. In connection with these legends are numerous other shorter stories of the same class, one of the most curious of which is part of a description of the Creation, which I found in the north palace at Kouyunjik, it is however too mutilated for translation. I believe that the legends current in Babylonia in the time of Izdubar were the foundation for the Chaldean accounts of the origin of the world, the antediluvians, the flood, and various other stories of primitive time.

There are in the British Museum fragments of inscriptions stated to have been written in the time of Izdubar, and I think the myths and wonders related of his reign, while they prove the ignorance and superstition of the time, do not warrant us in regarding his reign as unhistorical. A theory has been advanced by Sir Henry Rawlinson, that the legends of Izdubar describe the passage of the sun through the signs of the zodiac. There is no foundation whatever for this opinion, which is contradicted by the plain narrative of the legends. The history of Izdubar is poetical and exaggerated, and like all early histories abounds in miracles; but I believe it contains a basis of truth, and that this monarch really reigned and founded the Babylonian kingdom.

Chapter XII.

EARLY BABYLONIAN TEXTS.

Elamite conquest.—Sargon of Akkad.—His birth.—Concealed in ark.—Agu.—Temple of Bel.—Prayer for the king.—Dungi king of Ur.—Kudurmabuk.—Hammurabi.—Conquest of Babylonia. — Early bilingual text. — Turanian writing. — Semitic writing.—Riagu.—Text from Kouyunjik.—Kurigalzu.—Merodach Baladan I.—Royal grant.—Boundary stone.—Curses.

AMONG the new texts discovered during my expeditions to the valley of the Euphrates are several inscriptions of great importance belonging to the early kings of Babylonia. One of these is a new text of Assurbanipal relating to the restoration of the image of the goddess Nana. In the book of Genesis it is stated that in the time of Abraham Babylonia was under the dominion of the kingdom of Elam, and the monarch of that country bore the name of Chedorlaomar or Kudurlagamar. In the inscriptions of Assurbanipal, who reigned B.C. 668 to 626, we are told that when that Assyrian monarch took the city of Shushan, the capital of Elam, B.C. 645, he brought away from the city an image of the goddess Nana, which had been carried off from the city of Erech by Kudur-nanhundi, the Elamite monarch at the time of the Elamite conquest of Babylonia 1,635 years before (or B.C. 2280), thus confirming the statement of Genesis, that there was an early conquest of Babylonia by the Elamites. The new text which I discovered in the north palace, Kouyunjik, differs only slightly from the ones I formerly published: the variant passage in it reads—

" 1. The goddess Nana who for these 1,635 years

2. had been desecrated, and had dwelt in a place unsuitable to her,

3. until the days of her captivity were full.

4. Her journey to Erech, her entry to Bit-anna,

5. she had commanded to my majesty."

The rest of the inscription, describing the restoration of the image, is similar to those in my "History of Assurbanipal," pages 234-6 and 249-51. In the palace of Sennacherib at Kouyunjik I found another fragment of the curious history of Sargon, a translation of which I published in the "Transactions of the Society of Biblical Archæology," vol. i. part i. page 46. This text relates, that Sargon, an early Babylonian monarch, was born of royal parents, but concealed by his mother, who placed him on the Euphrates in an ark of rushes, coated with bitumen, like that in which the mother of Moses hid her child, see Exodus ii. Sargon was discovered by a man named Akki, a water-carrier, who adopted him as his son, and he afterwards became king of Babylonia. The capital of Sargon was the great city of Agadi, called by the Semites Akkad,[1] mentioned in Genesis as a capital of Nimrod (Genesis x. 10), and here he reigned for forty-five years. Akkad lay near the city of Sippara on the Euphrates and north of Babylon. The date of Sargon, who may be termed the Babylonian Moses, was in the sixteenth century B.C. or perhaps earlier.

Another inscription I discovered at Kouyunjik, belonged to an early Babylonian monarch named Agu, who restored the temple of Merodach at Babylon. A portion of this tablet was already in the British Museum, but not sufficient to enable us to judge of the date or importance of the inscription. The genealogy and essential parts of the text are, however, found in the new fragment which I obtained from the north palace, Kouyunjik. This copy belongs to the time of Assurbanipal, king of Assyria, and was taken as usual from an earlier document. The original was of great antiquity, being inscribed most probably more than 2,000 years before the Christian era. There are six Babylonian monarchs mentioned in the inscription, all of them kings not previously known, although one of the names, Suqamunu, is known as a god at a later period. This inscription will give some idea of the worship

---

[1] I have only recently discovered the identity of Akkad with the capital of Sargon.

of the Babylonian gods at this early period. It commences—

Column I.

" 1. Agu-kak-rimi
2. the son of Tassi-gurubar,
3. the noble seed
4. of Suqamunu,
5. named by the gods Anu and Bel
6. Hea and Meroach
7. Sin and Shamas.
8. The powerful chief
9. of Ishtar the archer
10. of the goddesses am I.

11. The king judicious and wise
12. the king learned and friendly,
13. the son of Tassi-gurubar,
14. the grandson
15. of Abi . . . .
16. the powerful warrior
17. devouring his enemies,
18. the eldest son
19. of Agu-rabi,
20. the noble seed the royal seed
21. of Ummih-zirriti,
22. The ruler of men
23. the powerful one am I
24. The ruler of
25. many peoples,
26. the warrior

27. of rulers
28. the establisher
29. of the throne of his father
30. am I.

---

31. The king of the Kassi
32. and Akkadi,
33. the king of Babylon
34. the great.
35. The settler of
36. the land of Asnunnak the people
37. numerous of Padan,
38. and Alman, king of Goim,
39. the people mighty,
40. the king the director
41. of the four races,
42. the follower of the great gods
43. am I.

---

44. When Merodach
45. the lord of the temple of Saggal,
46. and the lady of Babylon,
47. the great gods,
48. in their noble mouth
49. to the city of Babylon
50. his return commanded;
51. the god Merodach to Babylon
52. his city set his face.
53. . . . . the god Merodach
54. . . . . my . . . .

Column II.

1. I honoured, I glorified, and
2. to carry the god Merodach
3. to the city of Babylon,
4. his face I set and
5. in the will of Merodach
6. lover of my reign
7. I walked.

---

8. Saru-samas- the officer I called, and
9. to a remote country to the land of Hani
10. I sent him, and he the gods Merodach
11. and Zirat-banit
12. took, and
13. Merodach and Zirat-banit
14. lovers of my reign.
15. to the temple of Saggal
16. and Babylon
17. I restored them.
18. In the temple of the sun
19. for now and after time,
20. I established,
21. I restored them.

The country of Hani, to which the images of Merodach and Zirat-banit had been carried, lay north-east of Babylonia, and was early incorporated with Assyria. It is most likely that the Babylonians were worsted in war when they lost these sacred images.

The record then describes that the monarch gave costly robes to these gods, adorned with purple and gold, together with many precious stones which were given to the temple. A crown and diadem full of beauty and splendidly adorned, together with other valuable offerings, were also given to Merodach and his consort, and the king restored the temple of Saggal, the great house of Bel at Babylon, and built a papaha, or shrine, for the god, called the temple of Kua. The Babylonian monarch also dedicated some people, a house, grounds, and plantations, for the service of the temple, and the tablet gives a long list of blessings invoked by the priests on the head of the pious king.

1. To the king Agu
2. who the shrine of Merodach
3. had built,
4. and the temple of Merodach had restored,

Column VII.

1. the god Merodach
2. to his seat
3. had caused to enter,
4. the whole of
5. the sons of the people
6. those of them
7. the portion of the house, ground, and plantation,
8. to the gods Merodach
9. and Zirat-banit
10. he had dedicated them.

11. Of the king Agu
12. may his days be many,
13. may his years be extended,
14. his reign in blessings
15. may it abound,
16. The spirit of heaven
17. wide
18. may it glorify him,
19. the increase of
20. the rain
21. may . . . . .
22. . . . .
23. god . . . . . .
24. spreading . . . .
25. for ever . . . .
26. in far off . . . . .
27. ennoble him.
28. To the good king
29. Agu,
30. who the shrine of Merodach
31. has built,
32. and the sons of the people
33. has dedicated.

---

34. The gods Anu and Anunitu
35. in heaven may they favour him,
36. The gods Bel and Belat
37. in the temple also excellent renown
38. may they give him.
39. The gods Hea

40. and Davkina
41. dwelling in the great deep,
42. days of vigour
43. extended,
44. may they give to him.
45. The goddess Ziru lady of the high mountains,

Column VIII.

1. plenty
2. may she give to him.
3. Sin the light of heaven,
4. the continuance of his kingdom
5. for many days,
6. may he grant him.
7. The prince Shamas
8. the ruler of Heaven
9. and earth,
10. stability to the throne
11. of his empire,
12. to days
13. remote,
14. may he fix.
15. Hea lord of mankind,
16. wisdom
17. may he grant to him.
18. Merodach lover of his reign
19. lord of fountains,
20. his fertility
21. may he give to him.

22. The inscription
23. of Agu.

The end of the inscription describes that the copy was made in the time of Assurbanipal, king of Assyria, B.C. 668. All these inscriptions are later documents, copies of earlier texts, or containing statements referring to ancient events; but those which follow are inscriptions of the early Chaldean period. The first of these is on a small oblong stone written in the old hieratic form of cuneiform characters, the language being the Turanian Babylonian, the tongue spoken in Chaldea before the Semitic period. This inscription belongs to Dungi, an early Chaldean monarch, whose age is quite unknown, but who may be placed in round numbers at at least B.C. 2000. Dungi was king of Ur, then the capital of Babylonia, he was son of Urukh, the earliest Babylonian monarch who has left any known monuments. This inscription belongs to the city of Babylon, and is dedicated to the lady or goddess of " Su-anna or Emuk-anu," one of the religious names of Babylon. The text reads—

1. To the goddess of Emukanu
2. his lady;
3. Dungi
4. the powerful hero,
5. the king of the city of Ur,
6. king of Sumir and Akkad;
7. her temple
8. has built.

The simple ancient style of the inscription re-

EARLY BABYLONIAN TEXTS. 233

sembles that of other texts of the earliest period, and its contents prove that Babylon was at that time under the dominion of the city of Ur, which some suppose to be the Ur of the Chaldees the birthplace of Abraham. Another new monument discovered at Babylon is a large heavy stone with a bilingual inscription of Hammurabi. This bilingual text is written in double columns, on one side the Turanian, and on the other side the corresponding Semitic text. Like the former inscription, it is in old hieratic Babylonian characters, and belongs to the reign of Hammurabi, an early Babylonian monarch.

The subject-matter of the text probably refers to some of the numerous public works executed by Hammurabi, but the inscription is mutilated; its great value consists in the fact that it is a bilingual inscription, at least 800 years earlier than any previously discovered text of the same class. On the right-hand half of every column of writing is the copy in what is called Akkad or Turanian or proto-Babylonian, for scholars are not agreed as to a name for this early tongue. On the left hand stands the copy in Semitic Babylonian, which is the translation and equivalent of the other. I here give two extracts from the tablet, the first with the titles of Hammurabi, the second the close of the tablet, asking for blessings upon him.

Hammurabi, so far as we know him, commenced his reign as king of Babylon at a time when the country was divided into several states, a ruler named Kudur-mabuk, an Elamite, governing the region near Bagdad on the east of the Tigris, and the son of Kudur-mabuk, named Rim-agu or Riagu, being king of Larsa (now Senkereh) in the south of the country. Hammurabi met and defeated the forces of Kudur-mabuk and Rim-agu and then united Babylonia under his own sceptre, making the city of Babylon the capital of the country. The martial titles in the first extract from this inscription most probably refer to his successful war with Kudur-mabuk and his son.

Extract from bilingual tablet:—
1. Hammurabi
2. the king, the powerful warrior
3. destroying the enemy,
4. sweeper away of opposition,
5. possessor of his enemies.
6. Maker of battle,
7. spreader of reverence.
8. The plunderer,
9. the warrior,
10. the destroyer.

The second extract is one of those prayers for the good and success of the monarch, which generally follow large inscriptions.
1. established
2. in the four regions,
3. and in the heights of heaven
4. thy glory may they proclaim.
5. With valour

6. may they bless thee,
7. may their faces be propitious,
8. riches and greatness
9. may they accumulate,
10. with great exaltation
11. may they exalt thee.

The date of Hammurabi the author of this text is uncertain, and we can only say at present that he reigned not later than the sixteenth century before the Christian era.

In the mound of Kouyunjik I found part of a stone memorial tablet, apparently belonging to Riagu, or Rimagu, the king who was defeated by Hammurabi. The royal name, however, is mutilated; it reads:—

1. Rim ?-agu,
2. the powerful hero,
3. the governor of Ur,
4. king of Larsa,
5. king of Sumir and Akkad.

On the reverse is a fragment recording the restoration of some building. It is curious to find a tablet of this age at Kouyunjik, but the most probable explanation of the circumstance is, that this was a tablet carried off from Babylonia by the Assyrians during one of their wars.

The next inscription of the early Babylonian period belongs to Kuri-galzu, a monarch of a foreign race, who reigned B.C. 1370. This race of kings is called by Berosus " Arabian." The princes of the line were on friendly terms with the kings of Assyria, and one of them, named Burna-buriyas, married Mu-balidat-serua, the daughter of Assur-ubalid king of Assyria, and Kara-hardas the fruit of this union ascended the Babylonian throne. The Babylonians, who were dissatisfied with this alliance, revolted against him, putting him to death and setting up in his place a man named Nazi-bugas. Bel-nirari the king of Assyria took up the cause of Kuri-galzu, another son of Burna-buriyas, and marched into Babylonia to his aid. The Assyrians and the followers of Kuri-galzu defeated and killed Nazi-bugas, and Kuri-galzu ascended the Babylonian throne about B.C. 1370. This monarch was a great and successful prince, and is called " the unrivalled king:" the new inscription belonging to him is small, written round the eye of a statue, and reads " To Vul his lord, Kuri-galzu son of Ki . . . ." It was customary in the Babylonian period to make statues of metal or stone and to inlay the eyes of the figures with gems or agates cut to resemble the shape and colour of the eyes: the eye in question is one of this class, which belonged to a statue of the god Vul dedicated by Kuri-galzu.

The latest inscription I discovered of this period is a monolith of the grandson of Kuri-galzu, who bore the name of Merodach Baladan.

This inscription is on a large white stone about three feet high, having on the face a rude picture containing the emblems of the gods, including the

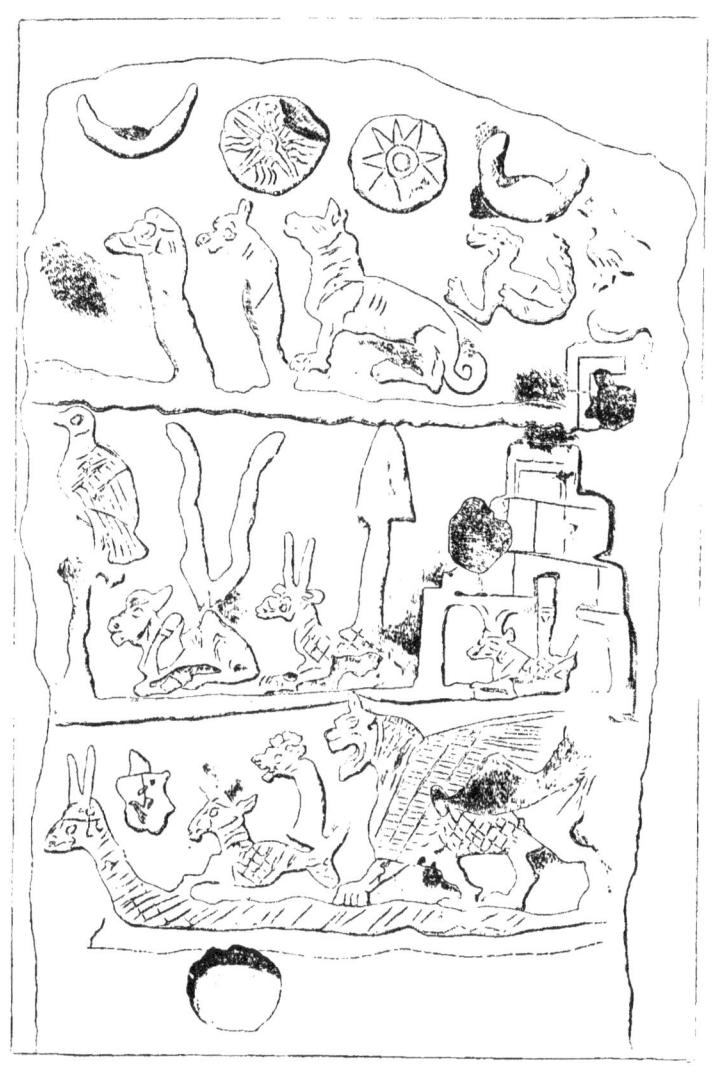

EMBLEMS OF THE GODS ON STONE OF MERODACH BALADAN I.

symbols of the sun and moon, a scorpion, dove, winged lion, a ziggurat or tower and many others. The back of the stone contains an inscription in three columns of 115 lines of writing, giving an account of a field of which this was the boundary or memorial stone, and relating that this property was granted by Merodach Baladan the king to his servant Maraduk-zakir-izkur in return for services rendered to the state. The document closes with a series of curses against anyone who should object to the right of Maraduk-zakir-izkur over the ground, and the gods whose emblems are carved on the stone were invoked to punish the defrauder. This stone adds two new kings to the list of Babylonian monarchs already known. Our history formerly ended with the reign of Kuri-galzu, but we now know that he was succeeded by his son Mili-sıhu and he again by his son Merodach Baladan I., the date of whose reign and consequently of this stone being about B.C. 1320. The inscription on the stone reads—

Column I.

1. A plantation? of 90 *sekul*
2. in measurements of great cubits,
3. a field of the town of Dur-zizi
4. beside the river Tigris,
5. in the district of the city of Ziku-istar.
6. Its upper side being on the west
7. of the river Tigris;
8. its lower side being on the east,

9. by the boundary
10. of the house of Nazi-maruduk
11. of the city of Ziku-istar;
12. its upper end was on the north
13. of the boundary of the city of Ilu-zagari,
14. and the house of Tunamissaki
15. the leader;
16. its lower end was on the south
17. of the boundary of the ground in the district
18. of the city of Ziku-istar,
19. and the city of Dur-zizi;
20. which Merodach Baladan
21. the king of nations,
22. king of Sumir and Akkad,
23. son of Mili-sihu
24. king of Babylon,
25. grandson of Kuri-galzu
26. the unrivalled king;
27. to Maruduk-zakir-izkur
28. the governor of
29. . . . . the temple and country
30. of the city of Idbimutgal
31. of . . . . . heaven and earth,
32. son of Nabu-nadin-ahi,
33. of whom the father of his father
34. was Rimini-maruduk,

Column II.

1. heart of hearts (descendant)
2. of Uballad-su-maruduk,

3. the descendant of Arad-hea
4. his servant;
5. To praise the kingdom
6. taxes . . . . . .
7. to sing the glory
8. of the gods Nebo and Saru,
9. and praise Sarturda
10. the god who begot him,
11. . . . . . . of heaven and earth
12. . . . the house of the sun of Borsippa
13. the *sudusi*
14. and the preservation of the temple of Sidda
15. in the day of payment,
16. the day of going out,
17. with his lord
18. Merodach Baladan.
19. Appointed for
20. after days,
21. successive months,
22. and years
23. unbroken,
24. to that man
25. without fail,
26. I give for good
27. like the delight of heaven,
28. for a settlement,
29. in return for his work.
30. Making witness,
31. Ninip-pal-idina
32. son of Vul-nazir

33. governor of the city of Zaku-istar,
34. Nabu-nazir
35. son of Nazi-maruduk the attendant,
36. and Nabu-sanismu?
37. son of Arad-hea
38. the *dugab*.

Column III.

1. If a ruler or eunuch
2. or a citizen, the memorial stone
3. of this ground
4. takes and
5. destroys,
6. in a place where it cannot be seen
7. to any where
8. shall place it in,
9. and this stone tablet
10. if a *naka* or a brother,
11. or a *katu* or a . . .
12. or an evil one,
13. or an enemy,
14. or any other person,
15. or the son of the owner of this land,
16. shall act falsely,
17. and shall destroy it,
18. into the water or into the fire,
19. shall throw it,
20. with a stone shall break it,
21. from the hand of Maruduk-zakir-izkur
22. and his seed shall take it away,

EARLY BABYLONIAN TEXTS. 241

23. and above or below
24. shall send it;
25. The gods Anu, Bel, and Hea,
26. Ninip and Gula,
27. these lords
28. and all the gods
29. on this stone tablet
30. whose emblems are seen,
31. violently may they destroy his name,
32. a curse unmitigated
33. may they curse over him,
34. calamity ?
35. may they bring upon him.
36. May his seed be swept away
37. in evil,
38. and not in good,
39. and in the day of departing
40. of life may he expire,
41. and Shamas and Merodach
42. tear him asunder, and
43. may none mourn for him.

I believe the Babylonian measure of land called a *sekul* measured about 40,000 square feet, or rather less than an English acre. The stone containing this inscription was discovered on the western side of the Tigris, opposite the town of Baghdad. The smaller fragments of the new Assyrian collection introduce to us several details of other portions of early Babylonian history, but these come properly into the next division of early Assyrian texts.

R

Chapter XIII.

EARLY ASSYRIAN INSCRIPTIONS.

Early Pottery—Text of Vul-nirari I.—Shalmaneser.—Temple of Ishtar.—Tugulti-ninip.—Babylonian wars.—Mutagil-nusku.—Assur-risilim.—Tiglath Pileser I.—Assur-nazir-pal.

MY excavations at Kouyunjik and Nimroud, and the examination of Kalah Shergat, have brought to light numerous texts belonging to the period of the early Assyrian empire. At Kouyunjik, in the area of the temples of Ishtar, I found numerous inscriptions and fragments of all ages, the oldest of which were some fragments of votive dishes, which I should place at least as early as the nineteenth century B.C. After these comes a fragment of a tablet referring to the diplomatic relations of Assyria and Babylonia, and mentioning some very early monarchs; this fragment is, however, a later copy, and not an original document. Contemporary documents commence again with the reign of Vulnirari I., B.C. 1320. In the ruins of Kalah Shergat I saw many fragments of inscriptions belonging to

EARLY ASSYRIAN INSCRIPTIONS. 243

this monarch, who there repaired a great temple to Assur, and I purchased a fine stone tablet found at this spot, which was in the hands of the French consul. This tablet is inscribed on both sides, and contains eighty lines of cuneiform text relating to the reigns of Assur-ubalid, Bel-nirari, Budil, and Vul-nirari, four successive Assyrian monarchs who reigned in the fourteenth century B.C. This document gives us almost all our knowledge of these reigns, and shows the extent of the Assyrian territory and the tribes conquered during this period, which was previously an obscure epoch in Assyrian history. The tablet was inscribed during the reign of Vul-nirari I., king of Assyria, B.C. 1320, to commemorate the restoration of the causeway of the temple of Assur at that capital. The translation reads—

1. Vul-nirari the noble prince appointed by heaven,
2. the noble established by the gods,
3. founder of cities, conqueror (?)
4. of the armies of Kassi, Guti (Goim), Lulumi,
5. and Subari, destroyer of all
6. the upper and lower foreigners, trampling on
7. their countries from Lubdi and Rapiqu,
8. to . . . . Zabiddi and Nisi.
9. Remover of boundaries and landmarks,
10. . . . . . . kings and princes
11. the gods Anu, Assur, Samas, Vul,
12. and Istar, to his feet have subjected.
13. The mighty worshipper of Bel,

14. son of Pudil priest of Bel,
15. viceroy of Assur, conqueror of
16. Turuki and Nirhi,
17. to the extremity of all their land,
18. king of the mountains and forests
19. to the extremity of wide Guti,
20. Gunuhlami, and Suti
21. their streams and lands,
22. remover of boundaries and landmarks.
23. Grandson of Bel-nirari
24. viceroy of Assur also who the army of the Kassi
25. destroyed, and the spoil of his enemies
26. his hand captured, remover of boundaries
27. and landmarks. Great grandson of
28. Assur-ubalid the powerful king
29. of whom his worship in the temple was fixed,
30. the protection and alliance of his kingdom
31. afar off like a mountain extended,
32. sweeper away of the forces of
33. wide Subari,
34. remover of boundaries and landmarks.
35. When the ascent to the house of Assur my lord,
36. which was before the gate of the people of the country,
37. and the gate of the judges;
38. which in former time had been made, decayed,
39. was stopped up, and ruined;
40. that place I constructed,

41. its measure I took,
42. with clay and earth four gurs I made,
43. I built it, to its place I restored it,
44. and my tablet I placed
45. for after days. The future prince who
46. when this place
47. becomes old and decayed,
48. its damage repairs, and my tablet written with my name
49. to its place restores ; The god Assur
50. his prayer shall hear. Whoever the writing of my name
51. shall efface, and his own name shall write,
52. and my tablet shall cause to cover,
53. to destruction shall consign
54. into the flood shall throw, in the fire
55. shall burn, into the water shall hurl,
56. in the ground shall cover,
57. or into the storehouse the place not seen
58. shall send and shall place it,
59. then I appoint these curses
60. to the foreigner, the stranger, the enemy, the evil one,
61. the strange tongue and any one
62. a rival shall send and execute,
63. and anyone who desires shall perform them.
64. Assur the mighty god dwelling in the temple of Sadimatati,
65. Anu, Bel, Hea, and Ziru,
66. the great gods, the angels of heaven,

67. and the spirits of earth in their might
68. firmly may they seize him,
69. an evil curse quickly
70. may they curse on him ; his name, his seed, his forces,
71. and his family, from the country may they wipe out.
72. Sweeping his country, destroying his people,
73. and his landmarks. By their great mouth
74. it is uttered, and Vul in his storming-
75. evil, may he stir up a flood,
76. an evil wind, an injurious earthquake,
77. a destruction, a failure of food,
78. the curse of famine in his country may he make, rain in his country like a deluge may he send,
79. to mounds and ruins may he turn it, and Vul in his evil consumption, his country may he consume.
80. Month Muhur-ili, twentieth day, eponymy of Salmanurris.

This tablet is of the highest importance ; it shows that Assyria at this time had already taken a leading place in the world, and was the most powerful state in Asia ; the Kassi, who were defeated both by Belnirariand his grandson Vul-nirari, were the leading tribe in Babylonia at this time. Vul-nirari, after a prosperous reign, left his crown to his son, Shalmaneser I., about B.C. 1300. Of Shalmaneser I found several memorials, all in the temple area, in the centre of the mound of Kouyunjik. One of these is a brick from a palace which formerly stood in this locality. A short time back nothing was known of Nineveh as a royal seat before the time of Assur-bil-kala. I found, about seven years ago, several inscriptions showing that the city was built and had a temple to Ishtar as early as the nineteenth century B.C., and there is an unnoticed fragment of Assur-risilim, who reigned B.C. 1150, among Layard's inscriptions, plate 75 F, which shows that there was a palace at Nineveh in his time. Now, however, we know that Nineveh was a royal residence at least 150 years earlier, in the time of Shalmaneser I. This inscription reads—" Palace of Shalmaneser, king of nations, the son of Vul-nirari, king of nations also." Other fragments turned up belonging to the same palace, but nothing was obtained in position or perfect enough to give any idea of this building, probably the oldest royal residence in the city of Nineveh. I discovered also a number of relics of the same king from the temple of Ishtar; among these was a brick inscription, which reads—

1. To the goddess Ishtar
2. his lady Shalman-
3. -eser viceroy of Assur
4. king of nations

There is a curious peculiarity about this inscription; it divides the name Shalmaneser, part of which is in line 2 and the rest in line 3. The division of a word is very unusual in Assyrian inscriptions. Another inscription belonging to this monarch which I discovered at Kouyunjik, is part of a votive dish belonging to the temple of Ishtar; from this and some other fragments the early history of this ancient temple can be traced. It appears that this temple was founded in very early times and restored by Samsi-vul in the nineteenth century B.C. One fragment of this age from the temple I discovered on the spot. After the time of Samsi-vul the temple fell into decay, and was restored by Assur-ubalid, king of Assyria, B.C. 1400. Again after this becoming ruinous, it was restored by Shalmaneser I., B.C. 1300. I have prepared a restored translation of the votive

HEAD FROM STATUE OF THE GODDESS ISHTAR.
From her temple, Kouyunjik.

dish inscription of Shalmaneser; in parts the record is so mutilated that I have only given the general sense.

"Shalmaneser the powerful king, king of nations, king of Assyria; son of Vul-nirari, the powerful king, king of nations, king of Assyria; son of Budil, the powerful king, king of nations, king of Assyria also.

Conqueror of . . . Niri, Lulumi . . . and Muzri, who in the service of the goddess Ishtar, his lady, has marched and has no rival, who in the midst of battle has fought and has conquered their lands. When the temple of the goddess Ishtar, the lady of Nineveh, my lady, which Samsi-vul, the prince who went before me had built, and which had decayed, and Assur-ubalid, my father, had restored it; that temple in the course of my time had decayed, and from its foundation to its roof I rebuilt it. The prince who comes after me, who my cylinders shall see and restore to their place, like I the cylinders of Assur-ubalid have restored to their place, may Ishtar bless him; and whoever destroys my records, may Ishtar curse him, and his name and his seed from the country root out."

The rebuilding of the temple of Ishtar was continued after the death of Shalmaneser by his son, Tugulti-ninip, and from the same spot I recovered some of the inscriptions of this monarch. One on a brick states:

1. Tugulti-ninip king of nations
2. son of Shalmaneser king of nations also
3. who the temple of Ishtar the lady
4. powerful, completed

This Tugulti-ninip, king of Assyria, was one of the most memorable monarchs of the period; he conquered the Babylonians and put an end to the dominion of the race of Arabian kings, who according to Berosus had reigned in Babylonia for 245 years. The account of this war I found on a fragment of the synchronous history from the palace of Sennacherib at Kouyunjik; this fragment belongs to Column II. of the document, nearly in the position of the fragment printed in "Cuneiform Inscriptions," vol. iii. plate iv. No. 3. The following is a translation of the two fragments, the name of Tugulti-ninip being restored:

1. Tugulti-ninip king of Assyria and Nazi-murudas king of Karduniyas (Babylonia)
2. a battle in the vicinity of the city of Kar-istar-agarsalu fought
3. Tugulti-ninip the overthrow of Nazi-murudas accomplished
4. from . . . . . . to his camp by the city of Hu-ahi-rabati-su feared him
5. and over all these neighbouring provinces
6. he ruled from the neighbourhood of Pilazzi
7. his servants he appointed and from the river Tigris the city of Armanagarsal
8. to the city of Kullar the kingdom he possessed and established.

---

9. Bel-kudur-uzur king of Assyria Vul . . bi his son king of Karduniyas
10. Bel-kudur-uzur had slain and Vul . . bi fought in the midst of battle
11. in the midst of the fighting with Ninip-pal-eser king of Assyria and
12. to his country he returned. After his warriors numerous he gathered

13. and to the city of Assur to capture it he marched up. Ninip-pal-eser

14. in his camp attacked him and compelled him to return to his country

---

15. In the time of Zamama-zakir-idin king of Karduniyas

16. Assur-dan king of Assyria to Karduniyas went down

17. the cities of Zaba, Irriya and Agarsalu he captured and

18. their abundant spoil to Assyria he carried away.

This passage in the old Assyrian chronicle gives a curious account of the relations between Assyria and Karduniyas, or Babylonia, in the thirteenth century B.C.

Of Mutaggil-nusku, king of Assyria B.C. 1170, son of Assur-dan, king of Assyria, I found a black stone, the inscription on which when restored reads:—

1. Palace of Mutaggil-nusku
2. king of nations king of Assyria
3. son of Assur-dan
4. king of nations king of Assyria
5. son of Ninip-pal-eser
6. king of nations king of Assyria

This is the only inscription of this monarch yet discovered.

Mutagil nusku was succeeded by his son, Assur-risilim, B.C. 1150, of whom I discovered a clay tablet containing his annals. It is in ancient characters, and much worn. After Assur-risilim came his son, Tiglath Pileser I. Of this monarch I found part of a terra-cotta cylinder with his annals, but not perfect enough for translation. Coming down to the time of Assur-nazir-pal, B.C. 885, I found numerous inscriptions of this period both at Nineveh and at Kalah (Nimroud), and I learned from these that he rebuilt the palace at Nineveh and the temple of Ishtar, which had fallen into decay since it was repaired by Samsi-vul, king of Assyria, B.C. 1080. Similar inscriptions of Shalmaneser II., B.C. 860, the son of Assur-nazir-pal, record that he made additions to these various works of his father, both at the palace and temple of Nineveh. At Nimroud, while excavating in the temple of Nebo, I discovered two votive hands belonging to the period of Vul-nirari III., the grandson of Shalmaneser II., B.C. 812.

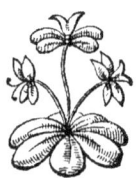

Chapter XIV.

INSCRIPTIONS OF TIGLATH PILESER II.
B.C. 745 TO 727.

Annals of Tiglath Pileser.—Their importance.—Tablet from Nimroud.—Babylonian wars.—Eastern wars.—Arabian wars.—Syrian tribute list.—Building of palace.—Fragments of annals.—Azariah.—Menahem.—Rezon.—His defeat.—War in Palestine. Pekah.—Hoshea.—Confirmation of Bible.

THE reign of Tiglath Pileser is an important epoch in Assyrian history, and his inscriptions are of the utmost value for comparison with the Biblical history. No less than five Hebrew kings are mentioned in the annals of this monarch, three of which I had discovered. Unfortunately the annals of Tiglath Pileser are all in a mutilated condition, so that it is difficult to make out some of the facts in his history. The importance of these inscriptions in reference to the Bible led me to search for additional fragments and evidence, and I discovered the remains of a palace of Tiglath Pileser at Nineveh, a part of a historical tablet at Nimroud, and I took paper impressions and copies of

some other inscriptions, so as to be able to give a better translation of these annals. From these sources I now give a translation of three copies of the annals of this monarch, commencing with the copy which I discovered in the temple of Nebo at Nimroud. There are among our fragments at least five versions of the annals of this monarch.

FRAGMENT OF ANNALS OF TIGLATH PILESER II. KING OF ASSYRIA, FROM A TABLET DISCOVERED IN THE TEMPLE OF NEBO (NIMROUD.)

1. Palace of Tiglath Pileser the great king the powerful king king of nations king of Assyria king of Babylon king of Sumir and Akkad king of the four regions.

2. The powerful warrior who in the service of Assur his lord the whole of his haters has trampled on like clay, swept like a flood and reduced to shadows.

3. The king who in the might of Nebo and Merodach the great gods has marched and from the sea of Bit-yakin to the land of Bikni by the rising sun

4. And the sea of the setting sun to Egypt; from the west to the east all countries possesses and rules their kingdoms.

---

5. From the beginning of my reign to my 17th year. The tribes of Ituha, Rubuha, Havaranu, Luhuatu, Harilu, Rubbu,

6. Rapiqu, Nabatu, Gurumu, Dunanu, Ubulu,

TIGLATH PILESER II.

Ruhua, Lihitau, and Marasu, the cities of Dur-kurigalzu,

7. Adini, Birtu of Sarragitu, and Birtu of Labbanat. The Arameans all of them who were beside the rivers Tigris, Euphrates,

8. Surappi and Ukru to the lower sea of the rising sun I conquered to the boundaries of Assyria I added.

9. My general prefect over them I made. In the cities of Sippara, Nipur, Babylon, Borsippa, Cutha Kisu, Kilmad? and Ur,

10. cities unrivalled noble offerings to Bel and Zirat-banit Nebo and Urmitu, Nergal and Laz the gods my lords I poured out and I increased in might.

11. Kar-duniyas the whole of it I possess and I rule its kingdom

12. Bit-amukkan and Bit-sahalli to their utmost border I swept. Nabuusabsi and Zaqaru their kings in hand I captured

13. The cities of Sarrapanu, Tarbazu Yapallu Durkassat and Malilatu their great capitals

14. with attacks? and missiles? I took, 155,000 people and children from them

15. their horses? and cattle without number I carried off, those countries to the boundaries of Assyria I added.

16. . . . . like clay I trampled and the assembly of their people to Assyria I sent. Kinziru their king in Sape his capital I besieged.

17. Pillutu on the borders of Elam to the boun-

daries of Assyria I added, in the hands of my general the governor of Arapha I placed it.

18. The tribute of the kings of the Chaldeans, Balasu son of Dakkuri, Nadin of Larancha, and

19. Merodach Baladan son of Yakin king of the sea coast, gold, the products of the country, silver, precious stones, strong wood Elutu wood oxen and sheep I received

---

20. The countries of Zimri, Bit-Sangibuti, Bit-hamban, Sumurzu, Bit-barrua, Bit-zualzas. . . . . .

Here the record is broken off, and although I searched carefully round the spot where this tablet was discovered I failed to find the rest of the inscription.

The second copy of the annals is translated from "Cuneiform Inscriptions," vol. ii. p. 67.

Historical tablet of Tiglath Pileser II.

("Cuneiform Inscriptions," vol. ii. p. 67.)

1. Palace of Tiglath Pileser, the great king, the powerful king, king of nations, king of Assyria, high priest of Babylon, king of Sumir and Akkad, king of the four regions.

2. The strong warrior who in the service of Assur his lord has marched through the countries and like a whirlwind has overspread and as captives has reckoned them.

3. The king who in the might of Assur, Shamas

and Merodach the great gods his lords, from the sea of Bit-yakin (the Persian Gulf) to Bikni of Shamsi

4. and the sea of the setting sun, to Muzri (Egypt), [from the] west to the east the countries he has possessed, and has ruled their kingdoms.

5. From the beginning of my kingdom to my 17th year. The tribes of Ituha, Rubuha Havarani (Hauran), Luhua, Harilu, Rubbu, Rapiqu, Hiranu, Rabilu,

6. Naziru, Gulusu, Nabatu (Nabateans), Rahiqu, Ka . . . Rummulusu, Adile, Kipre, Ubudu, Gurumu, Bagdadu, Hindaru,

7. Damunu, Dunanu, Nilqu, Rade, Da . . . ,Ubulu, Karmaha, Amlatu, Ruha, Qabiha, Lehitau, Marusu

8. Amatu (Hamath), Hagaranu (Hagarenes), and the cities of Dur-kurigalzu, Adili, Birtu of Sarragitu, Birtu of Labbanat, and Birtu of Kar-bel-matati.

9. The Aramcans all of them who are by the side of the rivers Tigris, Euphrates, Surappi, to the midst of the Ukni which is by the junction of the lower sea (Persian Gulf) I captured, their warriors I slew, their spoil I carried off.

10. The Aramu all there were to the borders of Assyria I added, and my generals prefects over them I made. Upon the mound of Kamri which the city Humut they call

11. a city I built, Kar-assur its name I called. People the conquests of my hand in the midst I

placed. In Sipara, Nipur, Babil (Babylon), Borsippa, Kutha, Kis, Chilmad, and Ur, cities unrivalled,

12. valuable sacrifices and libations to Bel and Zirubanit, Nebo and Urmitu, Nergal and Laz, the great gods my lords I poured out, and they strengthened my feet. The whole of Gan-dunias (Babylonia) to its utmost extent I possess, and

13. I rule its kingdom. The Puqudu (Pekod) like corn I swept away, their fighting men I slew, their abundant spoil I carried off. The Puqudu in the cities of Lahiru of Idibirina, Hilimmu, and

14. Pillutu, which border on Elam, to the boundaries of Assyria I added, and in the hands of my general the prefect of Arapha I placed them. The Kaldudu all there were I removed, and

15. in the midst of Assyria I placed them. Chaldea through its extent in hostility I swept. Nabu-usabsi, son of Silani, his fighting men on the walls of Sarrapani his city I slew,

16. and in front of the great gate of his city on a cross I raised him; I subdued his country, Sarrapanu to a heap of earth I reduced . . . I captured 5,500 of their people and children,

17. his spoil, his furniture, his goods, his wife, his sons, his daughters, and his gods, I carried off. That city and the cities round it, I pulled down, destroyed, in the fire I burned, and to mounds and ruins I reduced.

18. The cities of Tarbazu and Yapallu, I captured, 30,000 of their people and children, their furniture,

their goods, and their gods, I carried off. Those cities and the cities round them,

19. like a whirlwind I destroyed. Zaqiru son of Sahalli against the agreement of the great gods sinned, and with them set his face. Him and his great men in hand I took,

20. in bonds of iron I placed them, and to Assyria I brought. The people of Bit-sahalli feared and the tower . . . . them, for their stronghold they took.

21. That city by siege and famine I took and threw to the ground, 5,400 of their people and children, their spoil their furniture their goods, his wife, his sons, and his daughters, I carried off.

22. The city of Amlilatu I captured, the people and children, its spoil, its furniture, and its goods, I carried off. Bit-sahalli through its extent like a whirlwind I overspread, and I laid waste its districts.

23. Those countries to the boundaries of Assyria I added. Kinziru son of Amukkan in Sape his capital city I besieged him, his numerous fighting men in front of his great gate I slew.

24. The groves of palms which were in front of its wall I cut down, I did not leave one, its forests which extended over the country I destroyed, his enclosures I threw down, and filled up the interiors. All his cities

25. I pulled down, destroyed, and in the fire I burned, Bit-Silani, Bit-amukkan, and Bit-sahalli, through their extent like a whirlwind I destroyed, and to mounds and ruins I reduced.

26. The tribute of Balasu son of Dakkuri, and Nadini of Larrak (Larancha), silver, gold, and precious stones, I received. Maruduk-bal-iddina (Merodach Baladan), son of Yakin, king of the sea coast, from which to the kings my fathers, formerly none came and kissed their feet;

27. terrible fear of Assur my lord overwhelmed him, and to Sapiya he came, and kissed my feet, gold, the dust of his country in abundance,

28. cups of gold, instruments of gold, precious stones, the product of the sea, planks of wood . . carried by sailors (?) costly garments, gum, oxen, and sheep, his tribute, I received.

---

29. The countries of Zimri, Bit-sangibuti, Bit-hamban, Sumurzu, Barrua, Bit-zualzas, Bit-matti, Niqu of Umliyas, Bit-taranzai, Persia, Bitzatti,

30. Bit-abdadani, Bit-kipsi, Bit-sangi, Bit-urzikki, Bit-sa, Zikruti, Gizinikissi, Nissi, Zibur, Urimzan, Rahusan,

31. Niparia, Buztuz, Ararami, Burumi-sarri-izzuri, Saksukni, Araquettu, Kar-zipra, Gukinnana, Sakbat, Silhazi,

32. which the Babylonians call strong, Ruadi, Bit-munnatusqana, and Likra the heap of gold, districts of rugged Media, the whole of them in hostility I overwhelmed,

33. their numerous fighting men I slew, 60,500 of their people and children, horses, asses, mules, oxen, and sheep, without number I carried off,

34. their cities I pulled down, destroyed, burned in the fire, and to mounds and ruins reduced, the countries of Zimri, Bit-sangibuti, Bit-hamban, Sumurzu, Bit-barrua Bit-zualzas

35. Bit-matti, Niqqu of Umliyas, Bit-taranzai, Parsua, (Persia), Bit-zatti, Bit-abdadani, Bit-kipsi, Bit-sangi, Bit-urzikik, Bit-sa, and

36. Likruti of rugged Media, to the boundaries of Assyria I added, the cities in them anew I built, the soldiers of Assur my lord in them I set up, people captured by my hands in them I placed,

37. my generals prefects over them I appointed, my royal image in Tikrakki, Bit-sa, Zibur, Ararmi, Burumi-sarri-izzuri, and

38. Silhazi, which the Babylonians call strong, I set up. The tribute of Media, Illipa, and all the chiefs of the mountains to Bikni,

39. horses, asses, mules, oxen, and sheep, without number I received . . . . the great triumphs of Assur my lord, which were accomplished in all these countries he heard, and

40. the glory of Assur my lord overwhelmed him, and to Dur-tigulti-pal-esir the city which [I had built] . . . . to my presence he came, and kissed my feet,

41. Horses, asses, oxen, and sheep, instruments . . . . his tribute I received,

42. My general Assurdainani to rugged Media of the rising sun I sent, 5,000 horses, people, oxen, and sheep, without number he brought,

43. Ulluba, Kirhu, the whole of it I took, and to the boundaries of Assyria I added, an image of my majesty in the mountains of Limirra I set up, in the midst of Ullubi a city I built,

44. a palace my royal seat in the midst I placed, the soldiers of Assur my lord in it I set up, people captured by my hands in it I placed, my general prefect over it I appointed.

---

45. Saraduarri of Ararat, Sulumal of Milid, Tarhulara of Gamguna . . . . . .

46. . . . . Kustaspi of Kumuha, to take spoil . . .

47. . . . . near Kistan and Halpi districts of Kumuha . . . .

48. . . . . the river Sinzi the river like . . . .

49. . . . . I captured them in the midst of the fighting . . . .

50. . . . . royal images . . . .
[Many lines lost here.]

51. . . . . place . . . .

52. her tribute to my presence she brought, a guardian over her I appointed, and the men of . . . . I subdued to my yoke.

---

53. The tribes of Maza, Tema, Saba (Sabeans), Hiappa, Badana, Hatte, Idabahil, ... at the boundaries

54. of the setting sun, who knew no rivals, whose place was remote, the might of my dominion . . . . . they heard, and submitted to my dominion.

55. Gold, silver, camels, she camels, and gum, their tribute at once to my presence they brought, and kissed my feet.

56. Idibihil to the governorship over against Muzri (Egypt) I appointed. In all those countries which . . . of Assur in the midst I appointed.

57. The tribute of Kustaspi of Kumuha, Urik of Qua, Sibittibihil of Gubal, Pisiris of Gargamis (Carchemesh),

58. Eniil of Hamath, Panammu of Samhala, Tarhulara of Gauguma, Sulumal of Milid, Dadilu of Kaska,

59. Vassurmi of Tubal, Ushitti of Tuna, Urpalla of Tuhana, Tuhammi of Istunda, Urimmi of Husinna,

60. Mattanbahil of Arvad, Sanipu of Bit-ammana (Ammon), Salamanu of Moab . . . .

61. Metinti of Askelon, Yauhazi of Judah, Qavusmalaka of Edom, Muz . . . .

62. Hanun of Gaza, gold, silver, lead, iron, antimony, clothing the clothing of their country, lapis-lazuli (?) . . .

63. . . . produce of the sea and land, taken from their country, selected for my kingdom, horses and asses trained to the yoke.

---

64. Vassurmi of Tubal, in the service of Assyria delayed, and to my presence did not come, my general the rabshakeh . . . .

65. Hulli son of an unknown person on his throne I seated, 10 talents of gold, 1,000 talents of silver, 2,000 horses . . . .

66. My general the rabshekah to Tyre I sent. Of Metenna of Tyre, 150 talents of gold

---

67. In cunning ears, attentive and open, which the ruler of the gods the prince Nukimmut gave, a palace of planks . . .

68. And my decorated house, like a Syrian palace for my glory in the midst of Kahhi (Calah) I built . . .

69. extent of earth higher than the former palaces of my fathers, from the bed of the Tigris I caused to raise . . . . .

70. all my people the extent? of its drink failed and . . . .

71. 20 great cubits the strong foundations against the waters, the stone embankments I strengthened, like the mass of a mountain I filled . . . .

72. their mounds I made, their foundations I fixed, I raised their tops, $\frac{1}{2}$ gar and $\frac{2}{3}$ of a cubit . .

73. On the northern side I raised their gates, in ivory? hard wood? kakki, palm-tree planks? [cedar] and dapran.

74. The tribute of the kings of Syria, and princes of the Arameans and Chaldeans, whom by the force of my might I had subdued to my feet, I placed in them.

75. $5\frac{1}{2}$ gar 4 cubits from the embankment of the waters to the division of their boundary I enclosed, and beyond the palaces of the world I increased their work.

76. the beams of pine noble, like trees of *Hasur*

wood for... good ... from Lebanon and Ammanana.

77. I covered over them to last for ever, to appear the workmanship ... beautiful stones, burkullati I made, and I adorned the gates.

78. Doors of cedar planks in pairs closing, fixed at their entrances, of wood I made the interiors.

79. With *sibbu zahale* and *ibbi*, I covered, and in the gates I hung. Lions and winged lions and bulls, of gigantic workmanship, cunning, beautiful, valuable,

80. near I placed, and for admiration I set up, a pavement of paruti stone at their base I laid down, I adorned the entrance,

81. and figures carved in the likeness of the great gods around I made, and they inspired reverence.

82. Coats of karri, gold, silver, and copper to complete them I covered over them, I beautified their workmanship.

83. For my royal seat its building I raised, precious stones the product of sea? and land? I increased within it,

84. the palaces of rejoicing, carrying blessing and favour of the king their builder, as their name I gave.

---

85. The gates of the director of righteousness, the judge of the kings of the four races; receivers of the taxes of land and seas,

86. which cause to enter the production of adnati, to the presence of the king their lord, I proclaimed the names of their gates.

The third text or rather group of texts of the annals of Tiglath Pileser is from the stone slabs of his palace at Nimroud; it is in very fragmentary condition, and it is very difficult to arrange the fragments in their chronological order.

ANNALS OF TIGLATH PILESER FROM PALACE SLABS, NIMROUD.

First fragment.—The Babylonian Expedition, B.C. 745.

1. . . . Kalani?
2. . . . city of Sippara
3. . . . . Ruha
4. . . . . dain
5. . . . . Birtu in the plain,
6. and Birtu of Kar-belmatati, the Arameans all of them who are beside
7. the rivers Tigris, Euphrates, and Surappu,
8. to the midst of the river Ukni . . . . of the Arameans all of them
9. . . . . 9,000 men . . . thousand 500 oxen . . .
10. I pulled down, destroyed, and in the fire I burned. The tribe of Rahihu . . . .
11. the majesty of Assur my lord overwhelmed them . . . .
12. they came and kissed my feet . . . . . .
13. The priests of the temples of Saggal, Sidda, and Sidlam . . . .
14. the offerings of Bel, Nebo and Nergal to my presence brought . . . .

Second fragment.—Babylonian and Eastern Expeditions,
B.C. 745-4.

1. . . . . them and to their country they went, those cities a second time I built and upon the mound of Kamri

2. which the city of Humur is called, a city I built from its foundation to its top I constructed, and I finished it. A palace a seat of my royalty

3. within it I placed, Kar-assur its name I called. The soldiers of Assur my lord within it I set up, people of countries the conquests of my hand in the midst I placed,

4. taxes I appointed them, and with the men of Assyria I placed them. The river Patti . . . . which from days remote had been filled up and

5. . . . . . I excavated, and within it I brought refreshing waters . . . . the cities of Dur-kurigalzu, Sipar of Shamas,

6. . . . . Kisik, the tribes of Nakiri and Tane, the cities of Kalain by the river Sumandas, the city of Pazitu of the Dunani, Qirbutu

7. . . . . le, Budu, the cities of Pahhaz and Qinnipur, cities of Kar-duniyas to the midst of the river Ukni

8. . . . . I possess, to the borders of Assyria I added, my generals as governors over them I appointed, and from among their sheep and cattle

9. . . . . . I captured, 240 sheep as an offering to the

god Assur my lord I dedicated . . . . . those . . . .
which I had carried off,

10. in the government of the tartan, the government of the lord of the palace, the government of the rab-bitur, the government of Barhaziya, and the government of Mazamua,

11. . . . . I placed, of one speech I caused them to be, and with the men of Assyria I placed them; the yoke of Assur my lord like the Assyrians

12. . . . . filled . . . . my . . . . which in the time of the kings my fathers had become desert,

13. a second time I set in order, and the land of Assyria again . . . .

14. the city I built, a palace the seat of my royalty within it I placed . . . . . .

15. its name I called, the soldiers of Assur my lord within . . . . . .

16. with the people of Assyria I placed them. A statue of my majesty . . . .

17. which by the might of Assur my lord over the countries I had . . . .

18. 10 talents of gold as a gift, 1,000 talents of silver . . . .

19. his tribute I received. In my second year Assur my lord . . . .

20. the countries of Bit-zatti, Bit-abdadani, Bit-sangibuti . . . .

21. of my expedition saw, and the city of Nikur his fortress he abandoned . . . .

22. I protected, the city of Nikkur the soldiers . . .

23. his horses, his mules, his oxen . . . .
24. the cities of Sassiyas, Tutasdi . . .

Third fragment.—Eastern Wars, B.C. 774?

1. . . . . the cities of Kusianas, Harsu, Sanastiku, Kiskitara, Harsai, Aiubak

2. . . . . the mountains of Halihadri, the peaks of the mountains they took, after them I pursued, their overthrow I accomplished,

3. . . . . the defiles of the mountains they entered, in the fire I burned. The city of Uzhari of Bit-zatti I besieged, I captured. Kaki

4. . . . . city of Kitpattia of Bit-abdadan which Tunaku had captured, I besieged, I captured, its spoil

5. I carried off . . . . Nikur and the cities which were round it again I built, people the conquest of my hand in it I placed,

6. my general governor over them I appointed. The countries of Bit-kapsi, Bit-sangi, Bit-tazzakki like corn I swept; their warriors numerous

7. I slew . . . . ascended. The rest of their soldiers their limbs I cut off, and in the midst of their country I left.

8. . . . . their mules, their oxen, their sheep, and their people, without number I carried off. Mitaki

9. . . . . the city of Urdanika entered. The cities of Urdanika and Kitipal I captured, himself, his wife, his sons, his daughters,

10. . . . . those cities and the cities round them

I pulled down, destroyed, and in the fire I burned. Battanu son of Kapsi

11. .... submitted and took service, to prevent my wasting his district. The city Karkarhundir I left to him

12. .... I made. Erisaziasu which against Bizhadir of Kisira had revolted, I captured,

13. its spoil I carried off. Ramatiya of Aragi . . .

14. he quickly fled, and no one saw him . . . .

15. horses, oxen, sheep, good Ukni stone of . . .

16. the great gods my lords I offered. Tuni of Sumurza . . . .

17. I accomplished. His soldiers to escape ascended . . . .

18. Sumurza and Bit-hamban to the borders of Assyria I added . . . .

19. I placed. My general governor over them I made . . . .

20. to Assur my lord I devoted. The city Kizanti which in . . . .

21. I pulled down, destroyed, and in the fire I burned. The lords of those cities unsubmissive . . .

22. 300 talents of Ukni stone, 500 talents of ninzu of copper . . . .

23. the tribute of Mannukizabi of the city of Abdadan . . . .

24. Mikki of Halpi . . . . I devoted. Of . . . .

Fourth fragment.—Eastern and Northern Wars,
B.C. 744-3.

1. . . . . Bit-hamdan, Sumurzu, Bit-barrua,

2. Bit-zualzas, Bit-matti, and Niqu of Umliyas,

3. Bit-tarilai, Persia, Bit-kapsi, and the cities of Zakruti, Bit-istar

4. Nissa, Gizinkissi, Zibur, Urinna,

5. the countries of Sapira, Pustus, Ararmi, Darsarenihu,

6. Rua, the mountains to Bit-mun, Uskakka to Likraki, Silhazi

7. the fortress of the Babylonians, to the borders of Assyria I added.

8. My generals governors over them I made, and the tribute

9. of the lords of the Medes all of them to Bikni, I received.

10. My general Assur-dain-ani to the powerful Medes

11. who are at the rising of the sun, I sent. 5,000 horses, people, oxen,

12. and sheep without number he brought. Sarduri

13. of Ararat with me revolted, and with Matihilu

14. son of Agusi set his face. In the neighbourhood of Kastan and Halpi

15. districts of Kummuha, his overthrow I struck. His people

16. and all his camp I captured. The might of my servants he feared, and

17. to save his life on a mare he rode, and went off.

18. To the rugged mountains by night he rode and ascended them. Sarduri

19. of Ararat in the city of Turuspa his city

20. I besieged him, his numerous warriors in front of his great gate

21. I slew. An image of my majesty I made and in front of Turuspa

22. I raised. For 70 kaspu (about 450 miles) the land of Ararat entirely

23. from top to bottom I destroyed, and marched through with no resistance.

24. The lands of Ulluba, and Kirhu of Nahiri the whole of it

25. I took, to the borders of Assyria I added. An image of my majesty

26. in Kullimmir I set up. In Ulluba

27. a city I built, Assur-basa its name I called. People of countries the conquests of my hand

28. in the midst I placed. My general governor over it I appointed.

Fifth fragment.—Defeat of Northern Nations,
B.C. 743 ?

1. . . . . people the conquest of my hand in it I placed . . . .

2. .... in my .... year, Sarduarri of Ararat against me revolted ....

3. .... with Matihil .....

4. Sulumal of Milid, Tarhulara of Ganguma ...

5. .... Kustaspi of Kummuha, to each other's power they trusted ......

6. in the glory and might of Assur my lord with them I fought, their overthrow I accomplished ....

7. their warriors I slew, the clefts and hollows of the mountains I filled with them. Their chariots ......

8. their .... without number I carried off. In the midst of the fighting Sarduarri rode on his mare and escaped .....

9. my hand captured, 72,950 men ... people ....

10. Sarduarri to save his life by night rode away, and his road was not seen ....

11. .... to the bridge of the Euphrates, the boundary of his country I drove him, and a couch .....

12. his royal riding carriage, the seal of his neck, the necklace of his neck, his royal chariot ....

13. .... their .... all of it numerous, without number, his chariot, his horses his mules ....

14. .... his .... the army without number carried off, a great ship, a mace .....

15. .... his .... numerous in the midst of his camp, and in the fire I burned. His .....

16. ..... his couch to Ishtar the queen of Nineveh I dedicated .....

T

Sixth fragment.—Early Syrian Wars,
B.C. 743-40.

Lines 1 to 8 list of conquered cities in the north.
9. of Ma . . . .
10. over him I appointed. Of Rezon king of Syria
11. 18 talents of gold, 300 talents of silver, 200 talents of copper . . . . .
12. 20 talents of *simladunu* 300 . . . I appointed. The tribute
13. of Kustaspi of Kummuha, Rezon of Syria, . . . Hirom
14. of Tyre, Uriakki of Que . . . . . .
15. Pisiris of Carchemesh, Tarhulara of Gaugama, ... gold, silver, lead,
16. iron, skins of buffaloes, horns of buffaloes, blue . . . . black . . . . clothing of wool and linen, the production of their countries, numerous,
17. . . . . instruments and weapons . . . . in the midst of the city of Arpad I received.
18. Tutamu king of Unqi against my service was wicked, and forfeited his life,
19. . . . . went with me in strength.
20. . . . . of Tutamu and his great men
21. . . . . Kinalia his capital city I captured, people and their children
22. . . . . riding horses in my army like sheep I distributed.

23. .... in the midst of the palace of Tutamu my throne I placed,

24. 300 talents of silver .... 100 talents ....

25. .... clothing of wool and linen, *simi*, the furniture of his palace,

26. .... Kinalia a second time I took, Unqi to its utmost extent I conquered,

27. my general governor over them I appointed.

Seventh fragment.— War with Azariah of Judah, about B.C. 739.

("*Cuneiform Inscriptions*," vol. iii. p. 9, No. 2.)

1. .... course of my expedition the tribute of the kings ....

2. .... Azariah of Judah like a ....

3. .... Azariah of Judah in ....

4. .... without number to high heaven were raised ....

5. .... in their eyes which as from heaven ...

6. .... war and subdue the feet ....

7. .... of the great army of Assyria they heard, and their heart feared ....

8. .... their cities I pulled down, destroyed ...

9. .... to Azariah turned and strengthened him and ....

10. .... like an arch ....

11. .... fighting ....

12. .... he closed his camp ....

13. .... were placed and his exit ....

14. . . . . he brought down and . . . .
15. . . . . his soldiers he drew together to . . . .
16. . . . . made to surround them and . . . .
17. . . . . his great . . . like

Eighth fragment.—War in Syria and the East,
B.C. 738-7.

("*Cuneiform Inscriptions,*" vol. iii. p. 9, No. 3.)

1. . . . . Judah . . . .
2. . . . . of Azariah, my hand greatly captured . .
3. . . . . right . . . . tribute like that of . . . .
4. . . . . to his assistance the city of Ma . . . .
5. . . . . the cities of Uznu, Sihanu, Ma . . ka . . bu beside the sea, and the cities to Saua

6. the mountain which is in Lebanon were divided, the land of Bahalzephon to Ammana, the land of Izku and Saua, the whole of it, the district of Karrimmon,

7. Hadrach, the district of Nuqudina, Hazu, and the cities of the whole of them, the city of Ara . . . . cities helping them.

8. the cities of the whole of them the country of Sarbua, the mountain the whole of it, the cities of Ashani and Yadabi, of Yaraqu the mountain the whole of it

9. the cities of . . . . ri, Ellitarbi and Zitanu, to the midst of the city of Atinni . . . . Bumami 19 districts

10. of Hamath, and the cities which were round

TIGLATH PILESER II.

them, which are beside the sea of the setting sun, in sin and defiance to Azariah had turned,

11. to the boundaries of Assyria I added, and my generals governors over them I appointed. 30,300 . . . . .

12. . . . . in their cities and the city of Ku . . . . I caused to take. 1,223 people in the district of Ulluba I placed. The tribe of Qura . . . .

13. . . . . I took the road. The tribe of Qura . . . . across the river Zab to capture the Aklamiakkazi and the Gurumi . . . .

14. . . . . she and the Arameans who were beside the river, their warriors they slew, their cities they captured, and their spoil they carried off . . . .

15. . . . she and the Arameans in great numbers came, and a battle they made, and the Arameans his helpers they slew . . . .

16. . . . . to save his life alone he fled, and ascended to the city Birtu of Kiniya. The city of Saragitu . . . .

17. and the cities which were round them they took. 12,000 of their people and children, their oxen and sheep, Dira . . . .

18. to the land of the Hittites, to my presence they brought. My general the governor of Lulumi, the city of Mulugani . . . .

19. . . . . Kuri-dannitu of the people of Babylon and the cities which were round them he took, their warriors he slew . . . .

20. . . . . to the land of the Hittites to my pre-

sence they brought. My general the governor of Nahiri, the city of Subargillu

21. .... and the cities which were round them he took, their spoil he carried off. Siqila the commander of the fortress

22. .... to the land of the Hittites to my presence he brought. 600 women of the city of Amlate of the Damuni, 5,400 women of the city of Dur,

23. in the city of Kunalia .... cities of Huzarra, Tae, Tarmanazi, Kulmadara, Hatarra, Sangillu,

24. in the country of Unqi I placed .... women of Guti, Beth-sangibuti, 1,200 men of the tribe of Illil, 6,208 men of the tribes of Nakkap and Buda,

25. .... cities of Zimarra, Arqa, Uznu, and Siannu which were beside the sea I placed. 588 men of the Buda and Duna

26. .... 250 men of the Bela, 544 men of the Banita, 380 men of Sidu-ilu-ziri, 460 men of Sangillu,

27. .... men of the Illil, 457 women of the Quti, and Beth-sangibuti, in the district of Tuhimmi I placed, 555

28. women of Quti and Beth-sangibuti, in the city of Tul-garimi I placed, with the people of Assyria I joined them, and the performing of service like the Assyrians

29. I placed upon them. The tribute of Kustaspi of Kummuha, Rezon of Syria, Menahem of Samaria,

30. Hirom of Tyre, Sibitti-bahal of Gebal, Urikki of Qui, Pisiris of Carchemesh, Eniel

31. of Hamath, Panamma of Samhala, Tarhulara of Gauguma, Sulumal of Milid, Dadilu

TIGLATH PILESER II. 279

32. of Kaska, Vassurmi of Tubal, Ushitti of Tuna, Urpalla of Tuhana, Tuhammi of Istunda,

33. Urimmi of Husunna, and Zabibi queen of Arabia, gold, silver, lead, iron, skins of buffaloes, horns of buffaloes

34. clothing of wool and linen, violet wool, purple wool, strong wood, weapon wood, female slaves? royal treasures, the skins of sheep their fleece of

35. shining purple, birds of the sky, the feathers of their wings of shining violet, horses, riding horses, oxen and sheep, camels,

36. she camels and young ones, I received. In my 9th year Assur my lord protected me, and to the countries of Bit-kipsi, Bit-irangi,

37. Bit-tazakki, Media, Bit-zualzas, Bit-matti, and Umliyas I went. The cities of Bit-istar, Kingi-kangi, Kindigi-asu,

38. Kingi-alkasis, Kubushatedis, Ubusu, Ahsibuna, Girgira, Kimur-bazhatti and the cities

39. which are round them I captured. Their spoil I carried off, I pulled down, destroyed, and in the fire I burned. In those days a colossal monument of the god Ninip I made, and the glory of Assur my lord

40. upon it I wrote, and in the district of Baha of Bit-istar I set it up. Upas son of Kipsi his people gathered to the land of Abiruz. The mountains I ascended, after him

41. I pursued, his warriors I slew, his spoil I carried off. His cities I pulled down, destroyed, and in the fire I burned. Usura . . . . ruta and Burdada

42. of Vistakta feared and took to the mountains. After them I pursued, their warriors I slew, their spoil I carried off. Burdada in hand I captured

43. their cities I pulled down, destroyed, and in the fire I burned. The city of Zibur and the cities which were round it I captured, I carried off the spoil. Tanus

44. of . . . .

45. . . . .

46. . . . . their spoil I carried off . . . .

47. . . . he gathered and to the country of . . . . Dana the mountain . . . .

48. I ascended after them, their warriors I slew their spoil I carried off. Yahu-tarsi . . . .

49. . . . . of them who fled to the mountains of Amat, a district which is at the top of Rua, the mountain of . . . .

50. after them I pursued, their warriors I slew, like a single one I took them. The country of Kar-zipya in . . . .

51. they left. After them I pursued, and in the midst of battle like a storm with Vul, I raged over them . . . .

52. without number I carried off, not one among them got away, none got up the mountains, the people of Sangibuti . . . .

53. which the Babylonians had taken, after them I ascended, and their warriors I slew, their spoil I carried off . . . .

54. in the fire I burned. Over the country of Sil-

hazi which the Babylonians call the fortress, I . . . .

55. of the country of Tel-assur . . . . noble offerings to the god Merodach of Tel-assur I offered, the city of Argu . . . .

Ninth fragment.—Northern campaigns.
("*Cuneiform Inscriptions*," vol. iii. p. 10, No. 1.)

1. . . . . the cities of Hista, Harabisina, Barbaz, and Tasa, to the river Ulurus I captured, their warriors I slew. 8,650 people,

2. . . . . 300 horses, 660 asses, 1,350 oxen and 19,000 sheep I carried off, I pulled down, destroyed, and in the fire I burned.

3. And those cities to the borders of Assyria I added. Those cities a second time I built, and people the conquest of my hand in the midst of them I placed,

4. . . . . in the midst I raised, and to the government of Nairi I added. The cities of Daikangar, Sakka, Ippa, Elisansa,

5. . . . . Lugadangar, Quda, Elugia, Dania, Danziun, Ulai, Luqia, Abrania, Evasa,

6. . . . . their warriors I slew, 900 people, 150 oxen, 1,000 sheep, horses, riding horses, and asses I carried off

7. their cities I pulled down, destroyed, and in the fire I burned. The people of Muqan the collecting of my expedition saw, and the city of Ur

8. which is in the midst of Muqan . . . .

9. their sons, their daughters, their families . . . .
10. I cut off, and in their country . . . .
11. horses, riding horses . . . .
12. I pulled down, destroyed, and in the fire I burned . . .
13. I captured I pulled down, destroyed, and in the fire I burned . . . .
14. I captured, their warriors I slew . . . .

Tenth fragment.—Defeat of Rezon, king of Damascus.
(*Layard's "Inscriptions,"* plate 72.)

1. . . . . his warriors I captured . . . . with the sword I destroyed
2. . . . . *rusat* . . . . *luri* . . . . before him
3. . . . . the lords of chariots and . . . . their arms I broke and
4. . . . . their horses I captured . . . his warriors carrying bows . . . .
5. . . . . bearing shields and spears, in hand I captured them and their fighting
6. . . . . line of battle. He to save his life fled away alone and
7. . . . . like a deer, and into the great gate of his city he entered. His generals alive
8. in hand I captured, and on crosses I raised them. His country I subdued. 45 men of his camp
9. . . . . Damascus his city I besieged, and like a caged bird I enclosed him. His forests
10. . . . . the trees of which were without number, I cut down and I did not leave one.

11. . . . . Hadara the house of the father of Rezon of Syria,

12. . . . . the city of Samalla I besieged, I captured, 800 people and children of them

13. . . . . their oxen their sheep I carried captive, 750 women of the city of Kuruzza

14. . . . . the city Armai, 550 women of the city of Mituna I carried captive, 591 cities

15. . . . . of 16 districts of Syria like a flood I swept.

16. . . . . Samsi queen of Arabia who the oath of the sun god had broken, and . . . .

Eleventh fragment.— War in Palestine.

1. . . . . . sit . . . . ti
2. . . . . imbaka . . . .
3. of the city . . . .
4. of the city . . . . districts of Beth-gu . . . .
5. of 16 districts of . . . .
6. women of . . . . bara, 625 women of the city of . . . . a . . . .
7. 226 women of the city of . . . .
8. women of the city of . . . hinatuna, 650 women of the city of Qana . . . .
9. 400 women of the city of . . . . atbiti
10. 656 women of the city of Sasi . . . . making
11. 13,520 women of . . . .
12. and their children . . . . the cities of Aruma and Marum . . . .
13. the rugged mountains . . . .

14. Metinti of Azkelon in my service was wicked, and
15. with me revolted . . . . the defeat of Rezon
16. he saw, and in striking . . . .
17. his own fear overcame him, and . . . . he died ?
18. Rukiptu his son sat in his throne, to . . . .
19. he raised and prayed ? 500 . . . .
20. and to his city he entered. 15 cities . . . .
21. Idibihilu the Arabian . . . .

Twelfth fragment.—War in Palestine and Arabia.

("*Cuneiform Inscriptions,*" vol. iii. p. 10, No. 2.)

1. . . . . the city of Hadrach to the land of Saua
2. . . . . the cities of Zimirra, Arqa, and Zimarra
3. . . . . the cities of Uznu, Sihanu, Rihisuza
4. . . . . the cities beside the upper sea I possessed 6 of my generals
5. as governors over them I appointed . . . . asbuna which is beside the upper sea
6. the cities . . . . niti, Galhi . . . . abil . . . . which is the boundary of the land of Beth Omri
7. . . . . li wide the whole of it to the borders of Assyria I joined,
8. my generals governors over them I appointed. Hanun of Gaza
9. who before the face of my soldiers fled, and to Egypt got away; Gaza
10. I captured . . . his furniture, his gods . . . . and my royal couch

11. .... within his palace .... their gods I distributed and

12. .... I fixed them ...... him like a bird

13. .... to his place I restored him

14. .... gold, silver, clothing of wool and linen

15. .... great .... I received. The land of Beth Omri

16. .... *illut*, the tribe .... the goods of its people

17. and their furniture to Assyria I sent. Pekah their king .... and Hoshea

18. to the kingdom over them I appointed .... their tribute of them I received, and

19. to Assyria I sent. Samsi queen of Arabia ....

20. ...... slew, ... people, 30,000 camels, 20,000 oxen

21. ...... 5000 *simi* ... the country her gods

22. .... her goods I captured. She to save her life

23. ..... bazil an arid place like an ass of the desert

Thirteenth fragment.—*War in Palestine and Arabia*,
B.C. 734-2.

(*Layard's " Inscriptions," p. 66.*)

1. ..... the city ..

2. .... to the city Ezasi

3. .... Samsi queen of Arabia in the country of Saba

4. .... the people who were in the midst of her camp,

5. the might of my powerful soldiers overwhelmed her, and

6. camels and she camels .... her present to my presence she sent.

7. A governor over her I appointed, and the people of

8. Saba to my yoke I subdued. The cities of

9. Mazha and Tema, of the Sabeans, Hyappa,

10. Badana, and Hatte, of the Idibihilites,

11. ...... who are at the boundary of the lands of the setting sun (the west)

12. who have no rivals, and their country is remote; the renown of my dominion and account

13. of my victories they heard, and submitted to my dominion. Gold, silver, camels,

14. she camels, and *simi*, their tribute at once to my presence

15. they brought, and kissed my feet,

16. .... Idibihil to the governorship over the land of Egypt I appointed,

17. .... whom in my former campaigns all their cities I had reduced,

18. .... his helpers, Samaria alone I left. Pekah their king ....

In spite of the deplorable state in which the annals of this king still remain, the fragments of these records are of the highest interest, the names of Azaiah and Jehoahaz (Ahaz) kings of Judah, of Menahem, Pekah, and Hoshea kings of Israel, of Rezon of Damascus, and Hiram of Tyre, show at once their important connection with the book of Kings, while sufficient remains of the later campaigns to confirm the Biblical account of Tiglath Pileser's campaign into Syria, to assist Ahaz king of Judah. The defeat of Rezon king of Syria and the siege of Damascus are described in the tenth fragment; the conquest of the Philistines is given in the eleventh and twelfth fragments; the spoiling of Israel, death of Pekah king of Samaria, and accession of Hoshea, are given in the twelfth and thirteenth fragments; and the general submission of Syria and Palestine is given in the historical tablet, "Cuneiform Inscriptions," vol. ii. p. 67, lines 57 to 63. The details of these and many other events show the value of these annals. Further and systematic excavations at Nimroud would complete these, and so give us invaluable assistance in the study of Jewish history.

Chapter XV.

INSCRIPTIONS OF SARGON,

B.C. 722 TO 705.

Historical cylinder.—Median chiefs.—War with Ashdod.—Azuri.—Ahimiti.—Yavan.—Revolt.—Turning watercourses.—Judah.—Edom.—Moab.—Embassy to Pharaoh.—Egypt's weakness.—Advance of Sargon.—Flight of Yavan.—Seal of Sargon.

HE principal inscriptions of Sargon which I discovered are some fragments of an octagonal cylinder, containing a long text of the history of this reign and some dated monuments. The cylinder is full of matter valuable to the historian; but being very mutilated, I only here give two extracts, one a list of Median chiefs, the other an important campaign, namely, that against Ashdod, which I have restored in two places by comparison with Botta's Inscriptions.

The list of Median chiefs belongs to the year B.C. 713, and is curious as showing the divided state of Media at that time. These chiefs are:—

1. Pharnes chief of Sikrana,
2. Ziturna chief of Musana,

3. Uppamma chief of Katalina,
4. Vasdakku chief of Amakki,
5. Istesuki chief of Isteuppu,
6. Varzan chief of Vaqutti,
7. Aspabara chief of Kakkam,
8. Sataresu and Qururasu,
9. chiefs of Tabari,
10. and Luhbarri, rugged regions,
11. Satarparnu chief of Ubburia,
12. Parkuttu chief of Sidirpattianu,
13. Ariya chief of Bustu,
14. Vusra chief of Tutunenu,
15. Vastakku chief of Amista,
16. Hardukka chief of Harzianu,
17. Isteliku and Avariparnu,
18. chiefs of Kattanu,
19. Arbaku chief of Arnasia,
20. Karuti chief of Turzinu,
21. . . . panu chief of Barkanu,
22. . . . . . chief of Zazaknu,
23. . . . . of Garkasia,
24. . . . . of Partakanu.

On the next column this cylinder gives the war against Ashdod.

Account of the expedition of Sargon against Ashdod from the same cylinder completed from Khorsabad texts.

1. In my ninth expedition to the land beside
2. the great sea, to Philistia and

3. Ashdod I went.
4. Azuri king of Ashdod not to bring tribute,
5. his heart hardened, and to the kings round him
6. enemies of Assyria he sent, and did evil.
7. Over the people round him his dominion I broke,
8. and carried off . . . .
9. From that time
10. Ahimiti son of . . . .
11. his brother before his face over his kingdom
12. I raised and appointed him.
13. Taxes and tribute to Assyria
14. like that of the kings round him
15. over him I appointed. But the people
16. evil, not to bring taxes and tribute
17. their heart hardened and . . . .
18. their king they revolted against
19. and for the good he had done
20. they drove him away and . . . .
21. Yavan not heir to the throne,
22. to the kingdom over them they appointed. In the throne
23. of their lord they seated him,
24. and their cities they prepared
25. to make war . . . .
26. the dominion . . . .
27. against capture they fortified
28. its . . . . they faced . . . .
29. and around it a ditch they excavated.
30. Twenty cubits (34 feet) in its depth the made it,

31. and they brought the waters of the springs in front of the city.

32. The people of Philistia, Judah, Edom,

33. and Moab, dwelling beside the sea bringing tribute

34. and presents to Assur my lord,

35. were speaking treason. The people and their evil chiefs,

36. to fight against me unto Pharaoh

37. the king of Egypt, a monarch who could not save them,

38. their presents carried and besought his

39. alliance. I Sargon the noble prince

40. revering the oath of Assur and Merodach, guarding

41. the honour of Assur; the rivers Tigris and Euphrates

42. in their full flood my warriors of my guard

43. entirely I passed over. And he Yavan

44. their king, who in his own might

45. trusted, and did not submit to my dominion;

46. Of the advance of my expedition to the land of the Hittites heard, and

47. the majesty of Assur my lord overwhelmed him, and

48. to the border of Egypt, the shore of the river

49. at the boundary of Meroe . . . . under the waters

50. . . . . he took part

51. . . . . a place remote

52. . . . . he fled away

53. and his hiding-place was not discovered. The cities of Ashdod and

[Continued from Botta]

54. Gimzo of the Ashdodites

55. I besieged and captured. His gods, his wife, his sons, and his daughters,

56. his furniture, and goods, and the treasures of his palace, with the people of his country

57. as a spoil I counted, and those cities a second time

58. I built. People the conquests of my hands

59. from the midst of the countries of the rising sun, within them I seated; and with the people of Assyria I placed them, and they performed my pleasure.

This expedition against Ashdod took place B.C. 711, during the reign of Hezekiah king of Judah, and it is mentioned in the twentieth chapter of Isaiah, which is dated, verse 1, "In the year that Tartan came unto Ashdod (when Sargon the king of Assyria sent him), and fought against Ashdod and took it." Isaiah in this chapter denounces the conduct of Egypt, and the way in which he speaks of the Egyptians and Ethiopians in this and other chapters is remarkably verified by the account given by Sargon of his campaign against Ashdod. Egypt is described in the annals of Sargon as a weak power always stirring up revolts against Assyria, and unable to help or shield the revolters when the Assyrians attacked them. In those days Egypt was truly a broken reed. The account Sargon gives of the turning of the fountains and watercourses to protect the city of Ashdod strikingly parallels the similar preparations of Hezekiah when he expected an Assyrian invasion, Chronicles II. chap. xxxii. v. 3 and 4, and it is a curious fact that Hezekiah was reigning at this time, and his preparations were made according to the ordinary chronology B.C. 713, only two years before this invasion of Sargon.

It is also remarkable that the new text of this war gives it as happening in the ninth year of the monarch's reign, whereas the other records of Sargon state that it took place in the eleventh year. This makes a variation of two years as to the accession of Sargon, the one copy leading to the date B.C. 722, while the other favours B.C. 720. Shalmaneser, the predecessor of Sargon, had died B.C. 722, but it is possible that some heir to the throne may have stood in the way of Sargon during the first two years of his rule.

Among the other new inscriptions of Sargon is a curious inscribed seal, the device on which has the usual royal emblem of the king stabbing a rampant lion. The inscription round the seal reads:—Which Sargon king of Assyria gave to the governor of Irimuni, month Tebet, 25th day, eponymy of Taggil-ana-bel.

The date of this document was B.C. 715. Some other new and curious texts are on dated tablets, one of which leads to the conclusion that the district which the Assyrians called Mazamua (near the Babylonian frontier) was the Lulumu of the earlier inscriptions.

Chapter XVI.

INSCRIPTIONS OF SENNACHERIB.

B. C. 705 TO 681.

Cylinder C.—Intermediate record.—Titles.—War with Merodach Baladan.—Conquest of Babylonia.—Conquest of Kassi.—Ellipi.—War in Palestine.—Elulias of Zidon.—Zidga of Askelon.—Revolt of Ekron.—Battle with Egyptians.—Hezekiah.—Siege of Jerusalem.—Submission and tribute.—Second Babylonian war.—Letter from governor.

THE two expeditions to Assyria brought to light a considerable number of texts and fragments to complete texts of the reign of Sennacherib. Of these I shall choose two for notice; one a cylinder which I have named Cylinder C, the other a despatch from a local governor to the Assyrian monarch. Some fragments of Cylinder C were already in the British Museum, and I published a notice of them in my "Chronology of the reign of Sennacherib," London, 1871. In my excavations at the palace of Sennacherib I have discovered much larger portions of this text, which I am now able to entirely restore. This cylinder is in fact an octagonal prism, the text is very similar to that of the Taylor cylinder, and its value consists in the fact that it is intermediate in date between the Bellino and Taylor cylinders. The Bellino cylinder contains the records of two wars, and is dated in the eponymy of Nebu-liha governor of Arbela, B.C. 702, and the Taylor cylinder contains the records of eight wars, being dated in the eponymy of Bel-emur-ani, governor of Carchemesh, B.C. 691. Cylinder C has the records of four wars, two more than the Bellino, and four less than the Taylor, and it is dated in the eponymy of Nabu-dur-uzur governor of Dihnun, B.C. 697, five years later than the Bellino, and six years earlier than the Taylor text. I have here translated the historical portion of the cylinder on the first five faces of the document.

Column I.

1. Sennacherib the great king,
2. the powerful king, king of Assyria,
3. king of the four regions,
4. the appointed ruler,
5. worshipper of the great gods,
6. guardian of right, lover of justice,
7. maker of peace,
8. going the right way,
9. preserver of good. The powerful prince,
10. the warlike hero, leader among kings,
11. giant devouring the enemy
12. breaker of bonds.

SENNACHERIB. 297

13. Assur the great mountain an empire unequalled,
14. has committed to me, and
15. over all who dwell in palaces has exalted my servants.
16. From the upper sea of the setting sun,
17. to the lower sea of the rising sun,
18. all the dark races he has subdued to my feet.
19. and stubborn kings avoided war,
20. their countries abandoned and like Sudinni birds
21. . . . . . fled to desert places.

---

22. In my first expedition, of Merodach Baladan
23. king of Karduniyas, with the army of Elam his helpers,
24. in the vicinity of Kisu, I accomplished his overthrow.
25. In the midst of that battle he abandoned his camp,
26. alone he fled, and his life he saved.
27. Chariots, horses, carriages, and mules,
28. which in the midst of the fight he had abandoned, my hand captured.
29. Into his palace which is in Babylon, joyfully I entered and
30. I opened also his treasure house; gold, silver,
31. instruments of gold, silver, precious stones, everything,

32. furniture, and goods without number, abundant, his consort, the eunuchs of his palace,

33. the great men, those who stand in the presence, male musicians, female musicians,

34. the whole of the people, all there were,

35. living in his palace, I brought out, and

36. as spoil I counted. By the might of Assur my lord,

37. 75 of his strong cities, fortresses of Chaldea,

38. and 420 small cities which were round them,

39. I besieged, I captured, I carried off their spoil.

40. The Urbi, Arameans, and Chaldeans,

41. who were within Erech, Nipur, Kisu,

42. Harriskalama, Cutha, and Sippara,

43. with the sons of the rebel cities,

44. I brought out and as spoil I counted.

45. On my return the Tuhumuna,

46. Rihihu, Yadaqqu,

47. Ubudu, Kipre,

48. Malahu, Gurumu,

49. Ubulu, Damunu,

50. Gambulu, Hindaru,

51. Ruhua, Pekod,

52. Hamranu, Hagarenes,

53. Nabateans, Lihitau,

54. and Arameans, not submissive, forcibly

55. I captured. 208,000 people, small and great, male and female,

56. horses, mules, asses,

57. camels, oxen, and sheep,
58. which were without number, a great spoil
59. I carried off to the midst of Assyria.
60. In the course of my expedition, of Nabu-bel-zikri
61. governor of Hararati, gold, silver,
62. great palms, asses, camels, oxen,

Column II.

1. and sheep, his great present,
2. I received. The people of Hirimmi, obstinate rebels,
3. with the sword I destroyed, and one I did not leave. Their corpses
4. in the dust I threw down, and the whole
5. of that city I quieted. That district
6. a second time
7. I took; 1 ox, 10 sheep, 10 omers of wine,
8. and 20 omers of first fruits,
9. to the gods of Assyria
10. my lords, I appointed for ever.

---

11. In my second expedition, Assur my lord protected me, and
12. to Kassi and Yasubigalla
13. who from of old to the kings my fathers
14. were not submissive, I went. In the vast forests
15. and rugged ground, on a horse I rode;

16. my chariots and foot soldiers in waggons I caused to carry;

17. difficult places on my feet like a bull I pressed into.

18. Bit-kilamzah, Hardispi, and Bit-kubatti,

19. their cities, strong fortresses, I besieged, I captured.

20. People, horses, mules, asses,

21. oxen, and sheep, from the midst of them

22. I brought out, and as spoil I counted, and their small cities

23. which were without number, I pulled down, destroyed, and reduced to heaps.

24. The tents, the pavilions, their dwellings, in the fire I burned and

25. to ruins I brought. The city of Kilamzah,

26. that for a fortress I took, more than in former days

27. its walls I strengthened, and people of countries

28. conquered by my hand in the midst I placed.

29. The people of Kassi and Yasubigalla

30. who from the face of my soldiers fled,

31. from the midst of the mountains I brought down, and

32. into Hardispi and Bit-kubatti I drove,

33. to the hand of my general the governor of Arrapha

34. I appointed them. A tablet I caused to make, and

SENNACHERIB.

35. the glory acquired by my hand, which over them

36. I had gained, upon it I caused to write, and

37. in the midst of the city I set up. The front of my feet

38. I turned, and to Ellipi I took the road.

39. Before me Izpabara their king his strong cities

40. his treasure house he abandoned, and to a distance

41. he fled. The whole of his wide country like a hailstorm I swept.

42. Marubisti and Akkad, cities

43. the house of his kingdom with 34 small cities which were round them,

44. I besieged, I captured, I pulled down, I destroyed, in the fire I burned.

45. People small and great, male and female, horses,

46. mules, asses, camels,

47. oxen, and sheep, without number

48. I carried off, and until none were left

49. I caused it to be, and I reduced his country.

50. The cities of Zizirtu and Kummahlu

51. strong cities, with the small cities

52. which were round them, Bit-barru

53. the district the whole of it,

54. from the midst of his country I detached, and to the boundaries

55. of Assyria I added. Elinzas

56. for a royal city and fortress, that district

57. I took, and its former name I abolished, and
58. Kar-sennacherib I called its name.
59. People of countries conquered by my hand,
60. in the midst I placed, in the hand of my general
61. the governor of Harhar I appointed.
62. On my return,
63. of the Medes remote,
64. of whom among the kings my fathers,
65. anyone had not heard the fame of their country,
66. their great tribute I received;
67. to the yoke of my dominion I subjected them.

Column III.

1. In my third expedition to the land of the Hittites I went.
2. Elulias king of Zidon,
3. fear of the might of my dominion overwhelmed him, and
4. to a distance in the midst of the sea,
5. he fled, and his country I took.
6. Great Zidon,
7. Lesser Zidon,
8. Bit-sette, Zarephath,
9. Mahalliba, Hosah,
10. Achzib, and Accho,
11. his strong cities, fortresses, walled
12. and enclosed, his castles; the might of the soldiers

SENNACHERIB.

13. of Assur my lord overwhelmed them, and they submitted

14. to my feet. Tubahal in the throne of the kingdom

15. over them I seated, and taxes and tribute to my dominion

16. yearly, unceasing, I fixed upon him.

17. Of Menahem of Samaria,

18. Tubahal of Zidon,

19. Abdilihiti of Arvad,

20. Urumelek of Gubal,

21. Metinti of Ashdod,

22. Buduil of Beth Ammon,

23. Kemoshnatbi of Moab,

24. Airammu of Edom,

25. kings of the Hittites, all of them of the coast,

26. the whole, their great presents and furniture,

27. to my presence they carried, and kissed my feet.

28. And Zidqa king of Askelon,

29. who did not submit to my yoke; the gods of the house of his father, himself,

30. his wife, his sons, his daughters, and his brothers, the seed of the house of his father,

31. I removed, and to Assyria I sent him.

32. Sarludari son of Rukibti their former king,

33. over the people of Askelon I appointed,

34. and the gift of taxes due to my dominion,

35. I fixed on him, and he performed my pleasure.

36. In the course of my expedition, Beth Dagon, Joppa,

37. Bene-berak and Azor,
38. cities of Zidqa,
39. which to my feet homage did not render,
40. I besieged, I captured, I carried off their spoil.
41. The priests, princes, and people of Ekron,
42. who Padi their king, faithful
43. and stedfast to Assyria, in bonds of iron
44. placed and to Hezekiah
45. king of Judah gave him as an enemy;
46. for the evil they did their hearts feared.
47. The kings of Egypt, and the archers,
48. chariots, and horses, of the king of Meroe,
49. a force without number gathered and
50. came to their help.
51. In the vicinity of Eltekeh,
52. before me their lines were placed,
53. and they urged on their soldiers.
54. In the service of Assur my lord, with them
55. I fought, and I accomplished their overthrow.
56. the charioteers and sons of the kings of Egypt,
57. and the charioteers of the king of Meroe,
58. alive in the midst of the battle my hand captured.
59. Eltekeh and Timnah I besieged, I captured,
60. I carried off their spoil. To Ekron
61. I approached; the priests and princes,
62. who the rebellion had made, with the sword I slew,
63. and in heaps over the whole of the city I threw down their bodies.

SENNACHERIB.

64. The sons of the city doing this and the revilers
65. into slavery I gave; the rest of them
66. not making rebellion and defiance,
67. who of their section were not,

Column IV.

1. their innocence I proclaimed. Padi their king
2. from the midst of Jerusalem
3. I brought out and on the throne of dominion
4. over them I seated, and tribute
5. to my dominion I fixed upon him.
6. And Hezekiah of Judah,
7. who did not submit to my yoke,
8. 46 of his strong cities, fortresses, and small cities
9. which were round them, which were without number,
10. with the marching of a host and surrounding of a multitude,
11. attack of ranks, force of battering rams, mining and missiles,
12. I besieged, I captured. 200,150 people, small and great, male and female,
13. horses, mules, asses, camels, oxen,
14. and sheep, which were without number, from the midst of them I brought out, and
15. as spoil I counted. Him like a caged bird within Jerusalem
16. his royal city I had made, towers round him

17. I raised, and the exit of the great gate of his city I shut and

18. he was conquered. His cities which I spoiled from the midst of his country

19. I detached, to Metinti king of Ashdod,

20. Padi king of Ekron, and Zillibel

21. king of Gaza, I gave, and I reduced his country.

22. Beside their former taxes, their annual gift

23. the tribute due to my dominion I added and

24. fixed upon them. He Hezekiah

25. fear of the might of my dominion overwhelmed him, and

26. the Urbi and his good soldiers

27. whom to be preserved within Jerusalem

28. he had caused to enter, and they inclined

29. to submission, with 30 talents of gold,

30. 800 talents of silver, precious carbuncles,

31. daggasi, great .... stones,

32. couches of ivory, elevated thrones of ivory,

33. skins of buffaloes, horns of buffaloes, izdan, izku,

34. everything a great treasure, and

35. his daughters, the eunuchs of his palace, male musicians, and female musicians

36. to the midst of Nineveh the city of my dominion

37. after me he sent, and

38. to give tribute

39. and make submission, he sent his messenger.

---

40. In my fourth expedition Assur my lord

SENNACHERIB.

41. protected me, and my army
42. powerful I gathered and to the land of Bit-yakin
43. I commanded to go. In the course of my expedition,
44. of Suzub the Chaldean, dwelling within the lakes,
45. in the city of Bit-tut I accomplished his overthrow.
46. He the might of my attack
47. against him found, and his heart was cast down;
48. like a bird, alone he fled, and his place was not seen.
49. The front of my feet I turned and
50. to Bit-yakin I took the road.
51. He Merodach Baladan, of whom in the course
52. of my former expedition his overthrow I had accomplished, and
53. dispersed his forces;
54. the march of my powerful soldiers,
55. and the shock of my fierce attack he avoided, and
56. the gods ruling in his country in their shrines he gathered, and
57. in ships he caused to sail, and
58. to Nagiti-raqqi which is in the midst of the sea,
59. like a bird he fled.
60. His brothers the seed of the house of his father,
61. whom he had left beside the sea, and the rest of the people of his country,

Column V.

1. from Bit-yakin in the lakes and swamps
2. I brought out and as spoil I counted. I returned, and his cities I pulled down,
3. destroyed, and reduced to ruins. Upon his ally
4. the king of Elam terror I struck.
5. On my return, Assur-nadin-sum
6. my eldest son the child of my knees,
7. on the throne of his dominion I seated, and the extent of Sumir and Akkad
8. I entrusted to him.
9. Among the spoil of those countries which I carried off,
10. 15,000 bows and 15,000 spears
11. from the midst of them I selected and
12. over the body of my kingdom I spread.
13. The rest of the spoil of the rebels abundant,
14. to the whole of my camp, my governors,
15. and the people of my great cities,
16. like sheep I distributed.

The remainder of this text describes the neglect into which the city of Nineveh had fallen, and the works undertaken by Sennacherib to restore it. In this labour he used the captives taken in his expeditions, and he gives these as the Chaldeans, Arameans, Mannians, people of Que and Cilicia, the Philistines, and the Tyrians.

There is in the new collection a curious despatch to Sennacherib from Pahir-bel the governor of Amida (Amadiya) the first part of which I have translated.

Lintel of Doorway
Great Court of Sennecherib's Palace

S. Thompson

Despatch from Pahir-bel to Sennacherib.

1. To the king my lord, thy servant Pahir-bel.
2. May there be peace to the king my lord,
3. peace to the country of the king,
4. peace to the fortresses.
5. May the heart of the king my lord be well.
6. Concerning the news of Ararat (Armenia)
7. the *daili* I send.
8. He came here with this,
9. and told that the governor
10. of Butunni, and the second in command,
11. sent him. In the city of Harda
12. before the officer a watch they kept,
13. and from city to city, to the city of Turuspa.
14. Before that thou writest,
15. and the messenger of Argisti came
16. also about the matter, the news
17. I sent to thee; and the matter
18. also thou didst not decide, and thy horses
19. which were committed to the messenger,
20. I sent.

Amida, the head of the government of Pahir-bel was near the Armenian frontier; Butunni, the district mentioned, was in the same region, the city of Turuspa was near the modern city of Van, on the lake of Van. It was the capital of Ararat or Armenia, a country generally hostile to Assyria. Argisti was king of Armenia in the time of Sennacherib. After the murder of Sennacherib by his two sons, they fled into the land of Armenia.

The new collection contains several other documents of the reign of Sennacherib.

Chapter XVII.

INSCRIPTIONS OF ESARHADDON,

B.C. 681 TO 668.

New texts.—Wars with Tirhakah.—Bahal of Tyre.—March through Palestine.—Meroe.—Desert.—Want of water.—Long marches.—Conquest of Egypt.—Wars of Sennacherib.—Suzub. —Elamites.—Plunder of temple of Bel.—Babylonian dated tablet.

THERE are several new and important texts of Esarhaddon in the new collection. Most of these are not yet copied and translated; I have therefore only chosen two for my present work, which I have joined together, partly from the old collection and partly from the new. The first text gives an account of the operations of Esarhaddon against Tirhakah king of Egypt and Ethiopia, whom he conquered in his tenth expedition (about B.C. 672).

1. That . . . . a second time I . . . .
2. . . . . I placed. Bihilu . . . .
3. Bel-idina in the city of Kullimmir . . . .
4. to the borders of Assyria added . . . .
5. tribute to my dominion . . . .

6. In my 10th expedition the God . . . .

7. I set my face to the country of Magan (and Miluhha?) . . . .

8. which in the language of the people of Kush (Ethiopia) and Muzur (Egypt) are called . . . .

9. I collected my powerful army which within . . .

10. In the month Nisan the first month, from my city Assur I departed, the rivers Tigris and Euphrates in their flood I crossed over,

11. difficult countries like a bull I passed through.

12. In the course of my expedition against Bahal king of Tyre who to Tirhakah king of Kush his country entrusted, and

13. the yoke of Assur my lord threw off and made defiance;

14. fortresses over against him I built and food and drink to save their lives, I cut off.

15. From the land of Muzur (Egypt) my camp I collected, and to the country of Miluhha (Meroe) I directed the march,

16. 30 kaspu of ground (200 miles) from the city of Aphek which is at the border of Samaria to the city of Raphia,

17. to the boundary of the stream of Muzur (Egypt), a place where there was no water, a very great desert.

18. Water from wells in buckets for my army I caused to carry.

19. When the will of Assur my lord into my ears entered . . . . my mind,

20. The camels of the kings of Arabia all of them . . . . them

21. 30 kaspu of ground a journey of 15 days in . . . I pursued

22. 4 kaspu of ground with boulder stones . . . . I went

23. 4 kaspu of ground a journey of 2 days, with serpents having two heads . . . . death and

24. I trampled on and passed. 4 kaspu of ground a journey of 2 days . . . . burning . . . .

25. of winged flies. 4 kaspu of ground a journey of 2 days . . . . full

26. 15 kaspu of ground a journey of 8 days I pursued . . . . a journey.

27. Merodach the great lord to my aid came . . . .

28. and saved the lives of my soldiers. 27 days . . .

29. of the border of Egypt the city of Magan . . . .

30. From the city of Makan to . . . .

31. a measure of 20 kaspu of ground I pursued . . . .

32. that ground was like stone . . . .

33. like fowl with maces . . . .

34. blood and marrow . . . .

35. The obstinate enemy to . . . .

36. to the city it swept . . . .

This text, unfortunately fragmentary, gives the description of Esarhaddon's campaign, commencing with his starting from Assyria; he crossed the Tigris and Euphrates, and first attacked the city of Tyre. After blockading Tyre, which had joined Tirhakah king of Ethiopia against the Assyrian power, Esarhaddon marched from Aphek in the north of Palestine to Raphia on the Egyptian border. Already here he felt the want of water; but yet he tried a march through the desert to reach Miluhha or Meroe. In this journey the Assyrian army suffered severely from the nature of the ground travelled over, the noxious animals met with, and the want of water. It is uncertain if Esarhaddon succeeded in his expedition against Meroe, the stronghold of Tirhakah; and it is probable, at least, that the expedition produced no permanent results, and that Esarhaddon had to content himself with the possession of Egypt from the sea up to Thebes, which he appears to have gained in his previous expedition B.C. 673, the expedition in B.C. 672 being his second against Tirhakah.

Among the other new texts of Esarhaddon are long descriptions of his father's wars in Chaldea against Suzub, the Chaldean and Umman-minan king of Elam, of the plundering of the Babylonian temples to satisfy the Elamite allies of the Babylonians, of the ruin of Babylon in the time of Sennacherib, and of his own restoration of the temples and city.

The following is a translation of the principal of these texts:—

1. The Chaldean . . . . . rebels disregarding agreements,

2. a chief subject to the governor of the city of Lahiri, who in the midst of the days of my father

3. before the face of the advance and attack of the Assyrian generals, like a bird had fled and

4. came to misfortune; in revolt and .... to the city of Babylon entered and

5. joined with them. Over them they raised him, and the empire of Sumir and Akkad they committed to him.

6. To Babylon with many sinners he joined, and he Suzub the Chaldean of unknown parentage

7. the low chief, who possessed no power, to the kingdom of Babylon was appointed.

8. The sons of Babylon who revolt had made, the Chaldeans, Arameans, ... Arabuku, fugitives,

9. who by force and bribes, with them they caused to unite, ... and made agreement;

10. the house of the furniture of the temples of Saggal they opened, and silver, gold, and precious stones, of the gods Bel and Zirit-banit

11. and the gifts of furniture and goods they brought out, and sent to Umman-minan king of Elam

12. who knew not wisdom and judgment. An agreement with them he made and the present took and

13. made a promise to gather his people, to prepare his camp and assemble his chariots ....

14. His people he gathered, his chariots and carriages he prepared, his horses and mules he fastened to his yoke,

15. The countries of Persia Anzan, Pasiru Ellipu (here follows the list of countries subject to Elam the people of which came with Umman-minan to assist the Babylonians against Sennacherib father of

Esarhaddon. The text in this part is mutilated, but the rest of the history is given on the Taylor cylinder, "Cuneiform Inscriptions" vol. i. p. 41).

Esarhaddon proclaimed himself king of Babylon as well as Assyria, and the Babylonian contract tablets of his time are dated in the years of his reign. I procured one of these from Babylon, dated "In the city of Babylon, month Iyyar, day 22nd, 4th year of Esarhaddon king of Babylon." Another tablet I purchased in Hillah is the only known text of the reign of Saulmugina, son of Esarhaddon, who succeeded his father on the Babylonian throne, B.C. 668; this is dated City of Babylon, month . . . . 29th day, 14th year of Saulmugina . . . . .

Late in his reign, Esarhaddon associated with himself on the Assyrian throne his eldest son, Assurbanipal, who is mentioned with his father on some of the new texts.

Chapter XVIII.

INSCRIPTIONS OF ASSURBANIPAL,

B.C. 668 TO 626.

Greek Sardanapalus. — Library. — Former publication. — Egyptian history. — Sabako. — Tirhakah. — Undamane. — Text. — Titles. — Campaign against Tirhakah. — Revolt of Egypt. — Death of Tirhakah. — Undamane. — Second Egyptian campaign. — Siege of Tyre. — Arvad. — Gyges of Lydia. — Psammitichus. — War with Minni. — War with Elam. — Revolt of Babylon. — Wars with Elam. — Restoration of Nana. — Arabian war. — Armenian embassy. — Restoration of palace. — Restoration of temples. — Brick from Babylon.

ASSURBANIPAL, the Sardanapalus of the Greeks, was the greatest and most celebrated of Assyrian monarchs. He was the principal patron of Assyrian literature, and the greater part of the grand library at Nineveh was written during his reign. The fragments and texts of Assurbanipal in the new collection are very numerous. I only select two of these, to show the character of these records,—one the cylinder containing his history, which I have named

Cylinder A, and the other his account of the restoration of the Babylonian temples.

Cylinder A I have twice published previously,—once in my history of Assurbanipal, and a second time, with the additions and corrections derived from my first journey to Assyria, in the "Records of the Past," vol. i. I have now some important copies of this text, giving new information and variant passages, one remarkable new point being that Sabako the Ethiopian king of Egypt is mentioned, and his relationship to the other monarchs of this dynasty is stated; the result of this information may be shown by the following table:

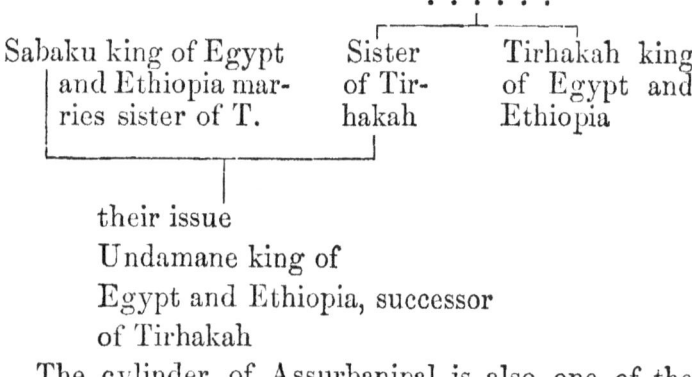

The cylinder of Assurbanipal is also one of the finest Assyrian historical documents, and shows the Assyrian view of the politics of that day.

History of Assurbanipal on Cylinder A (new text, with variants from other copies).

COLUMN I.

1. I am Assurbanipal the progeny of Assur and Beltis,
2. son of the great king of Riduti,
3. whom Assur and Sin lord of crowns from days remote
4. prophesying his name, have raised to the kingdom;
5. and in the womb of his mother, have created him to rule Assyria.
6. Shamas, Vul, and Ishtar, in their supreme power,
7. commanded the making of his kingdom.
8. Esarhaddon king of Assyria the father my begetter,
9. the will of Assur and Beltis the gods his protectors, praised,
10. who commanded him to make my kingdom.
11. In the month Iyyar, the month of Hea lord of mankind,
12. on the 12th day, a fortunate day, the festival of Bel;
13. in performance of the important message which Assur,
14. Beltis, Sin, Shamas, Vul, Bel, Nebo,
15. Ishtar of Ninevah, Sarrat-kitmuri,

16. Ishtar of Arbela, Ninip, Nergal, and Nusku, had spoken,

17. he gathered the people of Assyria, small and great,

18. and of the upper and lower sea,

19. to the consecration of my royal sonship;

20. and afterwards the kingdom of Assyria I ruled.

21. The worship of the great gods I caused to be offered to them,

22. I confirmed the covenants.

23. With joy and shouting

24. I entered into Riduti the palace,

25. the royal property of Sennacherib the grandfather my begetter,

26. the son of the great king who ruled the kingdom within it,

27. the place where Esarhaddon the father my begetter,

28. within it grew up and ruled the dominion of Assyria.

29. . . . . and the family increased

30. . . . .

31. I Assurbanipal within it preserved

32. the wisdom of Nebo all the royal tablets,

33. the whole of the clay tablets all there were, their subjects I studied.

34. I collected arrows, bows, carriages, horses,

35. chariots, their furniture, and fittings. By the will of the great gods

ASSURBANIPAL.

36. who . . . . I proclaimed their laws,

37. they commanded the making of my kingdom,

38. the embellishing of their temples they entrusted to me,

39. for me they exalted my dominion, and destroyed my enemies.

40. The man of war, the delight of Assur and Ishtar,

41. the royal offspring am I.

42. When Assur, Sin, Shamas, Vul, Bel, Nebo, Ishtar of Nineveh,

43. Sarrat-kitmuri, Ishtar of Arbela, Ninip, Nergal, and Nusku,

44. firmly seated me on the throne of the father my begetter,

45. Vul poured down his rain, Hea feasted his people.

46. fivefold the seed bore in its ear,

47. the surplus grain was two-thirds, the crops were excellent,

48. the corn abundant, my face was pleased with the raising of the harvest,

49. . . . . cattle were good in multiplying,

50. in my seasons there was plenty, in my years famine was ended.

---

51. In my first expedition to Makan

52. and Miluhha I went. Tirhakah king of Egypt and Ethiopia,

53. of whom Esarhaddon king of Assyria, the

father my begetter, his overthrow had accomplished,

54. and had taken possession of his country; he Tirhakah

55. the power of Assur, Ishtar and the great gods my lords

56. despised, and trusted to his own might.

57. Of the kings and governors, whom in the midst of Egypt,

58. the father my begetter had appointed; to slay, plunder,

59. and to capture Egypt, he came against them.

60. He entered and sat in Memphis,

61. the city which the father my begetter had taken, and to the boundaries

62. of Assyria had added. I was going in state in the midst of Nineveh,

63. and one came and repeated this to me.

64. Over these things

65. my heart was bitter, and much afflicted.

66. By command of Assur and the goddess Assuritu

67. I gathered my powerful forces,

68. which Assur and Ishtar had placed in my hands;

69. to Egypt and Ethiopia I directed the march.

70. In the course of my expedition, 22 kings

71. of the side of the sea, and middle of the sea, all

72. tributaries dependent upon me,

73. to my presence came and kissed my feet.
74. Those kings .... of them,
75. on sea and land their roads I took,
76. the level path .... them
77. for the restoration of the kings and governors,
78. who in the midst of Egypt were tributaries dependent on me;
79. quickly I descended and went to Karbanit.
80. Tirhakah king of Egypt and Ethiopia, in the midst of Memphis,
81. of the progress of my expedition heard; and to make war,
82. fighting, and battle, to my presence he gathered the men of his army.
83. In the service of Assur, Ishtar, and the great gods my lords,
84. On the wide battle-field I accomplished the overthrow of his army.
85. Tirhakah in the midst of Memphis, heard of the defeat of his army;
86. the terror of Assur and Ishtar overcame him, and
87. he went forward, fear of my kingdom
88. overwhelmed him, and his gods glorified me before my camp.
89. Memphis he abandoned, and to save his life
90. he fled into Thebes. That city I took,
91. my army I caused to enter and rest in the midst of it.
92. Necho king of Memphis and Sais,

93. Sar-ludari king of Pelusium,
94. Pisan-hor king of Natho,
95. Paqruru king of Pi-supt,
96. Pukkunanni-hapi king of Athribis,
97. Nech-ke king of Henins,
98. Petubastes king of Tanis,
99. Unamuna king of Natho,
100. Horsiesis king of Sebennytus,
101. Buaiuva king of Mendes,
102. Sheshonk king of Busiris,
103. Tnephachthus king of Bunubu,
104. Pukkunanni-hapi king of Akhni,
105. Iptihardesu king of Pi-zattihurunpiku,
106. Necht-hor-ansini king of Pi-sabdinut,
107. Bukur-ninip king of Pachnut,
108. Zikha king of Siyout,
109. Lamintu king of Chemmis,
110. Ispimathu king of Abydos,
111. Munti-mi-anche king of Thebes.
112. These kings, prefects, and governors,
113. whom in the midst of Egypt, the father my begetter had appointed;
114. who before the advance of Tirhakah
115. their appointments had left, and fled to the desert,
116. I restored, and the places of their appointments
117. in their possessions, I appointed them.
118. Egypt and Ethiopia, which the father my begetter had captured,

ASSURBANIPAL.

119. again I took, the bonds more than in former days
120. I strengthened, and I made covenants.
121. With abundant plunder and much spoil
122. in peace I returned to Nineveh.
123. Afterwards all those kings whom I had appointed,
124. sinned against me, they did not keep the oath of the great gods,

Column II.

1. the good I did to them they despised,
2. and their hearts devised evil.
3. Seditious words they spoke, and
4. evil council they counselled among themselves,
5. thus: "Tirhakah from the midst of Egypt
6. is cut off, and to us our seats are numbered."
7. Unto Tirhakah king of Ethiopia
8. to make agreement and alliance
9. they directed their messengers,
10. thus: "May an alliance by this treaty be established, and
11. we will help each other.
12. The country on the other side we will strengthen, and
13. may there not be in this treaty, any other lord."
14. Against the army of Assyria the force of my dominion,

15. which to their aid had been raised, they devised

16. a wicked plot. My generals of this plot

17. heard; their messengers

18. and their despatches they captured, and saw

19. their seditious work. These kings

20. they took, and in bonds of iron and fetters of iron,

21. bound their hands and feet. The oath of Assur king of the gods,

22. took those who sinned

23. against the great gods, who had sought the good of their hands, and

24. who had given them favours;

25. and the people of Sais, Mendes, Zoan

26. and the rest of the cities, all with them revolted and

27. devised an evil design. Small and great with the sword they caused to be destroyed,

28. one they did not leave in the midst.

29. Their corpses they threw down in the dust,

30. . . . . they destroyed the towers of the cities.

31. These kings who had devised evil

32. against the army of Assyria, alive to Nineveh

33. into my presence they brought.

34. To Necho . . . . of them,

35. favour I granted him, and a covenant . . . .

36. observances stronger than before I caused to be restored, and with him I sent

37. costly garments I placed upon him, ornaments of gold

38. his royal image I made for him, bracelets of gold I fastened on his limbs,

39. a steel sword its sheath of gold,

40. in the glory of my name more than I write, I gave him.

41. Chariots, horses, and mules,

42. for his royal riding I appointed him,

43. my generals as governors

44. to assist him, with him I sent.

45. The place where the father my begetter, in Sais to the kingdom had appointed him,

46. to his district I restored him,

47. and Neboshazban his son, in Athribes I appointed.

48. Benefits and favours, beyond those of the father my begetter,

49. I caused to restore and gave to him.

50. Tirhakah from the place fled,

51. the might of the soldiers of Assur my lord overwhelmed him, and

52. he went to his place of Night (*i.e.* died).

53. Afterwards, Undamane son of Sabako

54. sat on his royal throne.

55. The cities of Thebes and Hermopolis his fortresses he made,

56. and gathered his forces

57. to fight the army of the sons of Assyria,

58. who within Memphis gathered in the midst of it.

59 Those people he besieged and took the whole of them, and

60. a swift messenger to Nineveh came and told me.

---

61. In my second expedition to Egypt and Ethiopia

62. I directed the march. Undamane

63. of the progress of my expedition heard, and that I had crossed over

64. the borders of Egypt. Memphis he abandoned, and

65. to save his life he fled into Thebes.

66. The kings, prefects, and governors, whom in Egypt I had set up,

67. to my presence came, and kissed my feet.

68. After Undamane the road I took,

69. I went to Thebes the strong city.

70. The approach of my powerful army he saw, and Thebes he abandoned,

71. and fled to Kipkip. That city (Thebes)

72. the whole of it, in the service of Assur and Ishtar my hands took;

73. silver, gold, precious stones, the furniture of his palace, all there was,

74. garments of wool and linen, great horses,

75. people male and female,

76. two lofty obelisks covered with beautiful carving,

77. 2,500 talents (*over* 90 *tons*) their weight, standing before the gate of a temple,

78. from their places I removed and brought to Assyria.

79. The spoil great and unnumbered, I carried off from the midst of Thebes.

80. Over Egypt and Ethiopia,

81. my soldiers I caused to march, and

82. I acquired glory. With a full hand

83. peacefully I returned to Nineveh the city of my dominion.

---

84. In my third expedition, against Bahal king of Tyre,

85. dwelling in the midst of the sea, I went; who my royal will

86. disregarded, and did not hear the words of my lips.

87. Towers round him I raised,

88. on sea and land his roads I took,

89. their spirits I humbled and caused to melt away,

90. to my yoke I made them submissive.

91. The daughter proceeding from his body, and the daughters of his brothers,

92. for concubines he brought to my presence.

93. Yahimilek his son, the glory of the country, of unsurpassed renown,

94. at once he sent forward, to make obeisance to me.

95. His daughter and the daughters of his brothers,

96. with their great dowries I received.

97. Favour I granted him, and the son proceeding from his body,

98. I restored and gave him. Yakinlu

99. King of Arvad, dwelling in the midst of the sea,

100. who to the kings my fathers was not submissive,

101. submitted to my yoke. His daughter

102. with many gifts, for a concubine

103. to Nineveh he brought, and kissed my feet.

104. Mugallu king of Tubal, who against the kings my fathers

105. made attacks, the daughter proceeding from his body,

106. and her great dowry, for a concubine

107. to Nineveh he brought, and kissed my feet.

108. Over Mugallu great horses

109. an annual tribute I fixed upon him.

110. Sandasarmi of Cilicia,

111. who to the kings my fathers did not submit,

112. and did not perform their pleasure,

113. the daughter proceeding from his body, with many

114. gifts, for a concubine

115. to Nineveh he brought, and kissed my feet.

116. When Yakinlu king of Arvad

117. had met his death. Azibahal, Abibahal,

118. Adonibahal, Sapadibahal, Pudibahal,

119. Bahalyasup, Bahalhanun,

120. Bahalmaluk, Abimelek and Ahimelek

121. sons of Yakinlu, dwelling in the midst
122. of the sea, from the midst of the sea arose, and
123. with their numerous presents
124. came and kissed my feet.
125. Azibahal gladly I perceived and
126. to the kingdom of Arvad appointed.
127. Abibahal, Adonibahal, Sapadibahal,

COLUMN III.

1. Pudibahal, Bahalyasup, Bahalhanon,
2. Bahalmelek, Abimelek, and Ahimelek
3. clothing of wool and linen I placed on them, bracelets of gold I made and fastened on their limbs,
4. in my presence . . . . them.
5. Gyges king of Lydia
6. a district which is across the sea, a remote place;
7. of which the kings my fathers had not heard speak of its name;
8. the account of my grand kingdom in a dream was related to him, by Assur the god my creator,
9. thus: "The yoke . . . .
10. when in remembrance . . . .
11. the day he saw that dream,
12. his messenger he sent to pray for my friendship.
13. That dream which he saw,
14. by the hand of his envoy he sent, and repeated to me.

15. From the midst of the day when he took the yoke of my kingdom,

16. the Cimmerians wasters of the people of his country,

17. who did not fear my fathers

18. and me, and did not take the yoke of my kingdom; he captured.

19. In the service of Assur and Ishtar the gods my lords,

20. from the midst of the chiefs of the Cimmerians whom he had taken,

21. two chiefs in strong fetters of iron, and bonds of iron,

22. he bound, and with numerous presents

23. he caused to bring to my presence.

24. His messengers, whom to pray for my friendship

25. he was constantly sending, he wilfully discontinued,

26. as the will of Assur the god my creator, he had disregarded;

27. to his own power he trusted and hardened his heart.

28. His forces to the aid of Psammitichus king of Egypt,

29. who had thrown off the yoke of my dominion, he sent; and

30. I heard of it, and prayed to Assur and Ishtar,

31. thus: "Before his enemies his corpse may they cast, and

32. may they carry captive his servants." When thus to Assur

33. I had prayed, he requited me, before his enemies his corpse

34. was thrown down, and they carried captive his servants.

35. The Cimmerians whom by the glory of my name, he had trodden under him;

36. came and swept the whole of his country. After him his son

37. sat on his throne. That evil work, at the lifting up of my hands;

38. the gods my protectors in the time of the father his begetter had destroyed.

39. By the hand of his envoy he sent and took

40. the yoke of my kingdom, thus: "The king whom God has blessed, art thou;

41. my father from thee departed, and evil was done in his time;

42. I am thy devoted servant; and my people all perform thy pleasure."

---

43. In my fourth expedition, I gathered my army;
44. against Akhsera king of Minni
45. I directed the march.
46. By command of Assur, Sin, Shamas, Vul, Bel, Nebo,
47. Ishtar of Nineveh, Sarrat-Kitmuri,
48. Ishtar of Arbela, Ninip, Nergal, and Nusku,
49. into Minni I entered, and marched victoriously.

50. His strong cities and smaller ones which were without number,

51. to the midst of Izirtu, I took,

52. I threw down, destroyed, and in the fire I burned. People, horses,

53. asses, oxen, and sheep, from the midst of those

54. cities I brought out, and as spoil I counted.

55. Akhsera of the progress of my expedition heard, and

56. abandoned Izirtu his royal city,

57. to Istatti his castle he fled, and

58. took refuge. That district I took,

59. for fifteen days' journey I laid waste, and

60. the highlands I conquered.

61. Akhsera not fearing my power,

62. by the will of Ishtar dwelling in Arbela, who from the first had spoken,

63. thus: "I am the destroyer of Akhsera king of Minni,

64. as I have commanded it, it shall be accomplished." Into the hand of his servants

65. she delivered him, and the people of his country a revolt against him made and

66. in front of his city his servants threw down and

67. tore in pieces his corpse. His brothers, his relatives,

68. and the seed of the house of his father, they destroyed with the sword.

69. Afterwards Vaalli his son sat on his throne,

70. the power of Assur, Sin, Shamas, Vul, Bel, Nebo,

ASSURBANIPAL.

71. Ishtar of Nineveh, Sarrat-kitmuri,

72. Ishtar of Arbela, Ninip, Nergal, and Nusku,

73. the great gods my lords, he saw, and submitted to my yoke.

74. To preserve his life his hand he opened, and besought

75. my power. Erisinni his eldest son

76. to Nineveh he sent, and kissed my feet.

77. Favour I granted him, and my messenger for friendship

78. I sent to him. The daughter proceeding from his body

79. he sent for a concubine.

80. The former tribute, which in the time of the kings my fathers,

81. they had broken off, he brought to my presence.

82. Thirty horses beside the former tribute I added and fixed upon him.

---

83. In my fifth expedition, to Elam I directed

84. the march. By the command of Assur, Sin, Shamas, Vul, Bel, Nebo,

85. Ishtar of Nineveh, Sarrat-kitmuri,

86. Ishtar of Arbela, Ninip, Nergal, and Nusku,

87. in the month Elul, the month of the king of the gods Assur,

88. the father of the gods the glorious prince; like the shock of a terrible storm,

89. I overwhelmed Elam through its extent.

90. I cut off the head of Te-umman, their wicked king,

91. who devised evil. Beyond number I slew his soldiers,

 92. alive in hand I captured his fighting men.
 93. their bodies like bows and arrows
 94. filled the vicinity of Shushan.
 95. Their corpses the river Ulai I caused to take,
 96. its waters I made to consume them like chaff.
 97. Umman-igas son of Urtaki king of Elam,
 98. who from the face of Te-umman to Assyria
 99. fled, and had taken my yoke;
 100. with me I brought him to Elam, and
 101. I seated him on the throne of Te-umman.
 102. Tammaritu his third brother, who with him
 103. fled; in Hidalu I appointed to the kingdom.
 104. Then the servants of Assur and Ishtar over Elam

 105. I caused to march, I acquired power
 106. and glory. On my return
 107. against Dunanu the Gambulian, who to Elam
 108. trusted; I set my face. Sapibel
 109. the fortified city of Gambuli I took;
 110. into that city I entered, its people entirely
 111. I carried off. Dunanu and Samgunu
 112. opposers of the work of my kingdom,
 113. in strong fetters of iron, and bonds of iron,

114. I bound their hands and feet. The rest of the sons of Belbasa,

115. his kin, the seed of his father's house, all there were,

116. Nabonidus and Beledir sons of Nabu-zikir-esses

117. the tigenna, and the servants of the father their begetter,

Column IV.

1. with the . . . . and Tebe,

2. people of Gambuli, oxen, sheep, asses,

3. horses, and mules; from the midst of Gambuli

4. I carried off to Assyria. Sapibel

5. his fortified city, I pulled down, destroyed, and into the waters I turned.

---

6. Saulmagina my younger brother, benefits I had given to him, and

7. had appointed him to the kingdom of Babylon . . . . and gave him

8. . . . . chariots I fixed and

9. . . . . cities, fields, and plantations.

10. Tribute and taxes I caused to return, and more than the father my begetter,

11. I did for him. And he these favours

12. disregarded, and devised evil.

13. He spoke of good,

14. but within his heart he was choosing evil.

15. The sons of Babylon whom in Assyria I benefited,

16. servants dependent upon me, sinned and

17. wrong speech they spoke with them

18. and cunningly to pray for my friendship,

19. to Nineveh to my presence he sent them.

20. I Assurbanipal king of Assyria to whom the great gods excellent fame

21. have renowned, and have created to him right and justice;

22. the sons of Babylon of them in state chairs

23. I set them up, costly garments

24. I placed upon them, rings of gold I fastened on

25. their feet, and the sons of Babylon of them

26. in Assyria they were set up, they were honoured

27. before the giving of my command. And he Saulmugina

28. my younger brother, who did not keep my agreement,

29. the people of Akkad, Chaldea, Aram, and the sea-coast,

30. from Aqaba to Bab-salimitu,

31. tributaries dependent on me, he caused to revolt against my hand.

32. And Umman-igas the fugitive who took

33. the yoke of my kingdom, of whom in Elam

34. I had appointed him to the kingdom; and the kings of Goim,

35. Syria, and Ethiopia,

36. which by command of Assur and Beltis my hands held;

37. all of them, he caused to rebel and

38. with him they set their faces. The great gates of Sippara,

39. Babylon, Borsippa, and Cutha, they raised and broke off the brotherhood,

40. and the walls of those cities, his fighting men

41. he caused to raise. With me they made war and

42. the making of my sacrifices and libations, before the presence of Bel son of Bel,

43. the light of the gods Shamas, the warrior Ninip he stopped, and

44. caused to cease the gifts of my fingers.

45. To turn away the cities, seats of the great gods, of whom their temples

46. I had restored, adorned with gold and silver, and

47. within them had fixed images; he devised evil.

48. In those days then a seer in the beginning of the night slept, and

49. dreamed a dream, thus : " Concerning the matter which Sin was arranging and

50. of them who against Assurbanipal king of Assyria

51. devised evil; battle is prepared,

52. violent death I appoint for them. With the edge of the sword,

53. the burning of fire, famine, and the making of pestilence, I will destroy

54. their lives." This I heard and trusted to the will of Sin

55. my lord. In my sixth expedition I gathered my army,

56. against Saulmugina I directed the march.

57. Within Sippara, Babylon, Borsippa, and Cutha,

58. him and part of his fighting men I besieged and captured

59. the whole of them. In town and country without number

60. I accomplished his overthrow. The rest

61. with the making of pestilence, drought, and famine,

62. passed their lives. Umman-igas king of Elam,

63. appointed by my hand, who the bribe received and came to his aid;

64. Tammaritu against him revolted, and him

65. and part of his family he destroyed with the sword.

66. Afterwards Tammaritu, who after Umman-igas

67. sat on the throne of Elam,

68. did not seek alliance with my kingdom. To the help of

69. Saulmugina my rebellious brother he went, and

70. to fight my army he prepared his soldiers.

71. In prayer to Assur and Ishtar I prayed;

72. my supplications they received, and heard the words of my lips.

73. Inda-bigas his servant against him revolted, and

74. in the battle-field accomplished his overthrow. Tammaritu king of Elam,

75. who over the decapitated head of Te-umman untruth had spoken;

76. which he had cut off in the sight of my army,

77. thus; "I have not cut off the head of the king of Elam

78. .... in the assembly of his army." Again he said:

79. "And Umman-igas only kissed the ground,

80. in the presence of the envoys of Assurbanipal king of Assyria."

81. For these matters which he had mocked,

82. Assur and Ishtar turned from him; and Tammaritu

83. his brothers, his kin, the seed of his father's house, with 85 princes

84. going before him, from the face of Inda-bigas

85. fled, and their bitterness within their hearts

86. raged, and they came to Nineveh.

87. Tammaritu my royal feet kissed, and

88. earth he threw on his hair, standing at my footstool.

89. He to do my service himself set,

90. for the giving of his sentence, and going to his help.

91. By the command of Assur and Ishtar, he submitted to my dominion,

92. in my presence he stood up and glorified

93. the might of my powerful gods, who went to my help.

94. I Assurbanipal of generous heart,

95. of defection the remover, the forgiver of sin;
96. to Tammaritu favour I granted him, and
97. himself and part of the seed of his father's house, within my palace
98. I placed them. In those days the people of Akkad
99. who with Saulmugina were placed and
100. devised evil, famine took them;
101. for their food the flesh of their sons and their daughters
102. they did eat, and divided the . . . .
103. Assur, Sin, Shamas, Vul, Bel, Nebo
104. Ishtar of Nineveh, Sarrat-kitmuri,
105. Ishtar of Arbela, Ninip, Nergal, and Nusku,
106. who in my presence marched and destroyed my enemies;
107. Saulmugina my rebellious brother,
108. who made war with me; in the fierce burning fire
109. they threw him, and destroyed his life.
110. And the people who to Saulmugina
111. my rebellious brother, he had caused to join,
112. and these evil things did,
113. who death deserved; their lives
114. before them being precious:
115. with Saulmugina their lord
116. they did not burn in the fire. Before the edge of the sword,
117. dearth, famine, and the burning fire, they had fled, and

118. taken refuge. The stroke of the great gods
119. my lords, which was not removed,
120. overwhelmed them. One did not flee,
121. a sinner did not escape from my hands,
122. my hand held them. Powerful war chariots,
123. covered chariots, his concubines, and

Column V.

1. the goods of his palace, they brought to my presence.

2. Those men who the curses of their mouth,

3. against Assur my god curses uttered;

4. and against me the prince his worshipper, had devised evil:

5. their tongues I pulled out, their overthrow I accomplished.

6. The rest of the people alive among the stone lions and bulls,

7. which Sennacherib the grandfather my begetter, in the midst had thrown;

8. again I in that pit, those men

9. in the midst threw. Their limbs cut off

10. I caused to be eaten by dogs, bears, eagles,

11. vultures, birds of heaven, and fishes of the deep.

12. By these things which were done,

13. I satisfied the hearts of the great gods my lords.

14. The bodies of the men whom the pestilence had destroyed,

15. and who in drought, and famine, had passed their lives;

16. . . . . dogs, bears,

17. *saturi, burru*, ... grew fat.

18. Their attendants from the midst of Babylon,

19. Cutha, and Sippara, I brought out

20. and placed in slavery.

21. In splendour, the seats of their sanctuaries I built,

22. I raised their glorious towers.

23. Their gods dishonoured, their goddesses desecrated,

24. I rested in purple and hangings.

25. Their institutions which they had removed, like in days of old,

26. in peace I restored and settled.

27. The rest of the sons of Babylon, Cutha,

28. and Sippara, who under chastisement, suffering,

29. and privation had fled;

30. favour I granted them, the saving of their lives I commanded,

31. in Babylon I seated them.

32. The people of Akkad, and some of Chaldea, Aram,

33. and the sea coast, whom Saulmugina had gathered,

34. . . . . returned to their own districts.

35. They revolted against me, and by command of Assur and Beltis

36. and the great gods my protectors, on the whole of them I trampled,

37. the yoke of Assur which they had thrown off, I fixed on them;

38. governors and rulers appointed by my hand,

39. I established over them;

40. The institutions and high ordinances of Assur and Beltis,

41. and the gods of Assyria, I fixed upon them;

42. taxes and tribute to my dominion,

43. a yearly sum undiminished I fixed on them.

---

44. In my seventh expedition in the month Sivan the month of Sin lord of might,

45. eldest son and first of Bel: I gathered my army,

46. against Umman-aldas king of Elam I directed

47. the march. I brought with me Tammaritu king of Elam,

48. who from the face of Inda-bigas his servant had fled, and

49. taken my yoke. The people of Hilmi, Billati,

50. Dummuqu, Sulai, Lahira, and Dibirina,

51. the force of my fierce attack heard of, as I went to Elam.

52. The terror of Assur and Ishtar my lords, and the fear of my kingdom

53. overwhelmed them. They, their people, their oxen, and their sheep,

54. to do my service to Assyria they struck, and

55. took the yoke of my kingdom. Bitimbi the former

56. royal city, the fortress of Elam;

57. which like a wall the boundary of Elam divided,

58. which Sennacherib king of Assyria the grandfather my begetter,

59. my predecessor, had captured; and he the Elamite,

60. a city in front of Bitimbi,

61. another had built, and its wall he had strengthened, and

62. had raised its outer wall, Bitimbi

63. he had proclaimed its name: in the course of my expedition I took.

64. The people dwelling in it, who did not come out and did not pray

65. for alliance with my kingdom, I felled. Their heads I cut off, their lips

66. I tore out, and for the inspection of the people of my country, I brought to Assyria.

67. Imba-appi governor of Bitimbi,

68. the relative of Umman-aldas king of Elam;

69. alive from the midst of that city

70. I brought out, and hand and foot in bonds of iron I placed him, and

71. sent to Assyria. The women of the palace, and sons

72. of Te-umman king of Elam; whom by command of Assur,

73. in my former expedition I had cut off his head;
74. with the rest of the people dwelling in Bitimbi,
75. I brought out and as spoil I counted. Ummanaldas king of Elam
76. of the progress of my army which into Elam entered, heard and
77. Madaktu his royal city he abandoned, and fled, and his mountains ascended.
78. Umbagua who from Elam from a revolt,
79. to Bubilu had fled, and against Umman-aldas
80. had sat on the throne of Elam: like him also heard, and
81. Bubilu the city of his dominion he abandoned, and
82. like the fishes took to the depths of the remote waters.
83. Tammaritu who fled and took my yoke,
84. into Shushan I caused to enter, I appointed him to the kingdom.
85. The good I had done to him and sent to his aid, he rejected and
86. devised evil to capture my army.
87. Even he said in his heart thus: " The people of Elam
88. for a spoil have turned in the face of Assyria.
89. Their . . . has been entered and they have carried away
90. the plunder of Elam." Assur and Ishtar who before me march,
91. and exalt me over my enemies;

92. the heart of Tammaritu, hard and perverse, they broke, and

93. took hold of his hand, from the throne of his kingdom

94. they hurled him, a second time

95. they subdued him to my yoke.

96. Concerning these matters, in vexation was my heart;

97. which Tammaritu the younger offended.

98. In the glory and power of the great gods my lords,

99. within Elam, through its extent I marched victoriously.

100. On my return, peace and submission

101. to my yoke, I restored to Assyria.

102. Gatadu, Gataduma, Daeba,

103. Nadiha, Duramnani, Duramnanima,

104. Hamanu, Taraqu, Haiusi,

105. Bittagilbitsu, Bitarrabi,

106. Bitimbi, Madaktu, Shushan,

107. Bube, Temaruduksaranni,

108. Urdalika, Algariga,

109. Tubu, Tultubu,

110. Dunsar, Durundasi, Durundasima,

111. Bubilu, Samunu, Bunaki,

112. Qabrina, Qabrinama, and Haraba,

113. their cities I captured, pulled down, destroyed,

114. in the fire I burned; their gods, their people,

115. their oxen, their sheep, their furniture, their goods,

116. carriages, horses, mules,
117. and weapons instruments of war, I carried off to Assyria.

---

118. In my eighth expedition, by command of Assur and Ishtar,
119. I gathered my army, against Umman-aldas
120. king of Elam I directed the march.
121. Bitimbi, which in my former expedition
122. I had captured, again Rasi, Hamanu,
123. and that district I captured. And he Umman-aldas
124. king of Elam, of the capture of Rasi and Hamanu
125. heard, and fear of Assur and Ishtar going before me

Column VI.

1. overwhelmed him, and Madaktu his royal city
2. he abandoned, and fled to Durundasi.
3. The river Itite he crossed, and that river
4. for his stronghold he fixed, and
5. arranged in ranks to fight me.
6. Naditu the royal city, and its district I captured,
7. Bitbunaki the royal city ditto
8. Hardapanu the royal city ditto
9. Tubu the royal city ditto.
10. Beside all the river, Madaktu the royal city ditto,

11. Haltemas his royal city I captured,
12. Shushan his royal city I captured,
13. Dinsar, Sumuntunas ditto,
14. Pidilma his royal city, Bubilu ditto,
15. Kabinak his royal city ditto.
16. In the service of Assur and Ishtar, I marched and went
17. after Umman-aldas king of Elam,
18. who did not submit to my yoke. In the course of my expedition,
19. Durundasi his royal city I captured.
20. My army the Itite in high flood
21. saw, and feared the crossing.
22. Ishtar dwelling in Arbela, in the middle of the night to my army
23. a dream sent, and even told them,
24. thus: "I march in front of Assurbanipal, the king
25. whom my hands made." Over that vision
26. my army rejoiced, and the Itite crossed peacefully.
27. Fourteen cities royal seats, and smaller cities
28. the numbers unknown, and twelve districts
29. which are in Elam, all of them I took,
30. I pulled down, destroyed, in the fire I burned, and to mounds and heaps I reduced.
31. Without number I slew their warriors,
32. with the sword I destroyed his powerful fighting men.
33. Umman-aldas king of Elam

34. in his bitterness fled, and took to the mountains.

35. Banunu, and the districts of Tasara

36. all, twenty cities in the districts

37. of Hunnir, and the boundary of Hidalu, I captured.

38. Balimmu and the cities round it

39. I pulled down and destroyed. Of the people dwelling within them,

40. their misfortune I caused, I broke up their gods,

41. I set at liberty the great goddess of the lord of lords,

42. his gods, his goddesses, his furniture, his goods, people small and great,

43. I carried off to Assyria. Sixty kaspu of ground,

44. by the will of Assur and Ishtar, who sent me,

45. within Elam I entered and marched victoriously.

46. On my return, when Assur and Ishtar exalted me

47. over my enemies, Shushan the great city,

48. the seat of their gods, the place of their oracle, I captured.

49. By the will of Assur and Ishtar, into its palaces I entered

50. and sat with rejoicing. I opened also their treasure houses

51. of silver, gold, furniture, and goods, treasured within them;

52. which the kings of Elam the former,
53. and the kings who were to these days,
54. had gathered and made; which any other enemy
55. beside me, his hands had not put into them,
56. I brought out and as spoil I counted.
57. Silver, gold, furniture, and goods, of Sumir, Akkad,
58. and Ganduniyas, all that the kings of
59. Elam the former and latter, had carried off
60. and brought within Elam; bronze hammered,
61. hard, and pure, precious stones beautiful and valuable,
62. belonging to royalty; which former kings of Akkad
63. and Saulmugina, for their aid had paid
64. to Elam: garments beautiful belonging to royalty,
65. weapons of war, prepared for one to make battle,
66. suited to his hand, instruments furnishing his palaces,
67. all that within it was placed, with the food
68. in the midst which he ate and drank, and the couch he reclined on,
69. powerful war chariots,
70. of which their ornaments were bronze and paint,
71. horses and great mules,
72. of which their trappings were gold and silver, I carried off to Assyria.

73. The tower of Shushan, which in the lower part in marble was laid,

74. I destroyed. I broke through its top which was covered with shining bronze.

75. Susinaq the god of their oracle, who dwelt in the groves;

76. of whom, anyone had not seen the image of his divinity,

77. Sumudu, Lagomer, Partikira,

78. Ammankasibar, Uduran, and Sapak;

79. of whom, the kings of Elam worship their divinity.

80. Ragiba, Sumugursara, Karsa,

81. Kirsamas, Sudunu, Aipaksina,

82. Bilala, Panintimri, Silagara,

83. Napsa, Nabirtu, and Kindakarbu,

84. these gods and goddesses, with their valuables,

85. their goods, their furniture, and priests and

86. worshippers, I carried off to Assyria.

87. Thirty-two statues of kings, fashioned of silver gold, bronze,

88. and alabaster, from out of Shushan,

89. Madaktu, and Huradi,

90. and a statue of Umman-igas son of Umbadara,

91. a statue of Istar-nanhundi, a statue of Halludus

92. and a statue of Tammaritu the later,

93. who by command of Assur and Ishtar made submission to me,

94. I brought to Assyria. I broke the winged lions

95. and bulls watching over the temple, all there were.

96. I removed the winged bulls attached to the gates

97. of the temples of Elam, until they were not, I overturned.

98. His gods and his goddesses I sent into captivity.

99. their forest groves,

100. which any other had not penetrated into the midst of,

101. had not trodden their outskirts;

102. my men of war into them entered,

103. saw their groves, and burned them in the fire.

104. The high places of their kings, former and latter,

105. not fearing Assur and Ishtar my lords,

106. opposers of the kings my fathers,

107. I pulled down, destroyed and burned in the sun.

108. Their servants I brought to Assyria,

109. their leaders without shelter I placed.

110. The wells of drinking water I dried them up,

111. for a journey of a month and twenty-five days the districts of Elam I laid waste,

112. destruction, servitude, and drought, I poured over them.

113. The daughters of kings, consorts of kings,

114. and families former and latter

115. of the kings of Elam, the governors and

116. citizens of those cities,

117. all I had captured ; the commanders of archers, governors,

118. the directors of . . . three horse charioteers,

119. chariot drivers, archers, officers,

120. camp followers and the whole of the people all there were,

121. people male and female, small and great, horses,

122. mules, asses, oxen, and sheep,

123. beside much spoil, I carried off to Assyria.

Column VII.

1. The dust of Shushan, Madaktu,

2. Haltemas, and the rest of their cities,

3. entirely I brought to Assyria.

4. For a month and a day Elam to its utmost extent, I swept.

5. The passage of men, the treading of oxen and sheep,

6. and the springing up of good trees, I burned off the fields.

7. Wild asses, serpents, beasts of the desert, *Ugallu*,

8. safely I caused to lay down in them.

9. The goddess Nana who these 1,635 years

10. had been desecrated, had gone, and dwelt

11. in Elam, a place not suited to her.

12. And in these days, she and the gods her fathers,

13 proclaimed my name to the dominion of the earth.

14. The return of her divinity she entrusted to me,

15. thus: " Assurbanipal from the midst of Elam (wicked)

16. bring me out, and cause me to enter into the temple of Anna "

17. The will commanded by their divinity, which from days remote

18. they had uttered; again they spoke to later people.

19. The hands of her great divinity I took hold of, and

20. the straight road rejoicing in heart,

21. she took to the temple of Anna.

22. In the month Kislev, the first day, into Erech I caused her to enter, and

23. in the temple of Hilianni which she had delighted in,

24. I set her up an enduring sanctuary.

25. People and spoil of Elam,

26. which by command of Assur, Sin, Shamas, Vul, Bel, Nebo

27. Ishtar of Nineveh, Sarrat-kitmuri,.

28. Ishtar of Arbela, Ninip, Nergal and Nusku, I had carried away;

29. the first part to my gods I devoted.

30. The archers, footmen,

31. soldiers, and camp followers,

32. whom I carried off from the midst of Elam;

33. over the body of my kingdom I spread.

34. The rest to the cities, seats of my gods,

35. my prefects, my great men, and all my camp,
36. like sheep I caused to overflow.
37. Umman-aldas, king of Elam,
38. who the vigour of the powerful soldiers of Assur and Ishtar had seen;
39. from the mountains, the place of his refuge, he returned and
40. into Madaktu, the city which by command of Assur and Ishtar
41. I had pulled down, destroyed and carried off its spoil;
42. he entered and sat in sorrow, in a place dishonoured.
43. Concerning Nabu-bel-zikri the grandson of Merodach Baladan;
44. who against my agreement had sinned, and thrown off the yoke of my dominion;
45. who on the kings of Elam to strengthen him had relied,
46. had trusted to Umman-igas, Tammaritu,
47. Inda-bigas, and Umman-aldas,
48. kings who had ruled the dominion of Elam.
49. My envoy about the surrender of Nabu-bel-zikri,
50. with determination of purpose I sent,
51. to Umman-aldas. Nabu-bel-zikri grandson of Merodach Baladan
52. of the journey of my envoy, who into Elam had entered,
53. heard, and his heart was afflicted. He inclined to despair,

54. his life before him he did not regard, and
55. longed for death.
56. To his own armour-bearer he said also
57. thus: " Slay me with the sword."
58. He and his armour-bearer with the steel swords of their girdles pierced through
59. each other. Umman-aldas feared and
60. the corpse of that Nabu-bel-zikri who benefits trampled on,
61. with the head of his armour-bearer who destroyed him with the sword;
62. to my envoy he gave, and he sent it to my presence.
63. His corpse I would not give to burial,
64. more than before his death I returned, and
65. his head I cut off; round the neck of Nabu-qati-zabat
66. the *munmakir* of Saulmugina
67. my rebellious brother, who with him to pass into
68. Elam had gone; I hung it.
69. Pahe who against Umman-aldas
70. had ruled the dominion of Elam,
71. the terror of the powerful soldiers of Assur and Ishtar,
72. who the first, second, and third time, had trampled over Elam;
73. covered him, and he trusted to the goodness of my heart.
74. From the midst of Elam he fled and

75. took the yoke of my kingdom.
76. The people sinners of Bitimbi,
77. Kuzurtein, Dursar,
78. Masutu, Bube,
79. Bitunzai, Bitarrabi
80. Iprat, Zagar of Tapapa,
81. Akbarina, Gurukirra,
82. Dunnu-samas, Hamanu,
83. Kanizu, Aranzese,
84. Nakidati, Timinut of Simami,
85. Bit-qatatti, Sakisai,
86. Zubahe, and Tulhunba,
87. who in my former expedition, from the face of the powerful soldiers
88. of Assur and Ishtar fled, and
89. took to Saladri a rugged mountain;
90. those people who on Saladri
91. the mountain fixed their stronghold,
92. the terror of Assur and Ishtar my lords overwhelmed them,
93. from the mountain the place of their refuge they fled and
94. took my yoke. To the bow I appointed them,
95. over the body of my kingdom
96. which filled my hand, I spread.

---

97. In my ninth expedition I gathered my army,
98. against Vaiteh king of Arabia
99. I directed the march; who against my agree-

100. had sinned, the benefits done to him he did not regard, and

101. threw off the yoke of my dominion.

102. When Assur had set him up to perform my pleasure,

103. to seek my alliance his feet broke off, and

104. he ended his presents and great tribute.

105. When Elam was speaking sedition with Akkad, he heard and

106. disregarded my agreement. Of me Assurbanipal

107. the king, the noble priest, the powerful leader,

108. the work of the hands of Assur, he left me, and

109. to Abiyateh and Aimu sons of Tehari,

110. his forces with them to the help of

111. Saulmugina my rebellious brother he sent, and

112. set his face. The people of Arabia

113. with him he caused to revolt, and carried away the

114. plunder of the people, whom Assur, Ishtar, and the great gods,

115. had given me, their government I had ruled,

116. and they were in my hand.

117. By command of Assur and Ishtar my army in the regions

118. of Azaran, Hirataqaza

119. in Edom, in the neighbourhood of Yabrud,

120. in Beth-ammon, in the district of Hauran,

121. in Moab, in Saharri,

122. in Harze, and in the district of Zobah,

Column VIII.

1. his numerous fighting men I slew without number,.I accomplished

2. his overthrow. The people of Arabia, all who with him came,

3. I destroyed with the sword; and he from the face

4. of the powerful soldiers of Assur fled and got away

5. to a distance. The tents, the pavilions,

6. their dwellings, a fire they raised and burned in the flames.

7. Vaiteh misfortune happened to him, and

8. alone he fled to Nabatea.

9. Vaiteh son of Hazael was brother of the father

10. of Vaiteh son of Bir-daddi, whom the people of his country

11. appointed to the kingdom of Arabia.

12. Assur king of the gods the strong mountain, a decree

13. repeated, and he came to my presence.

14. To satisfy the law of Assur and the great gods

15. my lords, a heavy judgment took him, and

16. in chains I placed him, and with asi and dogs

17. I bound him, and caused him to be kept

18. in the great gate in the midst of Nineveh, Nirib-barnakti-adnati.

19. And he Ammuladi king of Kedar

20. brought to fight the kings of Syria;

21. whom Assur and Ishtar the great gods had entrusted to me.

22. In the service of Assur, Sin, Shamas, Vul, Bel, Nebo,

23. Ishtar of Nineveh, Sarrat-kitmuri,

24. Ishtar of Arbela, Ninip, Nergal, and Nusku,

25. his overthrow I accomplished. Himself alive with Adiya

26. the wife of Vaiteh king of Arabia,

27. they captured and brought to my presence.

28. By command of the great gods my lords, with the dogs

29. I placed him, and I caused him to be kept chained.

30. By command of Assur, Ishtar, and the great gods my lords,

31. of Abiyateh and Aimu sons of Tehari,

32. who to the help of Saulmugina my rebellious brother

33. to enter Babylon went;

34. his helpers I slew, his overthrow I accomplished. The remainder

35. who into Babylon entered, in want and

36. hunger ate the flesh of each other.

37. To save their lives, from the midst of Babylon

38. they came out, and my forces which around Saulmugina

39. were placed, a second time his overthrow accomplished; and

40. he alone fled, and to save his life

41. took my yoke. Favour I granted him and

42. an agreement to worship the great gods I caused him to swear, and

43. instead of Vaiteh or anyone

44. to the kingdom of Arabia I appointed.

45. And he with the Nabateans

46. his face set, and the worship of the great gods did not fear, and

47. carried away the plunder of the border of my country.

48. In the service of Assur, Sin, Shamas, Vul, Bel, Nebo,

49. Ishtar of Nineveh, Sarrat-kitmuri,

50. Ishtar of Arbela, Ninip, Nergal, and Nusku,

51. Nathan king of Nabatea whose place was remote,

52. of whom, Vaiteh to his presence had fled;

53. heard also of the power of Assur who protected me.

54. In the time past to the kings my fathers

55. his envoy he did not send, and did not seek

56. alliance with their kingdom; in fear of the soldiers of Assur

57. capturing him . . . he tore and sought alliance

58. with my kingdom. Abiyateh

59. son of Tehari did not . . . benefits, disregarding the

60. oath of the great gods, seditious words against me

61. he spoke, and his face with Nathan

62. king of Nabatea he set, and their forces

63. they gathered to commit evil against my border.

64. By command of Assur, Sin, Shamas, Vul, Bel, Nebo,

65. Ishtar of Nineveh, Sarrat-kitmuri,

66. Ishtar of Arbela, Ninip, Nergal, and Nusku,

67. my army I gathered, against Abiyateh

68. I directed the march. The Tigris

69. and the Euphrates in their strong flood, peacefully they crossed,

70. they marched, a distant path they took, they ascended

71. the lofty country, they passed through the forests,

72. of which their shadow was vast, bounded by trees great and strong,

73. and vines, a road of mighty woods.

74. They went to the rebels of Vas, a place arid and

75. very difficult, where the birds of heaven had not . . .

76. wild asses they found not in it.

77. 100 kaspu of ground from Nineveh

78. the city the delight of Ishtar wife of Bel;

79. against Vaiteh king of Arabia

80. and Abiyateh with the forces

81. of the Nabateans, they went.

82. They marched and went in the month **Sivan**, the month of **Sin**

83. the eldest son and first of Bel,
84. the 27th day, on the festival of the lady of Babylon,
85. the mighty one of the great gods.
86. From Hadatta I departed,
87. In Laribda a tower of stones,
88. over against lakes of water; I pitched my camp.
89. My army the waters for their drink desired, and
90. they marched and went over arid ground, a place very difficult
91. to Hurarina near Yarki,
92. and Aialla in Vas a place remote,
93. a place the beast of the desert was not in,
94. and a bird of heaven had not fixed a nest.
95. The overthrow of the Isammih, the servants
96. of Adar-samain, and the Nabateans,
97. I accomplished. People, asses, camels,
98. and sheep, their plunder innumerable; I carried away.
99. 8 kaspu of ground my army
100. marched victoriously, peacefully they returned, and
101. in Aialli they drank abundant waters.
102. From the midst of Aialli to Quraziti,
103. 6 kaspu of ground, a place arid and very difficult,
104. they marched and went. The worshippers of Adar-samain,

105. and the Kidri of Vaiteh
106. son of Bir-dadda king of Arabia, I besieged.
107. His gods, his mother, his sister, his wife, his kin,
108. the people in the midst all, the asses,
109. camels, and sheep;
110. all in the service of Assur and Ishtar my lords
111. my hands took. The road to Damascus
112. I caused their feet to take. In the month Ab the month of Sagittarius
113. daughter of Sin the archer, the third day, the festival
114. of the king of the gods Merodach, from Damascus
115. I departed. 6 kaspu of ground in their country all of it,
116. I marched and went to Hulhuliti.
117. In Hukkuruna the rugged mountain,
118. the servants of Abiyatch son of Tehari
119. of Kedar, I captured, his overthrow I accomplished,
120. I carried off his spoil. Abiyateh and Aimu
121. sons of Tehari, by command of Assur and Ishtar my lords,
122. in the midst of battle alive I captured in hand.
123. Hand and foot in bonds of iron I placed them, and

Column IX.

1. with the spoil of their country I brought them
2. to Assyria. The fugitives, who from the face of my soldiers

3. fled, ascended and took to

4. Hukkuruna the rugged mountain.

5. In Laanhabbi .... gathered

6. .... an ....

[Lines 7 to 25 are lost, only a few doubtful characters remaining.]

26. oxen, sheep, asses, camels

27. and men, they carried off without number.

28. The sweeping of all the country through its extent,

29. they collected through the whole of it.

30. Camels like sheep I distributed, and

31. caused to overflow to the people of Assyria

32. dwelling in my country. A camel

33. for half a shekel, in half shekels of silver, they valued in front of the gate.

34. The spoil in the sale of captives among the strong

35. .... which were gathered in droves,

36. they bartered camels and men.

37. Vaiteh and the Arabians,

38. who my agreement ....

39. who from the face of the soldiers of Assur my lord,

40. fled and got away;

41. Ninip the warrior destroyed,

42. in want and famine their lives were spent, and

43. for their food they ate the flesh of their children.

44. with a curse .... mud of the earth
45. in the house of Assur father of the gods ....
them.
46. Assur, Sin, Shamas, Vul, Bel, Nebo,
47. Ishtar of Nineveh, Sarrat-kitmuri,
48. Ishtar of Arbela, Ninip, Nergal, and Nusku,
49. camels strong, oxen and sheep,
50. more than seven the sacrificers sacrificed, and
51. for eating they did not eat their carcases.
52. The people of Arabia one to another, addressed each other
53. thus: " Concerning the number of these
54. evil things which happened to Arabia,
55. because the great agreements with Assur we have not regarded,
56. and we have sinned against the benefits of Assurbanipal
57. the king, the delight of the heart of Bel."
58. Beltis the consort of Bel,
59. the guardian of divinity;
60. who with Anu and Bel in dominion
61. is established: pierced my enemies with horns of iron.
62. Ishtar dwelling in Arbela, with fire clothed;
63. .... drought upon Arabia poured down.
64. Dabara the warrior, mourning caused and
65. destroyed mine enemies.
66. Ninip fierce, the great warrior,
67. the son of Bel; with his mighty arrows
68. destroyed the life of my enemies.

69. Nusku the glorious attendant, sitting in dominion;

70. who by command of Assur and Beltis . . . .

71. the archer, the goddess of . . . .

72. my forces preceded, and . . . . place of my kingdom,

73. the front of my army took and

74. destroyed my enemies.

75. The stroke . . . . Assur, Ishtar,

76. and the great gods my lords,

77. who in making war, went to the help

78. of my army: Vaiteh heard of, and

79. over these things feared, and

80. from Nabatea I brought him out, and

81. in the service of Assur, Sin, Shamas, Vul, Bel, Nebo,

82. Ishtar of Nineveh, Sarrat-kitmuri,

83. Ishtar of Arbela, Ninip, Nergal, and Nusku,

84. . . . . him and sent him to Assyria.

85. . . . . who to capture my enemies

86. . . . . fought. By command of Assur and Beltis

87. with a mace which was grasped by my hand,

88. the flesh coming out of him, his son,

89. in the sight of his eyes I struck down.

90. With the dogs I did not place him,

91. in the gate of the rising sun, in the midst of Nineveh,

92. which, Nirib-parnakti-adnati its name is called;

93. I caused to keep him chained,

94. to exalt the will of Assur, Ishtar, and the great gods

95. my lords. Favour I granted him and saved his life.

96. On my return Hosah,

97. which by the side of the sea has its place, I captured.

98. The people of Hosah who to their governors

99. were not reverent, and did not give the tribute,

100. the gift of their country, I slew. Amongst the people

101. unsubmissive, chastisement I inflicted.

102. Their gods and their people I carried off to Assyria.

103. The people of Accho unsubmissive, I destroyed.

104. Their bodies in the dust I threw down, the whole of the city

105. I quieted. The rest of them I brought

106. to Assyria, in rank I arranged, and

107. over my numerous army,

108. which Assur strengthened, I spread.

109. Aimu son of Tehari, with Abiyateh

110. his brother had risen, and with my army had made war.

111. In the midst of battle, alive in hand I captured him;

112. and in Nineveh the city of my dominion, his skin I tore off.

113. Umman-aldas king of Elam,
114. whom from of old Assur and Ishtar my lords
115. had commanded to make submission to me;
116. by command of their great divinities who were unchanged,
117. afterwards his country against him revolted, and
118. from the face of the tumult of his servants, which they made against him,
119. alone he fled, and took to the mountains.
120. From the mountains the house of his refuge,
121. the place he fled to;
122. like a raven I caught him, and

Column X.

1. alive I brought him to Assyria.
2. Tammaritu, Pahe, and Umman-aldas,
3. who after each other ruled the dominion of Elam;
4. whom, by the power of Assur and Ishtar my lords,
5. I subjugated to my yoke. Vaiteh
6. king of Arabia, of whom, by command of Assur and Ishtar his overthrow
7. I had accomplished; from his country I brought him to Assyria.
8. When to . . . . sacrifices and libations I had offered up
9. in Masmasu, the seat of their power,
10. before Beltis, mother of the great gods,

11. beloved wife of Assur, I had made to the gods of
12. Idkid. To the yoke of my war chariot
13. I caused to fasten them, and to the gate of the temple
14. they drew it. On my feet I made invocation,
15. I glorified their divinity, I praised
16. their power in the assembly of my army; of Assur, Sin,
17. Shamas, Vul, Bel, Nebo, Ishtar of Nineveh,
18. Sarrat-kitmuri, Ishtar of Arbela,
19. Ninip, Nergal, and Nusku, who the unsubmissive to me
20. subjugated to my yoke, and in glory
21. and power, established me over my enemies.

22. Saduri king of Ararat; of whom the kings his fathers
23. to my fathers had sent in fellowship.
24. Again Saduri, the mighty things
25. for which the great gods had caused renown to me, heard, and
26. like a son to a father, he sent to my dominion;
27. and he in these words sent
28. thus: " Salutation to the king my lord."
29. Reverently and submissively, his numerous presents
30. he sent to my presence

31. Now Riduti the private palace of Nineveh,
32. the grand city, the delight of Ishtar;

33. which Sennacherib king of Assyria, the grandfather my begetter,

34. built for his royal seat;

35. that Riduti in my days

36. became old, and its chamber walls decayed.

37. I Assurbanipal the great king, the powerful king,

38. king of nations, king of Assyria, king of the four regions,

39. within that Ridutu grew up.

40. Assur, Sin, Shamas, Vul, Bel, Nebo, Ishtar of Nineveh, Sarrat-kitmuri.

41. Ishtar of Arbela, Ninip, Nergal, and Nusku,

42. my royal sonship . . . .

43. . . . . their good protection,

44. . . . . over me

45. fixed, when on the throne of the father my begetter I sat.

46. They were made . . . . and many people

47. . . . . my hands

48. . . . . me within it.

49. On my couch at night . . . . my

50. in . . . .

51. that mastaku . . . .

52. the great gods its renown have heard . . . . good

53. its decay . . . . to enlarge it

54. . . . . the whole of it I destroyed.

55. . . . . fifty tipki the building of its sculpture

56. . . . . the work of the mound I completed.

57. Before the temples of the great gods my lords
58. I worshipped .... of that mound
59. its sculpture, I did not cut down its top.
60. In a good month and a prosperous day upon that mound,
61. its foundation I placed, I fixed its brickwork.
62. In *biris* and *kamis* its face I ....
63. I divided in three ....
64. In carriages of Elam,
65. which by command of the great gods my lords,
66. I had carried off; to make that Riduti,
67. the people of my country, in the midst of them carried its bricks.
68. The kings of Arabia who against my agreement sinned,
69. whom in the midst of battle alive I had captured in hand,
70. to build that Riduti,
71. heavy burdens I caused them to carry, and
72. I caused them to take ....
73. building its brickwork ....
74. with dancing and music ....
75. with joy and shouting, from its foundation to its roof,
76. I built. More than before ....
77. I extended ....
78. Beams and great planks from Sirara,
79. and Lebanon, I fixed over it.
80. Doors of forest trees, their wood excellent,
81. a covering of copper I spread over and hung in its gates.

82. Great columns of bronze . . . .
83. at the sides of the gates . . . .
84. That Riduti, my royal seat,
85. the whole of it I finished, entirely
86. I completed. Plantations choice,
87. . . . . for the glory of
88. my kingdom I planted like walls.
89. Sacrifices and libations precious I poured out to the gods my lords,
90. with joy and shouting I completed it,
91. I entered into it in a state palanquin.
92. In after days, among the kings my sons,
93. whomever Assur and Ishtar to the dominion of the country and people
94. shall proclaim his name;
95. when this Riduti becomes old and
96. decays, its decay he shall repair,
97. the inscription written of my name my father's and my grandfather's,
98. the remote descendant who . . . . may he see, and
99. a box may he make, sacrifice and libations may he pour out,
100. and with the inscription written of his name may he place them.
101. May the great gods, all who in this inscription are named,
102. like me also, establish to him
103. power and glory.
104. Whoever the inscription written of my name,

105. my father's and my grandfather's, shall destroy,

106. and with his inscription shall not place;

107. Assur, Sin, Shamas, Vul, Bel, Nebo,

108. Ishtar of Nineveh, Sarrat-kitmuri,

109. Ishtar of Arbela, Ninip, Nergal, and Nusku,

110. a judgment equal to the renown of my name, may they pass on him.

Date of document.

111. Month Nisan, 1st day,

112. in the eponymy of Shamas-dain-ani governor of Akkad.

Variant passages from other copies of the cylinder.

Column II., line 50, " Afterwards Undamane son of his sister "

Column II., line 55, " Thebes his fortified city he made "

Column V., line 67, " Imbaappa commander of the archers "

Column V., line 78, " Ambagua who from Elam, from a revolt,"

Column VII., lines 9 to 24, *see page* 224.

Variant for data of documents.

1. Month Elul, 28th day,

2. in the eponymy of Shamas-dain-ani governor of Babylon.

This document is one of the finest Assyrian texts we possess, and it gives the official history of Assyria, from the accession of Assurbanipal, B.C. 671, down to about B.C. 645. The cylinder opens with the account of Assurbanipal being proclaimed King of Assyria by his father, Esarhaddon, and then relates his various campaigns against surrounding nations. The first two of these campaigns were against Egypt, the third against Tyre, the fourth against Minni in the mountains east of Assyria, the fifth, seventh, and eighth against Elam or Susiana, the sixth against Babylon, and the ninth against Arabia.

The other document of Assurbanipal noticed here is the opening portion of a cylinder which I have named cylinder C, a text I have nearly completed from my excavations. This text refers to the restoration and adorning of the various temples; it runs:—

Assurbanipal the great king, the powerful king, king of nations, king of Assyria, king of the four regions, king of Babylon, king of Sumir and Akkad, son of Esarhaddon, king of nations, king of Assyria, grandson of Sennacherib, king of nations, king of Assyria.

The great gods in their assembly my glorious renown have heard, and over the kings who dwell in palaces, the glory of my name they have raised, and have exalted my kingdom.

The temples of Assyria and Babylonia which Esarhaddon, king of Assyria, had begun, their foundations he had built, but had not finished their tops; anew I built them : I finished their tops.

Sadi-rabu-matati (the great mountain of the earth), the temple of the god Assur my lord, completely I finished. Its chamber walls I adorned with gold and silver, great columns in it I fixed, and in its gate the productions of land and sea I placed. The god Assur into Sadi-rabu-matati I brought, and I raised him an everlasting sanctuary.

Saggal, the temple of Merodach, lord of the gods, I built, I completed its decorations; Bel and Beltis, the divinities of Babylon and Hea, the divine judge, from the temple of . . . . I brought out, and placed them in the city of Babylon. Its noble sanctuary a great . . . . with fifty talents of . . . . its brickwork I finished, and raised over it. I caused to make a ceiling (?) of sycamore durable wood, beautiful as the stars of heaven, adorned with beaten gold. Over Merodach the great lord I rejoiced in heart, I did his will. A noble chariot, the carriage of Merodach, ruler of the gods, lord of lords, in gold, silver, and precious stones, I finished its workmanship. To Merodach, king of the whole of heaven and earth, destroyer of my enemies, as a gift I gave it.

A couch of sycamore durable wood, for the sanctuary, covered with precious stones as ornaments, as the resting couch of Bel and Beltis, givers of favour, makers of friendship, skilfully I constructed. In the gate . . . . the seat of Zirat-banit, which adorned the wall, I placed.

Four bulls of silver, powerful, guarding my royal threshold, in the gate of the rising sun, in the greatest gate, in the gate of the temple Sidda which is in the midst of Borsippa, I set up.

Masmasu, the temple of the mistress of the world, beautifully I adorned, entirely . . . . the divine queen of Kitmuri, who . . . . her temple had left . . . . in my time . . . . which Assur had established . . . . to satisfy her divinity. . . .

The dwelling of the gods Sin and Nusku, which a former king, my predecessor, had built: from the beginning had been left, and that dwelling had become old. The dwelling of the gods Sin and Nusku, its damages I repaired, beyond what it was before, I enlarged its site, from its foundation to its roof I rebuilt, and finished it.

The temple of Melammi-sami (the worship of heaven) belonging to the god Nusku the great messenger, which a former king before me had built, and placed within it, great beams and planks I placed over it, and doors of Leari wood covered with plates of silver I hung in the gates.

Two bulls of silver, destroyers of my enemies, in the dwelling of Sin my lord I raised, two eagle-headed attendant figures placed together, protectors of my royal threshold, I set up. I caused to enter into it the productions of land and sea, and in the gate of the temple Hiduti I set them up. The hands of the gods Sin and Nusku I took, I brought them in, and seated them in everlasting sanctuaries. The temples of Assyria and Babylonia, the whole of them I finished, and the furniture of the temples all of it, of silver and gold I made.

Many of these grand works were executed at Babylon, and from the temple of Bel at that city I procured a brick bearing an inscription of Assurbanipal as follows:—

1. To the god Merodach his lord,
2. Assurbanipal
3. king of nations king of Assyria,
4. son of Esarhaddon
5. king of nations king of Assyria
6. king of Babylon,
7. the brickwork
8. of the temple of Te-an-ki
9. anew I caused to build.

From Babylon I procured inscriptions showing that Assurbanipal established a library there as well as in Assyria.

Chapter XIX.

INSCRIPTIONS OF BEL-ZAKIR-ISKUN, KING OF ASSYRIA, AND HIS SUCCESSORS.

Want of Monuments.—Obscurity of history.—Bel-zakir-iskun.—Cylinder.—Fall of Assyria.—Rise of Babylon.—Nebuchadnezzar.—Evil Merodach.—Nergalsharezer.—Method of dating.—Nabonidus. — Belshazzar. — Cyrus. — Cambyses. — Darius.— Trilingual text.— Artaxerxes.— Parthian date.— Important evidence.

HE present chapter is not a natural division of the history, as it includes texts of various ages and of distinct races of Assyrian, Babylonian, Persian, and Parthian kings, stretching from the date of the death of Assurbanipal, B.C. 626, down to the end of the second century before the Christian era. The new inscriptions of this long period were, however, not numerous enough to justify me in dividing it into chapters according to the empires that successively ruled in the country, and I was therefore obliged to class the inscriptions of all the successors of Assurbanipal under one head.

In the death of Assurbanipal the Assyrian power

declined, and it is not even certain who was his successor. It is probable, however, that the next monarch was a king named Bel-zakir-iskun, of whom I discovered part of a barrel cylinder near the centre of the mound of Kouyunjik. This fragment belongs to the text printed in "Cuneiform Inscriptions," vol. i. p. 8, No. 6. The text in question would not attract notice but for the fact that so few inscriptions of this period have been discovered, and that this is the longest one yet found. The translation of this text, so far as it can be restored, is:—

1. Bel-zakir-iskun the great king the powerful king, king of nations, king of Assyria,

2. . . . . of Assur and Belat, the delight of Merodach and Ziratbanit, joy of the heart of the lady of the temple,

3. the king who satisfies the heart of Nebo and Merodach, the follower . . . . of Nebo and Urmitu,

4. Whom Assur, Belat, Bel, Nebo, Sin, Ningal, Ishtar of Nineveh, Ishtar of Arbela, Ninip, Nergal, and Nusku,

5. . . . . him gladly perceived him, and proclaimed his name to the kingdom.

6. In all the holy cities the emblems of rule . . . his name they called,

7. . . . . they exalted him and destroyed his enemies, and struck down my enemies

8. who . . . . to supremacy and dominion they made him, and in all . . . . made me

9. to establish . . . . people a crown of dominion placed on him . . . . my birth

10. a sceptre of righteousness for the government of all people, Nebo my worship committed to my arm

11. . . . . destruction . . . . my officers

12. . . . . carrying the shrines of Bel and Nebo promoter of good

13. . . . . possessing knowledge and wisdom, rewarder of anyone with good

14. . . . . judging upright judgment to his people, over . . . . his blessing

15. . . . . not choosing the broken . . . . their might

16. . . . . they were divided, guarding . . . . his officers

17. son of . . . . the great king, the powerful king, king of nations, king of Assyria, king of the four regions,

18. son of . . . . king of Sumir and Akkad.

[Lines 19 to 46 very mutilated; they appear to describe the rebuilding of the temple of Nebo.]

47. . . . . I sent . . . . within it

48. . . . . unsubmissive to me they subdued to my feet.

49. In after days in the time of the kings my sons, whom Assur and Shamas shall call, and to the dominion of countries and peoples shall proclaim

50. his name. When this house decays and becomes old, who repairs its ruin and restores its decay;

51. the inscription written of my name may he see, may he in a receptacle enclose it, pour out a libation, and my name with his own name write.

52. may Nebo and Urmitu his prayer hear and bless him.

53. Whoever the writing of my name defaces, and with his name does not place it,

54. may they not establish him, and not hear his prayer, and

55. may they curse him, and his name and his seed from the country wipe out.

. . . . lines the written inscription, month . . . . 3rd day, in the eponymy of Daddi the great officer.

Such are the fragments of the last royal inscription of any length written in Assyria. The curious mixture of the first and third persons in the earlier lines, suggests that the king is speaking of another monarch as well as himself. I suspect that there was civil war in Assyria about this time, and Bel-zakir-iskun was succeeded after a short reign by Assur-ebil-ili-kain, the son of Assurbanipal. This prince, in a broken record which I recently discovered, tells us that when Assurbanipal died he himself was not called to the throne, but he ascended it at a later period. Of Assur-ebil-ili-kain I found several inscriptions at Nimroud, but these were only duplicates of the texts already known, recording his restoration of the temple of Nebo at that city.

The Assyrian empire was overthrown and succeeded by the Babylonian power under Nabopolassar, whose son and successor, Nebuchadnezzar, was one of the most famous monarchs in history. He reigned from B.C. 605 to 562, and left many memorials of his power. Some small texts of this king are in the new collection. One, of which I only obtained a cast, is the pupil of the eye of a statue of the god Nebo, inscribed with the following dedication:

1. To the god Nebo his lord,
2. Nebuchadnezzar
3. king of Babylon,
4. son of Nabopolassar
5. king of Babylon,
6. for his preservation he made.

The three other texts of the reign of Nebuchadnezzar are on dated contract tablets, and although the subject matter of these inscriptions is not of much interest, the dates attached to the documents are always valuable for confirming and proving the chronology of the reigns of the various monarchs. One of these has the following date in the reign of Nebuchadnezzar:—

City of Babylon, month Tammuz, 15th day, 20th year of Nebuchadnezzar king of Babylon.

The date of this document would be B.C. 585.

The two following texts are in the 37th year of the same monarch:—

City of Babylon, month Iyyar, 21st day, 37th year of Nebuchadnezzar king of Babylon.

City of Babylon, month Kislev, 8th day, 37th year of Nebuchadnezzar king of Babylon.

These tablets belong to the year B.C. 568.

I saw one text of Evil-merodach, the son of Nebuchadnezzar, the king who released Jehoiachim of

Judah from prison (2 Kings xxv. 27): this is dated,—

City of Dunrinu, month Tammuz, 22nd day, 1st year of Evil-merodach king of Babylon.

The date of this document is B.C. 561.

Another of these tablets presented to the British Museum belongs to the reign of Neriglissar, or Nergal-sharezer (Jeremiah xxxix. 3), who was a prince of Babylon in the time of Nebuchadnezzar, and ascended the throne on the death of Evil-merodach in B.C. 560. It is a curious fact that the kings of Assyria and Babylonia did not in general begin to count the years of their reign until the commencement of the new year following their accession. During the remainder of the year in which they ascended the throne, documents were dated, " In the year of the accession to the kingdom of so and so," and the first year of the reign commenced with the next new year's day, the first day of the month Nisan. The present document in the reign of Nergal-sharezer is dated in the accession year of that monarch, and will serve as a specimen of this style.

City of Babylon, month Elul, 16th day, in the year of the accession to the kingdom, of Nergal-sharezar king of Babylon.

This date was B.C. 560.

Another Babylonian date in an accession year is given in 2 Kings xxv. 27. " Evil-merodach king of Babylon in the year when he began to reign."

After the short reign of nine months of the son of

Nergal-sharezer, the throne of Babylon was occupied in B.C. 556 by Nabonidus the father of the Belshazzar of the Book of Daniel. The following dates are of his reign:—

City of Babylon, month Kislev 23rd day, 9th year of Nabonidus king of Babylon.

This document was written B.C. 547.

Another is dated,—

City of Babylon, month Iyyar, 13th day, 11th year of Nabonidus king of Babylon.

This corresponds to B.C. 545.

A third document has the date—

City of Babylon, month Elul, 10th day, 16th year of Nabonidus king of Babylon.

This belongs to the year B.C. 540.

Another text is dated,—

City of Babylon, month Nisan, 14th day, 17th year of Nabonidus king of Babylon.

This was the last year of Nabonidus, B.C. 539.

In the year B.C. 540 the Babylonians were attacked by the combined forces of the Medes and Persians under the leadership of Cyrus, and in B.C. 539 the city of Babylon was captured and the country added to the Persian empire.

There are no new inscriptions of the time of Cyrus, but there are two of the reign of his son and successor Cambyses, who ruled from B.C. 530 to 522. The first is dated,—

City of Babylon, month Elul, 6th day, 2nd year of Cambyses king of Babylon, king of countries.

Corresponding with the year B.C. 528.

The other tablet is dated,—

City of Babylon, month Tebet, 6th day 5th year of Cambyses.

Agreeing with B.C. 525.

The reign of Cambyses ended in B.C. 522; and after the usurpation of the Magi, Darius Hystaspes ascended the Persian throne the same year. The three following dates belong to the reign of Darius:—

City of Babylon, month Tebet, 9th day, 6th year of Darius king of Babylon, king of countries.

This tablet belongs to B.C. 516.

Another is dated,—

City of Kisu, month Ab, 7th day, 30th year of Darius king of Babylon, king of countries.

The date of this tablet is B.C. 492.

The third of these texts has the date,—

City of Babylon, month Elul, 24th day, 31st year of Darius king of Babylon and the countries.

This date is B.C. 491.

I saw at Baghdad a small conical stone of a black colour, in appearance like a weight, having a worn inscription of Darius in three languages, Persian, Medo-Scythic, and Babylonian.

The last inscription of the Persian period which I have to notice is dated in the "month Kislev, 2nd day, 39th year of Artaxerxes king of countries," which corresponds to B.C. 427.

The Persian empire was overthrown by Alexander the Great, and after his death his empire was divided among his generals. One of these, named Seleucus, obtained possession of Babylon, and from him an era was named which commenced B.C. 312. Some sixty years after this a chief named Arsaces revolted against the Seleucidæ and founded the Parthian monarchy and the dynasty of the Arsacidæ. The Parthians afterwards defeated the Greeks, and wrested Babylonia from them. From the time of the Parthian conquest it appears that the tablets were dated according to the Parthian style. There has always been a doubt as to the date of this revolt, and consequently of the Parthian monarchy, as the classical authorities have left no evidence as to the exact date of the rise of the Parthian power. I however obtained three Parthian tablets from Babylon, two of them contained double dates, one of which being found perfect supplied the required evidence, as it was dated according to the Seleucian era, and according also to the Parthian era, the 144th year of the Parthians being equal to the 208th year of the Seleucidæ, thus making the Parthian era to have commenced B.C. 248. This date is written:

Month . . . . 23rd day, 144th year, which is called the 208th year, Arsaces king of kings.

This tablet was inscribed B.C. 105, and is of considerable importance for the chronology of the period. Clinton, in his great work, has given the dates at which several authorities have stated that the Parthian monarchy arose. See Clinton's "Fasti Romani," vol. ii. appendix, p. 243. Justin, whom Clinton here follows, fixed on the year B.C. 250, and Eusebius gives the same date. Moses Chorenensis fixes on two dates, B.C. 251 and 252, and Suidas gives the year B.C. 246. On comparing the dates here given with that in the inscription, it appears that three of them, B.C. 252, 251, and 250, are too high, and one, B.C. 246, is too low, the true date being B.C. 248.

Many other dates in Parthian history are still undecided, but it is probable that evidence could be obtained by researches at Babylon, to settle these points of difficulty.

Chapter XX.

MISCELLANEOUS TEXTS.

Hymn to light.—Translation.—Invocation to Izdubar.—His worship.—Babylonian text.—Prayer to Bel.—Inundation.—Seven evil spirits.—Their work.—Bel.—Sin, Shamas, and Ishtar.—Attack on the moon.—War in heaven.—Message to Hea.—Mission of Merodach.—Comparison of legends.—Character of deities.—Astronomy.—Four seasons.—Intercalary month.—Astrolabe.—Observation of eclipse.—Respect for laws.—Epigraphs.—Letter.—Deed of sale.—Date of Assurbanipal.—Sale of slave.—Syllabaries.—Bilingual lists.

IN the previous chapters I have pointed out some of the principal historical inscriptions in the new collection. These, however, form only a small part of the discovered texts. There are besides inscriptions and parts of inscriptions of all classes on mythology, astronomy, astrology, geography, natural history, witchcraft, evil spirits, laws, contracts, letters, despatches, &c. I purpose noticing some of these texts as illustrations of the contents of the collection, but it would take a far larger work to exhaust or do justice to them. The first tablet I have chosen is the one photographed here, which I may describe as a hymn to the light of heaven. . . . This name, however, hardly describes the tablet, which abounds in abrupt transitions, and consists alternately of passages of praise of light and passages in which light personified as a goddess is speaking. The obverse of the tablet commences with the words, " Light of heaven, like a fire on the earth thou art kindled." The reverse, which is photographed, reads—

1. That which in the storehouse of heaven is kindled, and to the cities of men flies, my glory.

2. Queen of heaven above and below, may they call my glory.

3. Countries at once, I sweep in my glory.

4. Of countries their walls am I, their great defence am I in my glory.

---

5. May thy heart rejoice; may thy liver be satisfied;

6. O lord great Anu, may thy heart rejoice;

7. O lord great mountain Bel, may thy liver be satisfied;

8. O goddess lady of heaven, may thy heart rejoice;

9. O mistress lady of heaven, may thy liver be satisfied;

10. O mistress lady of the temple of Anna, may thy heart rejoice;

11. O mistress lady of Erech, may thy liver be satisfied;

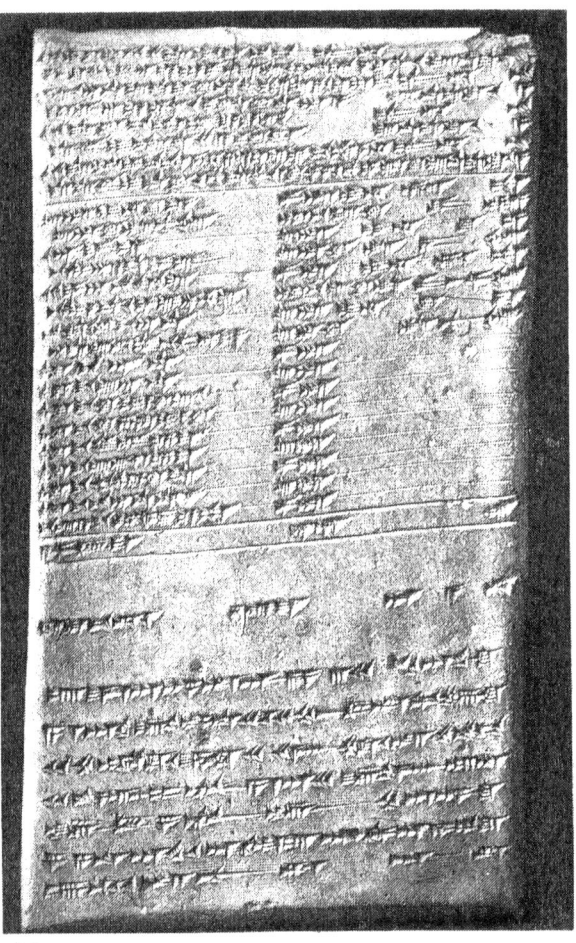

S. Thompson

Terra Cotta Bilingual Tablet

12. O mistress lady of Zasuh-erech, may thy heart rejoice.

13. O mistress lady of Harris-kalama (mount of the world) may thy liver be satisfied;

14. O mistress lady of Silim-kalama, may thy heart rejoice;

15. O mistress lady of Babylon, may thy liver be satisfied;

16. O mistress lady named Nana, may thy heart rejoice;

17. O lady of the temple, lady of the gods, may thy liver be satisfied.

---

18. The lament for the goddess

---

19. Like the old copy written and explained.

20. Palace of Assurbanipal king of Assyria,

21. son of Esarhaddon king of nations, king of Assyria, pontiff of Babylon,

22. king of Sumir and Akkad, king of the kings of Kush and Muzur,

23. king of the four regions, son of Sennacherib

24. king of nations, king of Assyria;

25. who to Assur and Beltis, Nebo and Urmit trusts.

26. Thy kingdom, light of the gods.

Here the first few lines are double, being one in the Turanian language, the other in the Assyrian. In the later lines the verb at the end is omitted, being indicated by a slight line across, to show that it is the same as those above. Line 18 contains the copy of the opening line of the next tablet in the series, and lines 19 to 26 contain the colophon, with the statement that the tablet is a true copy of the original, the genealogy of Assurbanipal, &c.

There is another curious tablet of this class in the new collection—an invocation to Izdubar, the hero of the flood legends, who was deified after his death. The idea of the power of this hero is forcibly shown in this tablet.

Invocation to Izdubar (Nimrod?).

1. Izdubar the giant king, judge of angels;
2. Noble prince great among men,
3. Conqueror of the world, ruler of the earth, lord of the lower regions;
4. Judge speaking like god. Thou dividest,
5. thou establishest in the earth, thou finishest judgment,
6. thy judgment is not changed, another exists not.
7. Thou spoilest, thou rejoicest, thou judgest, thou dividest, thou arrangest.
8. Shamas wisdom and power to thy hand has given,
9. kings, pontiffs, and princes before thee are subject.
10. Thou dividest their ways, their power thou breakest.
11. I so and so son of such an one, whom his god so and so and his goddess so and so,

12. with disease have covered, and have visited him with a judgment;

13. my strength to weakness before me turns,

14. Give judgment for me, &c., &c. . . . .

The remainder of the tablet is mutilated, and I have not yet had time to complete it, but I expect the rest of the inscription is in the collection. This portion, however, will show the popular idea of Izdubar, whom I think to be the giant hunter of Genesis. We must always remember that Izdubar is only a provisional name, which I proposed for this hero when I first discovered the account of his adventures; his real name we do not yet know, as we cannot read the characters of which it is composed; I believe when they are read they will turn out to be Nimrod. Beside this monarch, two other Babylonian kings were also deified, Suqamunu and Amaragu.

From Babylon I procured several tablets forming the first instalment of a Babylonian library attached to the temple of Bel; among these tablets were some curious records as to the rites in the Babylonian temples. The following translation is made from one written in the Turanian and Semitic Babylonian languages:—

Tablet from the Temple of Bel.

1. In the month Nisan, on the second day, one kaspu (2 hours) in the night,

2. the *amil-urgal* draws near and the water of the river he observes

3. to the presence of Bel he enters and measures, and in the presence of Bel

4. he marks it, and to Bel this prayer he prays:

---

5. " O lord, who in his might has no equal;

6. O lord, good sovereign, lord of the world;

7. Executor of the judgment of the great gods;

8. Lord who in his might is clothed with strength;

9. Lord king of mankind, establisher of glory;

10. Lord thy throne is Babylon, Borsippa is thy crown;

11. the wide heaven is the expanse of thy liver.

[12 and 13 of doubtful meaning.]

14. thy might thou . . . .

15. . . . . lord powerful,

16. returning reward . . . .

17. to those cast down, do thou give to them favour,

18. answer to the man who praises thy might.

19. O lord of the earth, of mankind, and spirits, speak good.

20. Who is there, whose mouth does not praise thy might,

21. and speak of thy law, and glorify thy dominion?

22. O lord of the earth dwelling in the temple of the sun, take hold of the hands which are lifted to thee,

23. to thy city Babylon grant favours,

24. to the temple of Saggal thy temple, incline thy face,

25. for the sons of Babylon and Borsippa grant blessings.

There are several of these tablets in the new collection giving directions for similar ceremonies on different days in the first month Nisan. From the wording of the tablets it appears that these rites were connected with the rise of the inundation, a matter of the utmost importance to the Babylonians. The officer called *amil-urgal* had to watch the stream and record in the temple the measure of the waters, praying at the same time to Bel, the great god of Babylon, to be propitious to the country.

Of the curious myths connected with the Babylonian religion there are several examples. I have already mentioned one, unfortunately too mutilated for translation, the account of the Creation. It appears to record that when the gods in their assembly made the universe there was confusion, and the gods sent out the spirit of life. They then create the beast of the field, the animal of the field, and the reptile or creeping thing of the field, and fix in them the spirit of life; next comes the creation of domestic animals and the creeping things of the city. There are in all fourteen mutilated lines remaining of the inscription.

The new collection has yielded another fine fragment of this class, which joins some others and helps to complete a curious myth relating to seven evil spirits. This tablet belongs to a series which appears to me likely to represent the tablets which Berosus states were buried by Xisithrus before the deluge, and recovered by the Babylonians after the waters had subsided. It is possible that these tablets were written by some Chaldean priest during the early Babylonian monarchy, and that their author endeavoured to increase their importance by representing them as works written before the flood. Among the known inscriptions there are no others likely to represent these supposed records. The tablet with the history of the seven evil gods or spirits is written in six columns, inscribed on both sides of a large clay tablet. Only the first three columns refer to the legend, the others being, however, on a similar subject.

Tablet with the story of the Seven Wicked Gods or Spirits.

Column I.

1. In the first days the evil gods
2. the angels who were in rebellion, who in the lower part of heaven
3. had been created,
4. they caused their evil work
5. devising with wicked heads . . .
6. ruling to the river . . . .
7. There were seven of them. The first was . . . .
8. the second was a great animal . . . .
9.   which anyone . . . .

MISCELLANEOUS TEXTS. 399

10. the third was a leopard . . . .

11. the fourth was a serpent . . . .

12. the fifth was a terrible . . . . which to . . . .

13. the sixth was a striker which to god and king did not submit,

14. the seventh was the messenger of the evil wind which . . . . made.

15. The seven of them messengers of the god Anu their king

16. from city to city went round

17. the tempest of heaven was strongly bound to them,

18. the flying clouds of heaven surrounded them,

19. the downpour of the skies which in the bright day

20. makes darkness, was attached to them

21. with a violent wind, an evil wind, they began,

22. the tempest of Vul was their might,

23. at the right hand of Vul they came,

24. from the surface of heaven like lightning they darted,

25. descending to the abyss of waters, at first they came.

26. In the wide heavens of the god Anu the king

27. evil they set up, and an opponent they had not.

28. At this time Bel of this matter heard and

29. the account sank into his heart.

30. With Hea the noble sage of the gods he took counsel, and

31. Sin (the moon), Shamas (the sun), and Ishtar

(Venus) in the lower part of heaven to control it he appointed.

32. With Anu to the government of the whole of heaven he set them up.

33. To the three of them the gods his children,

34. day and night to be united and not to break apart,

35. he urged them.

36. In those days those seven evil spirits

37. in the lower part of heaven commencing,

38. before the light of Sin fiercely they came,

39. the noble Shamas and Vul (the god of the atmosphere) the warrior to their side they turned and

40. Ishtar with Anu the king into a noble seat

41. they raised and in the government of heaven they fixed.

Column II.

1. The god . . . . . .
2. . . . . . .
3. The god . . . . . .
4. which . . . . . .
5. In those days the seven of them . . . . . .
6. at the head in the control to . . . . . .
7. evil . . . . . .
8. for the drinking of his noble mouth . . . . . .
9. The god Sin the ruler . . . . mankind
10. . . . . . . of the earth
11. . . . . . . troubled and on high he sat,

MISCELLANEOUS TEXTS. 401

12. night and day fearing, in the seat of his dominion he did not sit.

13. Those evil gods the messengers of Anu their king

14. devised with wicked heads to assist one another, and

15. evil they spake together, and

16. from the midst of heaven like a wind to the earth they came down.

17. The god Bel of the noble Sin, his trouble

18. in heaven, he saw and

19. Bel to his attendant the god Nusku said:

20. "Attendant Nusku this account to the ocean carry, and

21. the news of my child Sin who in heaven is greatly troubled;

22. to the god Hea in the ocean repeat.

23. Nusku the will of his lord obeyed, and

24. to Hea in the ocean descended and went.

25. To the prince, the noble sage, the lord, the god unfailing,

26. Nusku the message of his lord at once repeated.

27. Hea in the ocean that message heard, and

28. his lips spake, and with wisdom his mouth was filled.

29. Hea his son the god Merodach called, and this word he spake:

30. " Go my son Merodach

31. enter into the shining Sin who in heaven is greatly troubled;

32. his trouble from heaven expel.

33. Seven of them the evil gods, spirits of death, having no fear,

34. seven of them the evil gods, who like a flood

35. descend and sweep over the earth.

36. To the earth like a storm they come down.

37. Before the light of Sin fiercely they came

38. the noble Shamas and Vul the warrior, to their side they turned and . . . .

The next thirty lines of this curious legend are still lost; they probably contained the remainder of the speech of Hea, describing the events in heaven, and the mission of Merodach to his assistance. Of the following portion of the legend there remain six fragments, but these are not sufficient for the restoration of the text. This inscription gives us a curious picture of the myths prevalent in the Euphrates valley. They appeared to believe that in the early days of the world there was a chaos or confusion in heaven, and monstrous forms of animals ran riot as evil spirits in the universe, while the sun, moon, and stars had not been set in their places. In the upper regions of heaven ruled the god Anu, who corresponded in some senses to the Ouranos of the Greeks. He was god of heaven and king of the seven evil gods, and he had a son named Vul, who was god of the atmosphere and all its phenomena. On the earth ruled Bel, god of the middle region, and the principal object of Babylonian worship. Anu in heaven rather represented a passive divinity, overlooking all things, but seldom interfering. Bel on the other hand represents the acting principle moving in all matters, controlling and creating. The deep, or ocean, and region under the earth were ruled by Hea, who represents the mind or wisdom of the gods. Thus these three leading deities of the Babylonian pantheon represent in some sort a trinity, and exhibit the godhead under a threefold aspect. The seven wicked gods or spirits, with their monstrous forms, are probably the originals of the Titans of the Greeks, who were at war with Jupiter. Bel, seeing the confusion in heaven, resolves to place there the sun, the moon, and Venus, who typifies the stars, that these heavenly orbs might rule and direct the heavens. The evil spirits, emblems of chaos, resist this change, and make war on the Moon, the eldest son of Bel, drawing over to their side the Sun, Venus, and the atmospheric god, Vul. Bel hears of this, and then follows the mission to Hea for his advice. It is most probable that the legend closes with the destruction or punishment of the seven evil spirits, and the triumph of the Moon, who is considered the type of the good kings of the country; one later passage mentions: " The king the son of his god (*i.e.* the pious king) who like the glorious moon the life of the country sustains."

This legend of Bel ending the rule of the monsters, and setting the sun, moon, and stars in the heavens, forms a curious commentary on the description of the creation by Berosus, the Chaldean priest, who represents monsters as existing on the earth before Bel created light and the heavenly bodies. The details of the legend are, however, so different to those of the Greek translation of Berosus, that they suggest the idea that these myths had assumed various forms in Chaldea at an early period. Other fragments of similar legends are in the new collection, and when joined together and completed, will probably supply new and curious matter in the same direction.

In the division of tablets relating to astronomy and astrology there are many new and curious tablets. Some of these give us our first insight into the divisions of the heavens and positions of the fixed stars. One shows that the sky was divided into four regions, the passage of the sun through which marked the four seasons of the year. This fragment is the most valuable astronomical text that has yet been discovered, as it shows also the method of arranging the year. The following is a translation of the inscription, with some slight restorations, which are easily supplied by the regular character of the text:—

---

1. From the 1st day of the month Adar to the 30th day of the month Iyyar, the sun in the division (or season) of the great goddess,

2. is fixed and the time of showers and warmth

---

3. From the 1st day of the month Sivan to the 30th day of the month Ab, the sun

MISCELLANEOUS TEXTS.   405

4. in the division (or season) of Bel is fixed and the time of the crops and heat

---

5. From the 1st day of the month Elul to the 30th day of the month Marchesvan, the sun
6. in the division (or season) of Anu is fixed and the time of showers and warmth.

---

7. From the 1st day of the month Kislev to the 30th day of the month Sebat, the sun in the division (or season) of Hea is fixed and the time of cold.

---

8. When on the 1st day of the month Nisan the star of stars and the moon are parallel, that year is right (or normal).
9. When on the 3rd day of the month Nisan the star of stars and the moon are parallel, that year is full (*i.e.* has 13 months).

It appears by this that at the time this tablet was written the spring quarter was counted as extending through the months Adar (the last month of the year), Nisan (the first month), and Iyyar, that is, commencing in February and ending in May.

The summer quarter extended through the months Sivan, Tammuz, and Ab, commencing in May and ending in August. The autumn quarter extended through the months Elul, Tisri, and Marchesvan, commencing in August and ending in November. The winter quarter extended through the months

Kislev, Tebet, and Sebat, commencing in November and ending in February. To agree with and precisely mark these periods, the heavens were divided into four regions, and the passage of the sun from one of these to another served to mark the change of season. In this tablet I have according to usual custom translated the signs for " month " and " day," but I believe in this case the word " day " means a degree of the heavens, and the word " month " a sign of the zodiac, so that instead of " From the 1st day of the month Addar to the 30th day of the month Iyyar," I should propose, " From the 1st degree of the sign Pisces to the 30th degree of the sign Taurus," and so on through the translation. The Assyrian year consisted, like the Jewish, of twelve lunar months, and in order to keep it in proper relation to the solar year, an intercalary month was sometimes added. In order to know when to add the extra month, they watched a star called the " star of stars," which was just in advance of the sun when it crossed the vernal equinox. If the moon was parallel with that on the first day of the month, they made no intercalation; but if it did not reach the star until the third day, it showed that the year (from the fact that twelve lunar months were short of the solar year) began too far in advance of the equinox, and therefore an intercalary month was added to bring it round again. The information with respect to the divisions of the heavens and the names of some of the stars in the different divisions, will enable us in time to give something like precision to our knowledge of the Babylonian astronomy. I have been able already with these aids to fix approximately, and in some cases to identify, about thirty of the principal stars. Four of these are given on the fragment of the astrolabe, the stars Urbat and Addil, which were in the sign Scorpio, and the stars Nibat-anu and Udka-gaba, which were in the sign Sagittarius. The star Nibat-anu has hitherto been erroneously supposed to be a planet.

The fact that in this record the four quarters of the heavens do not commence with the new year, suggests the inquiry whether from the precession of the equinoxes the seasons had shifted since the first settlement of Babylonian astronomy. Another curious document of this class is an astrolabe, part of which I discovered in the palace of Sennacherib. In this the heavens and the year are represented by the circular form of the object, and round the circumference it was originally divided into twelve parts corresponding to the twelve signs of the zodiac and the twelve months of the year, the number of degrees in each being marked. Inside these there were twelve other divisions nearer the pole, forming a second and inner circle, and in each of the twenty-four divisions, the principal prominent star is inserted. The following diagram will give an idea of this work, remembering that the Assyrian copy is round a circle :—

Outer circle.

Arah-uru-gab-a *Month Marchesvan* (October) Star Ur-bat 140 degrees *	Arah-gan-gan-na *Month Kislev* (November) Star Nibat-anu 120 degrees *
Star Addil 70 degrees *	Star Ud-ka-gab-a 60 degrees *

Pole.

I am of opinion that the numbers under the month of Marchesvan, 140 and 70 degrees, are errors in the Assyrian copy, and should be 150 and 75 degrees.

These and some other similar documents will be of great value towards arranging the Babylonian names of stars, and ascertaining their divisions of the heavens. All investigations into the astronomy of the Assyrians and Babylonians are of little use until the positions of the stars according to their system are fixed.

In the valley of the Euphrates there were in those days observatories in most of the large cities, and professional astronomers regularly took observations of the heavens, copies of which were sent to the king, as each movement or appearance in the heaven was supposed to portend some good or evil to the kingdom. The following report was found in the palace of Sennacherib at Kouyunjik:—

1. To the king my lord, thy servant Abil-istar,

2. May there be peace to the king my lord. May Nebo and Merodach

3. to the king my lord be favourable. Length of days,

4. health of body, and joy of heart, may the great gods

5. to the king my lord grant. Concerning the eclipse of the moon

6. of which the king my lord sent to me; in the cities of Akkad,

7. Borsippa, and Nipur, observations

8. they made and then in the city of Akkad

9. we saw part . . . .

10. the observation was made and the eclipse took place

11. . . . . . .

12. . . . . the eclipse over . . . .

13. . . . . saw ? . . . .

14. which on the tablet was written . . . .

15. I made the observation . . . .

16. This to the king my lord I send.

17. And when for the eclipse of the sun we made

18. an observation, the observation was made and it did not take place.

19. That which I saw with my eyes to the king my lord

20. I send. This eclipse of the moon

21. which did happen, concerns the countries

22. with their god all. Over Syria

23. it closes, the country of Phœnicia,
24. of the Hittites, of the people of Chaldea,
25. but to the king my lord it sends peace, and according to
26. the observation, not the extending
27. of misfortune to the king my lord
28. may there be.

The care of these people about the laws and justice may be seen by the following inscription found in the north palace, Kouyunjik.

1. When the king according to judgment does not speak; his people decay, his country is depressed.
2. When according to the laws of his country he does not speak; the god Hea, lord of destiny,
3. his fate shall utter and he shall be set aside.
4. When according to good government he does not speak; his days shall be shortened.
5. When according to the good tablets he does not speak; his country shall know invasion.
6. When according to destruction he speaks; his country shall be broken up.
7. When according to the writings of the god Hea he speaks; the great gods
8. in glory and just praise shall seat him.
9. If the son of the city of Sippara, he beats and turns aside justice; Shamas the judge of heaven and earth,
10. another judge in his country shall place, and a just prince and just judge instead of unjust judges.
11. When the sons of the city of Nipur for judg-

ment shall come to him, and he shall take gifts and beat them;

12. The god Bel, lord of countries, another enemy
13. shall strengthen against him, and his army shall destroy.
14. The prince and his general in fetters like criminals shall be bound.
15. If silver the sons of Babylon bring and send presents, and
16. the judge of the Babylonians listens and turns to injustice;
17. Merodach lord of heaven and earth his enemy over him shall establish,
18. and his goods and furniture to his adversary shall give.
19. The sons of Nipur, Sippara, and Babylon, who shall do this;
20. to prison shall be sent.

There are several other lines to the same effect, and it appears that this is, like most of the tablets, a copy from a much older Babylonian original. The Assyrians had really little original literature of their own, almost all their writings being copies from early Babylonian texts.

Another curious class of tablets consists of small texts, apparently directions to the workmen as to what inscriptions are to be carved over the various sculptures in the palace. I have translated one which I found in the south-west palace, Kouyunjik.

Tablet containing copies of Epigraphs over Sculptures.

1. In front of the decapitated head of Te-umman king of Elam,

2. whom Ishtar my lady had delivered into my hands,

3. my entry into the city of Arbela I made with rejoicing.

---

4. Dunanu, Samgunu, and Paliya

5. in the regions of the rising sun and the setting sun,

6. to the astonishment of the people with me, I fettered them.

---

7. With the decapitated head of Te-umman king of Elam,

8. the road to Arbela I took with rejoicing

---

9. I am Assurbanipal king of Assyria. The great men of Ursa

10. king of Armenia, to ask for my alliance he sent.

11. Nabu-damiq and Umbadara great men of Elam

12. in bonds for the defiance I placed in their presence.

13. Before them Mannu-ki-ahi the second man *attazabni*

14. and Ninip-uzalli the prefect before the city their tongues I pulled out,

15. I tore off their skins

MISCELLANEOUS TEXTS. 413

16. Line of battle of Assurbanipal king of Assyria, who accomplished the overthrow of Elam

17. Line of battle of Te-umman king of Elam.

18. Head of Te-umman king of Elam.

19. I am Assurbanipal king of nations king of Assyria
20. conqueror of his enemies. The head of Te-umman into the city of Nineveh
21. of Assur, Sin, Shamas, Bel, Nebo, Ishtar of Nineveh,
22. Ishtar of Arbela, Ninip, and Nergal, into the city the men of my arms joyfully
23. carried, in front of the great gate and before the viceroy of Assur placed it,
24. in front of my footstool.

25. I am Assurbanipal king of nations, king of Assyria,
26. Nabu-damiq and Umbadara the great men
27 . . . .

Each space between the black lines contained an epigraph to go over the particular sculptured scene which it explained. All the epigraphs on this tablet belonged to the great war against Te-umman, which in the great cylinder is called the fifth campaign of the king. Similar epigraphs are found on the sculptures, and several of them are in the British Museum.

The following tablet is a request or petition found in the palace of Sennacherib. It is from an officer named Bel-basa connected with the palace of Kalzi, an Assyrian city on the site of the modern Shemamak. It appears that the palace there was assigned as a residence to the wives of the king and had become dangerous from want of repair.

Letter to the king of Assyria.

1. To the king my lord
2. from thy servant Bel-basa.
3. May there be peace to the king my lord,
4. Nebo and Merodach
5. the king my lord very
6. greatly bless.
7. Concerning the palace of the queen,
8. which is in the city of Kalzi
9. which the king my lord has appointed **us**;
10. the house is decaying,
11. the house the foundation is opening,
12. the foundations to bulge,
13. its bricks are bulging.
14. When will the king our lord command
15. the master of works?
16. An order let him make,
17. that he may come, and the foundation
18. that he may strengthen.

In connection with this tablet it may be noticed as a curious fact that Sennacherib mentions executing some works at the palace of Kalzi in B.C. 704.

The following inscription, which dates in the year B.C. 670, late in the reign of Esarhaddon, records the sale of a plantation or enclosure near the city of Lahiru, in the south-east of Assyria, and close to the Elamite frontier:—

Assyrian Deed of Sale.

1. Seal of Nergal-ilai the governor
2. of the city of Lahiru;
3. Seal of Sin-sar-uzur the second man in the same;
4. ditto of Musasu the third man in the same;
5. ditto of Zabinu the director of the . . . . ;
6. making four men owners of the enclosure sold.

[Here follow impressions of seals.]

---

7. The enclosure of Bahai, the whole of it;
8. measuring 500 of ground reckoned in *sekul* (acres),
9. bounded by the enclosure of Tabhari,
10. bounded by the ground of the enclosure of Zilli-bel the ruler of Sakullat,
11. bounded by the ground of the city of Paqut and of the city of Dur-mannai,
12. bounded by the ground of the enclosure of Ahiya-amnu and the enclosure of Zilli-bel;
13. they sold; and Adar-ili the officer
14.   of the son of the king of Babylon
15 from before these men,

16. for the sum of fourteen manas (15 lbs.) of silver

17. bought. . . . of the king

18. . . . . to be eaten

19. . . . . sekul (acres)

20. . . . . *kar abhi*

21. . . . . this year the silver on account of

22. . . . . placed, his ground

23. . . . . went out of that ground, the seed for its sowing

24. they had not sown; and its grain

25. he will not gather

---

26. Witness Sin-bel-uzur the great collector,

27. witness Salimha the third man

28.   of the palace,

29. witness Bel-nahid minister of the son of the king,

30. witness Mannu-ki-assur the scribe,

31. witness Maruduk-sarani . . . .

32. witness Ginai the Elamite

33. witness Nabu-musa the scribe

34. Month Iyyar, 1st day,

35. in the eponymy of Salmu-bel-lasmi

36. governor of the city of Diri.

         [On edge of tablet.]

37. Bounded by the ground of the enclosure

38. of La . . . .

In this inscription Esarhaddon is spoken of simply as the king of Babylon, which makes it probable that

MISCELLANEOUS TEXTS.

he had already associated his eldest son, Assurbanipal, with himself on the throne, and had resigned Assyria to him, retaining Babylon for himself. The accession of Assurbanipal will thus be some years earlier than I have formerly supposed, and probably took place in B.C. 671. Adar-ili, who purchased this field, was governor of Lahiru three years earlier; he was now promoted to be an officer of Assurbanipal, while Nergal-ilai replaced him at Lahiru. Bel-nahid, the third of the witnesses, was a few years later made tartan or commander-in-chief.

Another of these deeds of sale in the new collection is an illustration of the slavery which then as now existed in the Euphrates valley. This tablet records the sale of a girl to one of the women of the palace of Sennacherib, and it is dated in the monarch's one eponymy in the year B.C. 687. This girl was probably intended for the harem of the king.

Tablet with record of the sale of a female slave from the Palace of Sennacherib, Kouyunjik.

1. Seal of the woman Daliya
2. mistress of the girl who was sold.

Space for seals.

---

3. The girl Anadalati
4. daughter of Sayaradu
5. she sold, and Ahitilli
6. female of the palace, from the hand

7. of the woman Daliya for the price
8. of one half mana of silver bought.
9. The sale was complete and she gave
10. that girl
11. for the price she was bought,
12. and judgment was given
13. not to alter, which in . . . .

[Several lines lost here containing the names of the witnesses.]

[Date.]

a. Month Sebat, 22nd day

b. eponymy of Sennacherib king of Assyria.

Some of the syllabaries and bilingual lists in the new collection are of great value to students, but it is impossible to exhibit them properly in a work like the present without the cuneiform characters. Two of these include explanations of the ancient names of some of the capitals of Assyria and Babylonia; another explains the names of the various guards and watches, and the signs for classes of men. Another is the syllabary in four columns which I have before mentioned, p. 101. Among numerous other signs, it gives the following values of one which is usually read *im* :—

1. Pu-luh-tu, fear.
2. Ra-ma-nu, self.
3. E-mu-qu, power.
4. Zu-um-ru, back or skin.
5. Sa-mu, heaven.
6. Ir-zi-tu, earth.

7. A-hu-u, brother.
8. Di-du, friend.
9. Sa-a-ru, wind.
10. Zu-un-nu, rain.
11. Dup-pu, tablet.

Many inscriptions of this class, and others similar to those in this chapter, are not yet copied or translated, and further work on this part of the collection will, without doubt, reveal new and important texts.

Chapter XXI.

FOREIGN INSCRIPTIONS.

Baghdad lion.—Egyptian monarch.—Ra-set-nub or Saites.—Founder of Shepherd power.—Tablet of Rameses.—Date of monument.—Hyksos.—Expelled by Amosis.—Worship of Set.—Type of Lion.—Hamath inscription.—Seals at Nineveh.—Cypriote inscription.—Phœnician texts.—Contract tablets.—Pehlevi inscriptions.—Later texts.—Nisibin.—Destruction of monuments.

BESIDE the cuneiform inscriptions found in the Euphrates valley, I found or saw several inscriptions in other characters. One of these is an hieroglyphic inscription on a stone lion. This lion was discovered some years ago in an excavation at Baghdad, and a copy of the inscription upon it was published in "La Religion des Pré-Israélites, Recherches sur le Dieu Seth," by W. Pleyte, plate i. figs. 9 and 10.

I saw this antiquity when I was at Baghdad and purchased it for the British Museum. The lion is sitting down with the front legs stretched out, and the inscription containing the name and title of one of the Egyptian monarchs is carved on the breast. The royal name is read by Dr. Birch, Ra-set-nub. Ra-set-nub is the monarch called Saites by Manetho, who relates that he was the leader of the Hyksos, a foreign shepherd race who invaded Egypt and conquered all the lower part of the country. Ra-set-nub, or Saites, is mentioned on a tablet of Rameses II. king of Egypt, about B.C. 1300. Rameses relates that it was then 400 years after the era of Ra-set-nub, which would give about B.C. 1700 for the conquest of Egypt by the shepherd race, and this will, consequently, be the date of the lion.

The Hyksos are supposed to have been a Phœnician or Arabian race; they held the country until they were expelled by Amosis, an Egyptian prince who restored the native rule about B.C. 1500. The Hyksos worshipped Sut or Set, who is identified with Baal, instead of the supreme gods of the Egyptians, and the name of Set forms one of the elements in the cartouch of the monarch in whose reign the lion was carved. The feelings of the Egyptians against the foreigners on religious grounds were very strong, and few of their monuments have escaped to this day, but those that have been discovered show a peculiar type and style of art different to those of the native Egyptian periods. In style this lion resembles the other known works of the shepherd period, the character of the sculpture closely according with the inscription It is probable that this lion was removed from one of the Egyptian temples during the period of Nebuchadnezzar's conquest of that country B.C. 572, as it was the custom at that time to carry away monuments as trophies of victory.

Another hieroglyphic inscription which I saw at Aleppo is a new text in the so-called Hamath character. As yet very few texts have been found in this strange form of writing, and nothing whatever is known of the meaning of the inscriptions. Almost all the previous inscriptions of this class have been found at Hamath, and from this cause they have been provisionally called "Hamath inscriptions," but it is evident from the other specimens found that these characters were by no means confined to that locality. The characters are evidently hieroglyphic, but totally different to the hieroglyphics of Egypt. They contain representations of human figures, hands, boots, heads, fishes, trees, and various other signs. The race which used these hieroglyphics must have been spread over a large area in Syria, but which of the peoples who inhabited these regions were the authors of the inscriptions we are at present quite unable to say. The text which I found at Aleppo is on a black oblong stone, built into the wall of an old mosque now in ruins. The inscription is in two lines, the character in relief, closely resembling the specimens from Hamath.

It is a curious fact that among the seals found by Mr. Layard in the palace of Sennacherib were some inscribed with Hamath characters (see "Early Sassanian Inscriptions," by Edward Thomas, pp. 7 and 8), showing the use of these hieroglyphics during the Assyrian period, but the larger stone inscriptions appear older in style than the seals. Some scholars have supposed that this writing is connected with the Arabic kingdom, which was contemporary with the Assyrian empire, and attempts have been made to identify the names on the seals, but it is evident that the localities where the stone inscriptions are found are not within the limits of the Arabic kingdom; Hamath, Antioch, and Aleppo are all in Syria.

Among the antiquities which I discovered in the north palace at Kouyunjik, the residence of Assurbanipal, were several objects which appeared to have come from Cyprus, and one of these had three Cypriote characters upon it. This object is in the shape of a truncated cone with four sides, the characters being scratched on one of the faces. There is a hole for suspension, and the object appears to have been a curtain weight or something of that sort. Such objects are very common, but seldom marked with any characters. The principal of the foreign texts found in the Assyrian and Babylonian mounds are Phœnician, and are contemporary with the cuneiform inscriptions, and often found as dockets to the contract tablets of that period.

OBJECT WITH CYPRIOTE CHARACTERS.

FOREIGN INSCRIPTIONS.

The oldest Phœnician inscriptions I found belonged to the period of the dynasty of Sargon, who reigned from B.C. 722 to 609, and they came from the library of the south-west palace at Kouyunjik, the building raised by Sennacherib. The first of these is on an oblong tablet of dark clay inscribed on the front and back with cuneiform characters. It forms a contract between some persons of the poorer class, the parties not even possessing seals, but, after the custom of the country among the lower ranks of the population, impressing their finger nails on the document instead. The contract is with respect to a field the owner of which bore the name Ilu-malek. Ilu-malek sold this field, which measured 30 omers in extent, to a man named Mannu-ki- .... the price being 11 shekels of silver (about 6 oz.) The date is unfortunately wanting, but it probably belongs to the seventh century B.C. The Phœnician legend is beautifully incised along the edge of the tablet, and is very sharp and clear. Transcribed into Hebrew letters it reads

דנת ּ אלמלך ּ זי ּ ארק ּ טמת

The words are divided by dots and the meaning of the inscription is clear.

דנת is the word for "sale."

אלמלך, Almalak, is the proper name of the owner, answering to the Ilu-malak of the cuneiform text.

זי is a particle meaning "this" or "the," here to be rendered "of the."

ארק, a "field," this word is used for "earth" in Jer. x. 10.

שמט means "cultivated." Castelli translates this root "demersus." The meaning of the inscription will thus be: "The sale by Almalak of the cultivated field"— exactly agreeing with the statement of the cuneiform inscription on the tablet. The second of these inscriptions is obscure. It is on a beautiful conical shaped tablet, perfect, and inscribed with a cuneiform legend recording the sale of thirty omers of barley. There is a hole in the base of the tablet through which a cord appears to have been passed to fasten round the mouth of the sack containing the grain. On one side are impressions of a seal, and also along the edge and at the base, with a Phœnician legend. The date of the document is "Month Marchesvan, 17th day, in the eponymy of Mannu-ki-sari, officer of the king," about B.C. 665.

The Phœnician legend on the base in Hebrew letters reads:

קשדושעריא. Here the first part קשדו is obscure. The second שעריא is the name of barley.

On the side of the tablet the legend is

עלכנדרי 10 + 20: here are two numbers which together make 30, the number of the omers of barley; but the meaning of the following letters is altogether uncertain, the ע may be the initial letter of the word "omers" and may possibly be used as a contraction for that word, and the last letters דרי look like the end of the name Nabu-duri, which belongs to one of the contracting parties. Perhaps נדרי Naduri is used for Nabu-duri, and omitting the opening characters perhaps we may read: ". . . . the barley 30 o(mers) of Na(bu)duri."

From the same locality I procured part of a longer text in Phœnician, a small part only of which is legible, in Hebrew letters it is

1 . . . . ועל . . . . .   2 . . . . עכרי . . .   3 . . . . ט . . . . .

From the ruins of Babylon I brought copies of two Phœnician inscriptions on bricks probably belonging to the sixth century B.C. the first of which is:

וריעצבן apparently a proper name and the second in the same style reads: יבל. Beside these I saw at Aleppo a Phœnician inscription on a seal. There is a figure of a boar in the centre and a line of inscription above and below. The characters are not very certain, but appear to be,—

1. מלכסתר   2. אמפקיד

Here the first line may be the proper name of the owner of the seal, Melek-satur, and the second the title of the individual. פקיד is used in the Bible for an officer, overseer, or judge. This seal is the property of the Russian consul at Aleppo, who kindly allowed me to take an impression of it.

In the various alphabets current in the East after the fall of the Persian empire, I found several inscriptions. Most of these were in Pehlevi, a mode of writing derived from the Phœnician, and used in the East during the period of the Roman empire.

The principal Pehlevi inscriptions which I copied, or brought from Asiatic Turkey, are:—

I. An inscription in four lines on a circular pillar

now standing in the courtyard of the fort erected by the Turks on the north mound of Kalah Shergat.

II. An inscription on a column in the citadel at Orfa.

III. An inscription on a circular ornament with figures round it, like the signs of the zodiac.

IV. An inscription painted on a flat fragment of bone discovered in the palace of Sennacherib at Kouyunjik.

V. An inscription scratched on flat fragments of baked clay from the same locality.

The two last are in the new collection.

Greek, Roman, and Arabic inscriptions were also found in various places, but these were out of the limits of my researches, and I copied very few of them. I may, however, notice that there appears to be a rich store of inscriptions of all ages at Nisibin, and the natives were digging into the mounds there for stones when I passed. Large blocks, broken into fragments, covered with fine Latin inscriptions, were turned up; but as there was no one to look after them, I believe they will all be destroyed.

The Turkish officials, while always ready to oppose researches and prevent the discovery or removal of monuments, never hinder the natives from destroying antiquities.

Chapter XXII.

OBJECTS ILLUSTRATING ARTS AND CUSTOMS.

Larger sculptures already discovered.—Hand in wall.—Lintel.—Head of Ishtar.—Shoulder of statue.—Winged bull.—Assyrian columns.—Crystal throne.—Crystal vase.—Name of Sennacherib.—Lamps.—Lamp feeder.—Assyrian fork.—Glass.—Roman bottle.—Glass seal.—Pottery.—Cypriote style.—Chariot group.—Commerce.—Personal ornaments.—Rings.—Beads.—Seals.—Later occupation of mound.—Destruction of antiquities.

AMONG the things now brought from the Assyrian mounds there is a fair collection of new objects and types, throwing new light on the customs of Assyria and the advancement of the country in arts and sciences.

During the former excavations, most of the sculptured halls at Kouyunjik and Nimroud had been discovered, and my excavations were undertaken in the centres of the rooms and the minor portions of the buildings, so that I had no opportunity of discovering large sculptures or portals, and the rooms I

OBJECTS ILLUSTRATING ARTS.   429

discovered in the domestic parts of the palaces were bare of sculpture and inferior in ornamentation. At Nimroud I found the position of those curious rude models of hands which were placed in the walls fist upwards, their object was probably to preserve the place against evil spirits. The inscription on one I found reads—

1. Palace of Assur-nazir-pal, king of nations, king of Assyria.
2. Son of Tugulti-ninip, king of nations, king of Assyria.
3. Son of Vul-nirari, king of nations, king of Assyria.

MODEL OF HAND FOUND IN WALL.

Assur-nazir-pal, B.C. 885, built the north-west palace at Nimroud. In the southern hall of the south-west palace, Kouyunjik, which is of the age of Sennacherib, B.C. 705, I discovered the lintel of a door which appeared to have covered one of the passages out of the hall. It was probably the custom of the Assyrians to construct the lintels and roofs of wood, and they have all been destroyed, but this one, spanning a narrow passage, was made of stone, and to this fact we probably owe its preservation. It had fallen from its original position, and lay broken into two on the floor of the hall. This lintel gives us our first satisfactory evidence as to the ornamentation of the tops of entrances in the palace. The stone is 6 ft. long and 10 inches deep; the principal ornament consists of two dragons lengthened out to suit the positions; they have wings over the back, and long curved necks. Each animal looks towards the centre of the lintel, where there stands a vase with two handles. All along the top over the vase and dragons is an ornament of honeysuckles, and above this a plain projecting ledge. The lintel is somewhat worn by the weather, but was originally roughly and boldly carved to suit its height from the ground. Of statues I only found fragments, but two of these are curious. One is the head of a female divinity, probably the Venus of Nineveh. The cheeks are plump, there is a band or fillet round the forehead, the hair is thrown back behind the ears, and falls in masses of curls on the shoulders. The statue to which this has belonged has been broken up, and the nose and lips injured. The height of the head is 9 inches, and the breadth of the face $5\frac{1}{2}$ inches. The second specimen is a fragment of a colossal statue belonging to the period of Assurbanipal. It is the left shoulder of a figure, made of a black stone full of fossils. There is an inscription on the back of the statue, giving the descent of Assurbanipal from Esarhaddon, Sennacherib, and Sargon. I discovered some remains of two black obelisks carved with bands of sculpture and cuneiform writing, but unfortunately, like the statues, broken into fragments. I conjecture that one of the obelisks belonged to Samsi-vul, king of Assyria, B.C. 825. A very curious and beautiful little specimen,

ARTS AND CUSTOMS.

discovered at Kouyunjik, is a small model in fine yellow stone of a winged cow or bull, with a human head, the neck adorned with a necklace, the head surmounted by a cylindrical cap adorned with horns and rosette ornaments, and wings over the back. On the top of the wings stands the base of a column, having the uniform pattern found on Assyrian bases. The dimensions of this figure are, length 3 inches, breadth $1\frac{1}{2}$ inches, present height (feet broken off) 3 inches, probable original height $3\frac{1}{2}$ inches, height of base of column $\frac{3}{4}$ inch, diameter of base of column $1\frac{1}{4}$ inches. This figure, although not precisely like them, reminds one strongly of the colossal winged man-headed bulls at the sides of Assyrian portals; it has probably formed part of an ornamental chair or couch, the pillars and legs of such furniture sometimes resting on the backs of animals. The disposition of columns over the backs of animals is in accordance with the known features of Assyrian architecture, as represented on the sculptures. At the ruined entrance of the north palace, Kouyunjik, I found two bases of columns. The pedestals were 14 inches by 10 inches and 3 inches high. Over these the circular work was $8\frac{1}{2}$ inches in diameter, with a flat circle to receive the column, the total height of base and pedestal being 8 inches. The furniture of the royal palace appears to have been very magnificent, skilful in execution, and often of valuable or beautiful material. Thrones and fragments of thrones have been found in bronze and ivory, and during my excavations in Sennacherib's palace I discovered several portions of a throne of rock crystal. This, so far as preserved, was similar in shape to the bronze throne, and beautifully turned and polished. As the crystal throne is too fragmentary to copy, I here give an engraving of the bronze throne found by Layard at Nimroud, to show

BRONZE THRONE,
Discovered by Mr. Layard at Nimroud.

the shape of these objects. Accompanying this were fragments of vases and cups in the same material, one of them bearing the name of Sennacherib in cuneiform characters. In my collection there are several lamps; but I have no satisfactory evidence that they are Assyrian. Some of them are Roman, but one or two appear Assyrian in style, and I believe belong

ARTS AND CUSTOMS. 433

to the time of that empire. There is one curious Assyrian object of this class, a lamp-feeder in the shape of a sitting bird. There is a curious neck over the back, through which it was filled with oil, and a

TERRA-COTTA LAMP.

TERRA-COTTA LAMP FEEDER.

beak in front of the breast, through which it discharged it into the lamp. I found two of these objects in the palace of Assurbanipal, one I brought to England, the other I gave to the Imperial Museum at Constantinople. One curious and unique specimen in the new collection is a bronze fork to which I have already called attention (p. 147); it is entirely Assyrian in style and ornament, and of very fine work. The end of the handle is terminated by the head of an ass, the ears stretched out and lying one on each side of the handle. This termination in the head of an animal is a feature seen in the Assyrian representations of ornamental implements. The handle of the fork is ornamented with a spiral cable ornament, and it expands and becomes flattened out at its junction with the prongs, forming a shoulder which is ornamented by small incised circles, and a fringe of lines. The length of the fork is 8 in., the breadth of the shoulder ⅞ in., and the length of the prongs 2½ in. This fork was found in the long gallery of the palace of Sennacherib, among the clay tablets on the floor. There are several other bronze ornaments and implements, including a bronze bracket, bronze dishes and ladles, and a specimen of the styles with which the cuneiform characters were inscribed. The glass in the collection belongs mostly to the post-Assyrian period, but there is one remarkable exception. This is a paste seal in shape of a scarab, with hole pierced through it longitudinally; the back is oval and the front has the device of the royal Assyrian seal, the king killing a rampant lion. Most of the figure of the king is, however,

BRONZE BRACKET.

BRONZE STYLE.

lost by a fracture. There are several beautiful specimens of iridescent glass bottles, including a fine blue glass Roman bottle with two faces, one on each side of the body. The pottery found in the course of the excavation is, as might be expected, very miscellaneous in character: Phœnician, Assyrian, Egyptian, Parthian, Persian, and early Arabic are all represented in the collection, and some of the specimens resemble the Lydian and Cypriote vases. From the temple area I obtained part of a chariot group in terra cotta similar to the early Cypriote specimens, the height of the charioteer being 5 in. without the legs, which are lost, and the diameter of the wheel 4 in. The extensive commerce of the Assyrians, and the influence of the empire on distant countries, accounts for the mixture of styles in these things, many of which may have come by way of barter or tribute.

The number of personal ornaments in the collection is small, consisting of beads in gold, silver, and stones, bracelets and rings in glass and carnelian, and a massive silver ring with an iron die set in it instead of a stone. Most of these ornaments are late, belonging to the Greek and some of them to the Arabic period; but two carnelian rings, one with an engraving of a scorpion, are Assyrian. Clay impressions of Assyrian seals are numerous and very fine. They include several royal seals, the royal seal of Sargon, B.C. 722, the royal seal of Assurbanipal, B.C. 668, beside many other specimens. Of other seals there are good specimens, among which are impressions of the king walking, with attendant behind holding umbrella. The miscellaneous objects from the mound of Kouyunjik serve evidently to show that Nineveh was not abandoned when the Assyrian monarchy was destroyed, but that the site continued to be inhabited for centuries afterwards, and the later inhabitants have in a great measure gradually destroyed the great works which their predecessors had raised.

Chapter XXIII.

CONCLUSION.

Difficulty of work.—Short time.—Good results.—Babylonian kings.—Assyrian kings.—New inscriptions.—Uncertainty of chronology.—Assyrian history.—Jewish history.—Pul.—New light on the Bible.—Origin of Babylonian civilization.—Turanian race.—Semitic conquest.—Flood legends.—Mythology.—Connection with Grecian mythology.—Astronomy.—Architecture.—Importance of future excavations.

IN the previous chapters I have described my travels and researches, and have given some account of the more prominent results of the expeditions. So far as my two visits to the East are concerned, they were both of such short duration that they could not yield such complete or satisfactory results as I could have wished; but the great number of interesting inscriptions I discovered under such difficulties, and in so limited a space of time, ought to speak strongly in favour of completer and systematic excavations on these ancient sites. My excavations at the two sites of Kouyunjik and Nimroud, taking out the period I was stopped by the Turkish officials altogether did not last four months, but so rich were these mines of antiquities that I obtained over 3,000 inscriptions and fragments of inscriptions, beside many other objects. These inscriptions and objects were not of slight interest, but included some texts and antiquities of first-class importance. In one great and valuable direction the expeditions have been quite successful, the majority of the fragments of inscriptions found form parts of texts the other portions of which were already in the British Museum, and the new fragments enable us either to complete or greatly enlarge several of these inscriptions.

Perhaps in no part of cuneiform enquiry have the late researches added more to our knowledge than in early Babylonian history. The list of monarchs in the second edition of Rawlinson's "Ancient Monarchies," published in 1871, after I had commenced my researches, only then contained twenty-eight kings from the inscriptions in the period before B.C. 747.[1] From B.C. 747 downwards the kings were well known from the canon of Ptolemy and other sources. As I have not yet published any complete list of the Babylonian and Assyrian monarchs, I will here give them so far as they are discovered, to show the advance made in the history and chronology of these early kingdoms.

List of Babylonian monarchs :—

See Rawlinson's "Ancient Monarchies," second edition, vol. i. p. 171, and vol. iii. p. 43.

MYTHICAL KINGS BEFORE THE FLOOD.

From the Inscriptions.	*From Berosus*
Adi-ur	Alorus
. . . . . .	Alaparus
. . . . . .	Almelon
. . . . . .	Ammenon
. . . . . .	Amegalarus
. . . . . .	Daonus
. . . . .	Aedorachus
. . . . . .	Amempsin
Ubara-tutu	Otiartes
Hasis-adra	Xisithrus

In whose time the deluge happened.

MYTHICAL KINGS AFTER THE DELUGE.

From Berosus.

Evechus.
Chomosbelus.

From the Inscriptions.

. . . . . . ili.
Ilu-kassat his son.
Bel-agu-nunna.
Abil-kisu.

HISTORICAL PERIOD.

Izdubar (probably the Nimrod of the Bible).

. . . .

Kings of Babylon.

Suqumuna.

Ummih-zirritu.
Agu-rabi.
Abi . . . . .
Tassi-gurubar.
Agu-kak-rimi (restored the temple of Bel)
. . . . . .
Sumu . . . . .
Zabu (built the temples of Venus and the sun at Sippara).
Abil . . . . .
Sin . . . . .

Viceroys.

Be-huk
Mi-sa-dimira-kalammi } viceroys of Eridu.

. . . . . .
Idadu   viceroy of Eridu,
. . . . . .
Adi-anu   viceroy of Zerghul,
. . . . . .
Gudea   viceroy of Zerghul,
. . . . . .
Ilu-mutabil viceroy of Diri.
. . . . . .

Kings of Ur (modern Mugheir).

Urukh (founded many temples).
Dungi his son (continued his works).
. . . . . .
Gunguna son of Ismi-dagan king of Karak.
. . . .

Su-agu.
Amar-agu (built the city of Abu-Shahrein).
Ibil-agu.

Kings of Karrak.

Gamil-ninip built a temple at Nipur.
Isbi-barra.
Libit-anunit.
Ismi-dagan built a palace at Ur.
Ilu-. . . zat.

Kings of Erech (modern Warka).

Belat-sunat (a queen).
Sin-gasit rebuilt the temple of Anna.

Kings of Larsa (modern Seukereh).

Nur-vul.
Gasin . . . . .
Sin-idina.
Rim-agu son of Kudur-mabuk.

Kings of Akkad.

Ai . . . . .
Amat-nim . . . . .
Sargon (the Babylonian Moses, reigned 45 years).
Naram-sin his son.
Ellat-gula (a female).

Elamite Kings.

Kudur-nanhundi (reigned B.C. 2280).
. . . . . .
Chedorlaomer (Genesis ch. xiv.)
. . . . . .
Simti-silhak.
Kudur-mabuk his son conquered Syria.

Native Kings Contemporary with the Elamites.

. . . . . zakir-idin
Bel-zakir-uzur } In time of Kudur-nanhundi.

. . . . . .

Amraphel king of Shinar ⎫ In time of
Arioch king of Elassar ⎬ Chedorlaomer
Tidal king of Goim   ⎭ (Genesis).

Kings of Babylon.

Hammu-rabi (conquered Kudur-mabuk and his son)
Samsu-itibna rebuilt temple of Babylon.
Ammi-dikaga.
Kuri-galzu I.
Simmas-sihu I.
Ulam-buriyas.
Nazi-murudas I. } 16th century B.C. ?
Mili-sihu I.
Burna-buriyas I.
Kara-bel.

. . . . . .

Saga-saltiyas (rebuilt the temples of Sippara).

. . . . . .

Harbi-sihu.

. . . . . .

Kari-indas, B.C. 1450 (made a treaty with Assyria).

Burna-buriyas II., B.C. 1430 (married daughter of king of Assyria).

Kara-hardas, B.C. 1410 (murdered).

Nazi-bugas, B.C. 1400 (an usurper).

Kuri-galzu II., B.C. 1380, son of Burna-buriyas.

Mili-sihu II. his son, B.C. 1350.
Merodach Baladan I. his son, B.C. 1325.
Nazi-murudas II., B.C. 1300.

Assyrian Dynasty.

Tugulti-ninip, B.C. 1271 (conquered Babylonia).
Vul . . . bi, B.C. 1230.
Zamama-zakir-idin, B.C. 1200.

Chaldean Kings.

Nebuchadnezzar I., B.C. 1150.
Kara-buriyas, B.C. 1120.
Maruduk-nadin-ahi, B.C. 1100.
Maruduk-sapik-zirrat, B.C. 1090.
. . . . sadua, B.C. 1080.
Simmas-sihu, reigned 17 years.
Hea-mukin-ziri (an usurper), reigned 3 months.
Kassu-nadin-ahu, reigned 6 years.
Ulbar-surki-idina, reigned 15 years.
Nebu?-chadnezzar II., reigned 2 years.
. . . . suqamuna, reigned 3 months.
(After these an Elamite, reigned 6 years.)

. . . . . .

Vul-pal-idina (built the wall of Nipur).

. . . . . .

Nabu-zakir-iskun at war with Assyria.

. . . . . .

Iriba-maruduk.
Merodach Baladan II. his son.

. . . . . .

Vul-zakir-uzur.

. . . . . .
Sibir invaded South Assyria.
. . . . . .
Nabu-bal-idina, B.C. 880 to 853.
Maruduk-zakir-izkur, B.C. 853.
Maruduk-balasu-ikbu, B.C. 820.
. . . . . .
Nabu-nazir (Nabonassur), B.C. 747.
Nabu-usabsi (Nabius), B.C. 734.
Kin-ziru (Chinzirus), B.C. 732.
Ilulæus (not in the inscriptions), B.C. 727.
Merodach Baladan III. (Mardokembad), B.C. 722.
Sargon (Arceanus), B.C. 710.
Hagisa (not in the inscriptions), B.C. 705.
Merodach Baladan III. (restored), B.C. 705.
Bel-ibni (Belibus), B.C. 703.
Assur-nadin-sum (Apronadissus), B.C. 700.
Irregibelus (not in the inscriptions), B.C. 694.
Suzub (Messesimordachus?), B.C. 693.
(Babylon destroyed, B.C. 689.)
Esarhaddon, restores Babylon B.C. 681.
Saul-mugina (Saosduchinus), B.C. 668.
Assurbanipal (Chiniladanus?), B.C. 648.
Bel-zakir-iskun, B.C. 626.
Nabu-pal-uzur (Nabopolassar), B.C. 626.
Nabu-kudur-uzur (Nebuchadnezzar III.), B.C. 605.
Amil-maruduk (Evil-merodach), B.C. 562.
Nergal-sar-uzur (Neriglissar), B.C. 560.
Ulbar-surki-idina (Labarosoarkodus?), B.C. 556.
Nabu-nahid (Nabonidus), B.C. 556.

CONCLUSION. 445

Bel-sar-uzur (Belshazzar) son of Nabonidus, associated with his father on the throne.

Cyrus conquers Babylon, B.C. 539.

In the period before Hammurabi there were several different kingdoms in the country, and it was only occasionally that Babylonia was united under one sceptre.

List of the Assyrian Kings with their Approximate Dates.

Ismi-dagan	B.C. 1850 to 1820.
Samsi-vul I.	,, 1820 ,, 1800.
Igur-kap-kapu Samsi-vul II.	about B.C. 1800.
Ilu-ba Iritak	about B.C. 1750.
Bel-kap-kapu	about B.C. 1700.
Adasi Bel-bani	about B.C. 1650.
Assur-zakir-esir Ninip-tugul-assuri	about B.C. 1600.
Iriba-vul Assur-nadin-ahi	about B.C. 1550.
Assur-nirari I. Nabu-dan	about B.C. 1500.
Assur-bel-nisisu	B.C. 1450 to 1420.
Buzur-assur	,, 1420 ,, 1400.
Assur-ubalid	,, 1400 ,, 1370.
Bel-nirari	,, 1370 ,, 1350.
Budil	,, 1350 ,, 1330.

Vul-nirari I.	B.C. 1330 to 1300.
Shalmaneser I.	,, 1300 ,, 1271.
Tugulti-ninip I.	,, 1271 ,, 1240.
Bel-kudur-uzur	,, 1240 ,, 1220.
Ninip-pal-esar	,, 1220 ,, 1200.
Assur-dan I.	,, 1200 ,, 1170.
Mugtagil-nusku	,, 1170 ,, 1150.
Assur-risilim	,, 1150 ,, 1120.
Tiglath-Pileser I.	,, 1120 ,, 1100.
Assur-bel-kala	,, 1100 ,, 1080.
Samsi-vul III.	,, 1080 ,, 1060.
Assur-rab-amar or Assur-rabbur	about B.C. 1050.
-nimati	about B.C. 1000.
Assur-dan II.	B.C. 930 to 913.
Vul-nirari II.	,, 913 ,, 891.
Tugulti-ninip II.	,, 891 ,, 885.
Assur-nazir-pal	,, 885 ,, 860.
Shalmaneser II.	,, 860 ,, 825.
Assur-dain-pal (rebel king) B.C. 827.	
Samsi-vul IV.	B.C. 825 to 812.
Vul-nirari III.	,, 812 ,, 783.
Shalmaneser III.	,, 783 ,, 773.
Assur-dan III.	,, 773 ,, 755.
Assur-nirari II.	,, 755 ,, 745.
Tiglath-Pileser II.	,, 745 ,, 727.
Shalmaneser IV.	,, 727 ,, 722.
Sargon	,, 722 ,, 705.
Sennacherib	,, 705 ,, 681.

Esarhaddon	B.C. 681 to 668.
Assur-bani-pal	,, 668 ,, 626.
Bel-zakir-iskun	,, 626 ,, 620.
Assur-ebil-ili	,, 620 ,, 607.

In the period of early Babylonian history the new inscriptions of Agu, Merodach Baladan I., and other monarchs, enable us to extend our knowledge in this direction, but an inspection of the list of kings given above shows how defective our information still remains on this subject. It is quite uncertain how far back the records of Babylonia reach, and the lists of kings are too imperfect to construct any satisfactory scheme from them; but it is certain that they reach up to the twenty-fourth century B.C., and some scholars are of opinion that they stretch nearly two thousand years beyond that time. Certainly a civilization, literature, and government like that which we find in Babylonia 2,000 years before the Christian era could not have arisen in a day, and it will probably require many expeditions to the country before we ascertain its primitive history.

The early history of Assyria is in little better condition than that of Babylonia, but the succession of the kings is clearer and the information fuller. The Assyrian power was a single monarchy from the beginning, and gradually grew by conquering the smaller states around it, and there is consequently a uniformity in its records and traditions which makes them easier to follow than those of the sister kingdom. The new inscriptions, particularly that of Vul-nirari I., give us new and welcome material for estimating the progress of Assyria in early times, and it appears that the country gained a prominent place in the world much earlier than some have supposed.

The period of Assyrian history contemporary with the kings of Judah and Israel is the most interesting and important epoch in their annals, and new and valuable material has been added to this part of the subject, the additions and corrections to the history of Tiglath-Pileser, the new portions of the annals of Sargon, giving his campaign against Ashdod and Palestine, the Sennacherib fragments, Esarhaddon's Egyptian and Syrian wars, the new texts of Assurbanipal mentioning Sabako, and the fragments of his successors, all help in this interesting but still in part obscure portion of Assyrian history.

On one much debated point, the comparative chronology of the Assyrian and Jewish kingdoms, the recent expeditions have added nothing to what we already know. The most remarkable circumstance in the whole matter is the fact that the Assyrian king Pul who first reduced the kingdom of Israel under regular taxation has never been discovered; this is the more curious as despatches have been found written by an officer who bore that name. One of the letters from the Assyrian officer Pul is in the new collection. The light already thrown by the Assyrian inscriptions on Biblical history forms one of the most interesting features in cuneiform inquiry, and there can be no question that further researches will settle many of the questions still in doubt, and give us new information in this field, of an important character.

Of the later Babylonian period, the time of Nebuchadnezzar and his successors, there are a few new dated documents and some useful inscriptions of the same sort belonging to the succeeding Persian empire; but the most valuable of the later inscriptions is the one which fixes the date of the rise of the Parthian empire, so long a point of doubt among chronologists.

Intimately connected with these historical studies is the question of the origin and history of the great Turanian race which first established civilization in the Euphrates valley. It is the opinion of the majority of Assyrian scholars that the civilization, literature, mythology, and science of Babylonia and Assyria, were not the work of a Semitic race, but of a totally different people, speaking a language quite distinct from that of all the Semitic tribes. There is, however, a more remarkable point than this; it is supposed that at a very early period the Akkad or Turanian population, with its high cultivation and remarkable civilization, was conquered by the Semitic race, and that the conquerors imposed only their language on the conquered, adopting from the subjugated people its mythology, laws, literature, and almost every art of civilization. Such a curious revolution would be without parallel in the history of the world, and the most singular point in connection with the subject is the entire silence of the inscriptions as to any such conquest. There does not appear any break in their traditions or change in the character of the country to mark this great revolution, and the question of how the change was effected or when it took place is at present quite obscure. The new syllabaries and bilingual tablets will assist in the discussion of these obscure and intricate questions, but we cannot hope that they will be settled until the study of the inscriptions is much further advanced.

On the subject of the myths and traditions current in the Euphrates valley, there is valuable new matter from the recent excavations. The most interesting of these legends, that of the flood, is now much more complete. A comparison of my first translation of the deluge tablet, made before I started for the East, with the new translation published in this volume, will show the additions and corrections gained through the new matter; and all the other legends connected with this tablet have benefited in an equal proportion. There is one point which I did not allude to in my account of the Izdubar legends, namely, the great antiquity claimed in it for the principal cities in Babylonia. In a fragment of this series of legends which I recently discovered, Izdubar, when lamenting the loss of Hea-bani, calls upon the principal cities in his dominion to join him in his mourning. Among the cities mentioned are Babylon, Cutha, Kisu, Harriskalamma, Erech, Nipur, and the list, when complete, evidently contained several other names. In the division of mythology there are

CONCLUSION.

new tablets of various classes, lists of gods, myths, prayers, hymns, and litanies, some that I have translated here being fair specimens of this class.

The value of the Assyrian and Babylonian mythology rests not only on its curiosity as the religious system of a great people, but on the fact that here we must look, if anywhere, for the origin and explanation of many of the obscure points in the mythology of Greece and Rome. It is evident that in every way the classical nations of antiquity borrowed far more from the valley of the Euphrates than that of the Nile, and Chaldea rather than Egypt, is the home even of the civilization of Europe.

In one line of science is the pre-eminence of Babylonia universally acknowledged, and that is astronomy.

The climate of the country, and the clearness of the atmosphere, with the vast unbroken plain of Chaldea, give every facility for the observation of the heavens, and here accordingly we find astronomy was early cultivated and reached a high state of perfection. The Chaldeans mapped out the heavens and arranged the stars, they traced the motions of the planets, and observed the appearance of comets, they fixed the signs of the zodiac and the constellations of the stars, and they studied the sun and moon and the periods of eclipses.

Among the new tablets on these points the one recording the division of the heavens according to the four seasons, and the rule for regulating the intercalary month of the year, and the fragment of the Assyrian astrolabe, are especially valuable.

In the other classes of tablets—the fables, the omen and witchcraft texts, those on the laws, geography, natural history, and the foreign texts—there are many additions which will hereafter engage the attention of scholars and throw new light on the manners and customs of the country.

Compared with former expeditions the last excavations have given little on the subjects of art and architecture; but there are some unique objects, particularly the lintel found in Sennacherib's palace, which show us a new and unexpected style of ornamenting the upper part of doorways.

Such are some of the results realized in the recent attempt to reopen excavations in the East. Much more remains to be accomplished, and I wish that any interest which may be taken in my labours may take the form of encouraging further and systematic exploration of this important field. My desire is that whatever has been accomplished may be taken as evidence of the greater and more important results which will inevitably follow complete excavations. How much there is to be done may be judged from the extent of the excavations on the site of the library of the palace of Sennacherib at Kouyunjik. I have calculated that there remain at least 20,000 fragments of this valuable collection, buried in the unexcavated portions of the palace, and it would require £5,000, and three years' work, to fairly recover this treasure.

INDEX.

BDI EFFENDI, 46, 136, 150, 151, 155.
Abdul Kareem, 40.
Abiyateh, 360, 362, 363, 364, 366, 370.
Aburumeha, 39.
Accho, 302, 370.
Achtareen, 122.
Achzib, 302.
Adana, 36, 112, 123.
Afrin, 30, 115, 120.
Agu, 225, 232.
Agurabi, 226.
Aimu, 360, 362, 366, 370.
Ain Bada, 29, 115, 120.
Akhsera of Minni, 333.
Akkad, 225, 227, 315, 352.
Aleppo, 31, 114, 120, 162.
Alexander, 388.
Alexandretta, 25, 117, 120, 164.
Ali Rahal, 135, 150.
Altar, building of, 191.
Altun Kupri, 67.
Amaragu, 391.

Amida, 308.
Amram mound, 58.
Amudia, 127, 128.
Aneiza, tribe, 95.
Anna, temple of, 356.
Antioch, plain of, 28, 116.
Anu, 173, 230, 399, 400, 401, 402.
Anunit, 173, 230.
Arabia, 313, 359. 361, 368, 371.
Arabian kings, 250.
Aram, 338.
Arameans, 308.
Ararat, 217.
Arbat, 132.
Arbela, 67, 334, 350.
Argisti, 309.
Ark, 185.
    building of, 186.
    filling of, 187.
    size of, 213.
    of Sargon, 224.
Armenia, 211, 309.
Army, Turkish, 125.
Arnold, Edwin, 16.

Arsaces, 389.
Artaxerxes, 388.
Arvad, 330.
Ashdod, 288, 289, 290, 292, 293, 306.
Assi, 44.
Assur, 291.
Assurbanipal, 11, 90, 93, 98, 141, 317.
    cylinder of, 319-377.
Assur-bel-kala, 247.
Assur-dain-pal, 92.
Assur-dan, 91, 251.
Assur-ebil-ili-kain, 73, 384.
Assur-nazir-pal, 72, 91, 103, 141, 252.
Assur-risilim, 247.
Assur-ubalid, 91, 244.
Assyrian monarchs, list of, 445-447.
    power, 447.
Astrolabe, 407, 408.
Astronomy, 404, 407, 451.
Athribis, 327.
Azariah, 12, 275, 286.
Azibahal, 330, 331.
Aznowa, 157.

Babil, 55, 56.
Babylon, 55, 59, 60, 61, 62, 166, 339, 340, 344, 376, 396, 410, 411.
Babylonian chronology, 120.
    monarchs, list of, 439-445.
    monarchy, antiquity of, 447.
Backsheesh, 153.
Baghdad, 53, 54, 64.

Baghdad lion, 420.
Bahal of Tyre, 312, 329.
Barimeh, 99.
Beglabeg, 32.
Behistun inscription, 5.
Beilan, 26, 116, 120.
Bel, 192, 201, 230, 339, 399, 401, 402, 403.
    temple of, 56, 229, 380.
Belat or Beltis, 230.
Belbasa, 336.
Belesu, 167.
Bel-kudur-uzur, 250.
Bellino cylinder, 296.
Bel-nirari, 236, 244.
Belshazzar, 387.
Bel-zazir-iskun, 103, 382, 384.
Berosus, 209, 211, 403.
Beth Ammon, 360.
Biblical account of flood, 208.
Bilingual list, 418.
    tablet, 143.
    text, 233.
Biradjik, 33, 114, 122, 161.
Birds from ark, 217.
Birs Nimrud, 58, 59.
Bitani, 172.
Bit-imbi, 345, 359.
Black obelisk, 10.
Borsippa, 338, 340, 396.
Botta, excavations of, 2, 3.
    works of, 6, 100, 288.
Brandis, 8.
Bronze bracket, 434.
    lamp, 140.
    style, 434.

INDEX. 455

Burial of warrior, 204.
Burial places, 206.
Burna-buriyas, 236.

Calah, 70.
Calendar, 404, 406.
Cambyses, 387, 388.
Canon, Assyrian, 5, 120.
Chaldea, 338, 344.
Chaldean account of deluge, 165.
Chaldeans, 308.
Chamber, 140.
Chariot group, 435.
Chief of Durnak, 155, 156.
Cilicia, 308, 330.
Cimmerians, 332, 333.
Circassian soldiers, 128, 157, 160.
City of ark, 168.
Clinton, 389.
Conquest of Erech, 168.
Conscription, 125.
Country of Noah, 214.
Creation, 397.
Cronos, 211.
Crystal throne, 432.
Cure of Izdubar, 194.
Curse of Ishtar, 174.
Cutha, 338, 340, 344.
Cyaxares, 93.
Cylinder of Sargon, 288.
Cypriote inscription, 423.
Cyrus, 387.

Dabun, 161.
"Daily Telegraph," 14, 15, 97, 100.

Dancing boy, 129.
Darius, 388.
Dashlook, 37, 112.
Davkina, a goddess, 231.
Deception, 137.
Deed of sale, 415, 416.
Delebekir, 28, 116, 120.
Delli Abas, 65.
Deluge, Chaldean account of, 13, 97, 100, 102.
    end of, 190.
Demands, Turkish, 138.
Deruneh, 109, 132.
Descent into Hades, 220.
Description of Creation, 222.
Destruction of North gate, Nineveh, 151.
Dinasar, 110, 124.
Discontent of soldiers, 155.
Divine bull, 167, 174.
Djezireh, 42, 43, 107, 133, 157.
Dove, 191.
Dragon, 170.
Dream of Heabani, 175.
Dunanu, 336, 412.
Dungi, 232.
Durnak, 155.
Dyke of Nimrod, 49.

Early Elamite conquest, 12, 102, 224.
Eclipses, 12, 408, 409.
Edom, 291, 360.
Egypt, 292, 304, 312, 322, 325, 328, 329.
    revolt of, 325.

456 INDEX.

Ekron, 304, 306.
Elam, 335, 338, 340, 354, 355, 356, 357, 374.
Elkod, 115.
Eltekeh, 304.
Engineers, Turkish, 116, 120.
Entertainment, Arabic, 83, 84.
Epigraphs, 412.
Erech, 166, 171, 356.
Ervil, 67.
Esarhaddon, 73, 93, 98, 311, 319, 321, 376, 416.
Ethiopia, 292, 312, 322, 325, 328, 329, 338.
Etna, 19.
Euphrates, 33, 114, 291, 312.
Evil-merodach, 386.
Exorbitant demands, 149.

Flood, the, 188.
   legend, 450.
   ravages of, 189.
Floods, 154, 157.
Fork, Assyrian, 147, 433.
Franck, M., British Consul, 25, 117, 120, 164.
Furniture, 431.

Gambuli, 336, 337.
Gaza, 306.
Gededa, 65.
Geography, absence of, 207.
Gershene, 105.
Ghost of Heabani, 220.
Goim, 338.
Grotefend, 5, 6.

Guides, abandoned by, 160.
Gulres, 155.
Gyges of Lydia, 331.

Hades, 201, 202.
Hagub, pastor, 35, 112.
Hamath inscriptions, 164, 422.
Hammum Ali, 94, 95.
Hammurabi, 233, 234.
Hani, Land of, 228.
Harimtu, 170, 174.
Hasisadra, 167, 179, 182.
Hazel river, 134, 155, 156.
Hea, the god, 185, 192, 201, 212, 230, 231, 399, 401, 402, 403.
Heabani, 167, 170, 175.
   death of, 183.
   resurrection of, 202.
Head of statue of goddess, 142, 420.
Heaven, 203, 205.
Hell, 205.
Herbert, Col., 54.
Hezekiah, 89, 292, 305.
Hieroglyphics, 422.
Hillah, 58, 62.
Hincks, 5, 7.
Harom, 274, 278, 287.
Hosah, 370.
Hoshea, 12, 285, 287.
Housebuilding, 81, 82.
Humbaba, 166, 171.
Hyksos, 421.
Hymer, 62.
Hymn to light, 391, 392.

Ibrahim, 157.

INDEX. 457

Imperial Museum, Constantinople, 143, 151.
Inda-bigas, 340, 341, 345, 357.
Irregular soldiers, 127, 128.
Ishtar, 91, 171, 172, 334, 350, 399, 400.
    amours of, 173.
Istar-nanhundi, 353.
Izdubar, 14, 167, 394.
    antiquity of legends of, 166.
    founded Babylonian monarchy, 222.
    illness of, 176.
    journey of, 178, 180, 181.
    lament of, 177, 199, 200.
    legends of, 14, 165.
    makeshift name, 166.
    probably historical, 222.
    probably Nimrod, 166.
    return of, 196, 197.
    third dream of, 176.
Izirtu, capital of Minni, 334.

Jebel Abjad, 44, 105, 106.
Jebel Djudi, 41, 106, 217.
Jehu, date of, 11.
Jerusalem, 305.
Jewish synchronisms, 448.
Judah, 291.
Justice, care of, 410.

Kalah Shergat, 50, 51, 242.
Kalata, 99.
Kalzi, 414.
Kanun musical instrument, 130.
Karajah Dagh Mountains, 37.
Karatapa, 65.

Karbanit, 323.
Kasr, 57.
Kassi, 227, 246, 299.
Kazekoi, 154.
Kedar, 361.
Kerkook, 66.
Kerook, 157.
Khabour, 43, 106, 155.
Khan Baleos, 153.
Khazil, 159.
Khorsabad, 98, 99.
Khosr river, 68.
Kobuk, 39, 41.
Korban, Bairam festival, 32.
Kouyunjik, 86-103, 382.
Kudur-nanhundi, 206.
Kufre, 65.
Kufru, 154.
Kuri-galzu, 235, 237.

Lagomer, Elamite god, 353.
Lamech, 212.
Lamp feeder, 433.
Lamps, 432, 433.
Later occupation of Nineveh, 139.
Layard, discoveries of, 4, 6, 70, 71, 88, 89.
Lenormant, M., 5, 8.
Library chamber, 144.
    of Nineveh, 452.
Lintel, 146, 429.
Loftus, 4, 6, 13.
Louvre collection, 16.
Lydia, 331.

Madaktu, 347, 349, 355.

INDEX.

Magan, or Makan, 312, 313.
Magician Arab, 123
Mahomedan tomb, 149.
Manitu, 184.
Mannians, 308.
Mannu-ki-ahi, 412.
Marseilles, 17.
Median chiefs, 288.
Memphis, 323, 327.
Menahem, 278, 286.
Menant, 5, 8.
Mendes, 326.
Merodach, 228, 231, 291, 401, 402.
Merodach Baladan, 236, 237, 256, 260, 297, 307.
Meroe, 291, 304.
Mersina, 25.
Mili-sihu, 237.
Minni, 333.
Mizir, 111.
Moab, 291, 360.
Model of hand, 429.
Modern objects, 146.
Mosul, 46, 68, 134, 153.
Mount of ark, 216.
Mua, 182.
Mugallu of Tubal, 330.
Mujelliba, 55.
Music, Arabic 129, 130.
Mutaggil-nusku, 91, 251.
Muzar, 33.
Mythology, 451.

Nabateans, 363, 365, 367.
Nabonidus, 387.
Nabopolassar, 93, 384.

Nabu-bel-zikri, 358.
Nabu-damiq, 412.
Naharwan, 43, 133.
Nana goddess, 206, 223, 355.
National poem, Babylonian, 205.
Navarino, 20.
Nazi-bugas, 236.
Nazi-murudas, 250.
Nebbi Yunas, 68, 89.
Nebuchadnezzar, 57, 384, 385.
Necho, 93, 323, 326.
Neriglisar, 386.
New fragments deluge tablets, 166.
Nimrod, 49.
Nimroud, 48, 70-85.
Nineveh, 46, 48, 86, 93, 134, 306, 337.
Ninip, 192, 339.
Ninip-uzalli, 412.
Ninip-pal-esar, 251.
Nipur, 410, 411.
Nisibin, 39, 109, 129, 157.
Nizir, mountains of, 190, 216.
Norris, Dr., 5, 7.
Nusku, 401.

Obelisks, 141, 328.
Obstructions, Turkish, 47, 115, 117, 131, 136, 149, 162, 163.
Officer, Turkish, 125.
Okusolderan, 114.
Oppert, Professor, 5, 7.
Orfa, 35, 112, 113, 123, 160.
Otiartes, or Ardates, 212.

Pacha of Orfa, 160.

Pahe, Elamite king, 358, 371.
Palermo, 18.
Paliya, 412.
Parthian era, 388, 389, 390.
Pedestal of column, 431.
Pehlevi inscriptions, 113, 426, 427.
Pekah, 12, 285, 286.
Pelusium, 324.
Pharaoh, 291.
Philistia, 289, 291.
Philistines, 308.
Phœnician inscriptions, 423, 424, 425, 426.
Place, M., 3, 6.
Pleyte, W., 420.
Pool of Abraham, 113.
Pottery, 141.
Prayer to Bel, 395, 396.
Primitive state of Babylonia, 166.
Procession of warriors, 142.
Proposed canal, 161.
Psammitichus, 332.
Pudil, 244.
Pul, 448.

Que, 308.

Raft, 48, 156.
Railway, 116.
Ra-set-nub, Egyptian king, 421.
Rassam, Mr. H., 4, 13.
Raven, 191.
Rawlinson, G., 8, 438.
Rawlinson, Sir H., 4, 5, 7, 59, 63.
Redif Pacha, 136.
Restoration of Nineveh, 308.

Results of excavations, 437.
Resurrection of Heabani, 202.
Rezon, 274, 278, 283, 287.
Rhodes, 24.
Riduti, palace of, 372, 373, 375.
Rimagu, 235.
Rings, 435.
Robber, Syrian, 30, 121.
Robbery attempted, 158.
Rock tombs at Orfa, 113.
Royal seal, 293.
Russian consul at Aleppo, 164.

Sabako, 318, 327.
Sabbath, Assyrian, 12.
Sabitu, 180.
Sadimatati temple, 245.
Saduri of Ararat, 372.
Saggal, temple of, 228.
Saites, 421.
Sais, 323, 326, 327.
Sale of slave, 417.
Samgunu, 412.
Samhati, 174.
Samsi-vul, 91.
Sargon, 73, 92, 98, 293.
— the Babylonian Moses, 224.
Sarturda, 175.
Sassanian vase, 143.
Saulmugina, 316, 337, 338, 339, 342, 344.
Saulcy, De, 8.
Sayce, 5, 8.
Schrader, 5, 8.
Seal of Sargon, 148.
Seals, 435.

INDEX.

Seasons, 404, 405.
Second expedition, 119.
Secul, a Babylonian measure, 241.
Seleucus, 389.
Semil, 105, 134, 155.
Semitic conquest, 449.
Sending out birds, 191.
Sennacherib, 90, 92, 98, 295, 320, 343, 346, 376, 414.
    palace of, 144.
Seven wicked spirits, 398-403.
Severe weather, 149.
Shalmaneser I., 72, 91, 140.
Shalmaneser II., 73, 74, 79, 91, 141, 252.
Shamas, 231, 339, 399, 400, 402.
Shammer revolt, 39, 40.
Sharabarazi, 157.
Shepherd kings, 421.
Shoulder of statue, 430.
Shushan, 336, 350, 351, 353, 355.
Siduri, 180.
Sin, 201, 231, 339, 345, 399, 400, 401, 402.
Sippara, 338, 340, 344, 410, 411.
Skene, Mr., Consul, 31, 162, 163.
Smyrna, 22, 23.
Soldiers, Turkish, 30.
Spoon, 147.
Stories of Nimrod, 168.
Storm, 154.
Style, 147.
Sumir, 315, 352.
Superstition, 161.
Suqamuna, 225, 395.
Surippak, 185, 212.

Suzub, 307, 314, 315.
Syllabaries, 101, 147, 418.
Synchronous history, 250.
Syra, 20, 21.
Syria, 338.
Swallow, 191.

Talbot, Mr. F., 5, 7.
Tammaritu the Elamite, 336, 340, 341, 342, 345, 347, 348, 353, 371.
Tammuz, 173.
Tanis, 324.
Tartar post, 133.
Taylor, Mr., 4.
Taylor cylinder, 296.
Tcharmelek, 34, 114, 122.
Tekrit, 52.
Tel Adas, 45, 105, 154, 155.
Tel Gauran, 37, 111.
Tel Ibrahim, 63.
Tel Karamel, 32, 114.
Tellibel, 41, 109.
Temple of Assur, 244.
    of Ishtar, 214.
Temples, building, 377, 378, 379.
Termanin, 31.
Terra-cotta tablets, 147.
Te-umman the Elamite, 336, 412, 413.
Thebes, 324, 328, 329, 376.
Thomas, E., 423.
Tiglath Pileser, 9, 73, 74, 92, 139, 253.
    annals of, 254-286.
Tigris, 42, 107, 153, 291, 312.

INDEX. 461

Tiha, 81.
Timnah, 304.
Tirhakah, 311, 312, 318, 321, 322, 323, 324, 325.
Toma, 69, 84, 85.
Tomazini, Dr., 164.
Tower of Nimroud, 75, 76, 77.
Trial by birds, 209.
Tubal, 330.
Tugulti-ninip, 91, 140, 249.
Turanian writing, 233.
Turanians in Babylonia, 449.
Turkish policy, 136.
Turuspa, capital of Armenia, 309.
Tyre, 312, 329.
Tyrians, 308.

Ubaratutu, 177.
Udder, Arab chief, 81.
Umbadara, an Elamite, 412.
Umman-aldas, king of Elam, 347, 349, 350, 357, 358, 371.
Umman-igas, 336, 338, 340, 357.
Umman-minan, 314.
Ummih-zirriti, 226.
Undamane, 318, 327, 376.
Ur, 232.
Ur of Chaldees, 233.
Urhamsi, 181, 195.
Urukh, 232.

Vaalli king of Minni, 334.
Vaiteh king of Arabia, 359, 361, 363, 366, 369, 371.
Van, 309.
Varenshaher, 37, 110, 124.

Varenshaher, sack of, 159.
Vul, 399, 402.
Vul-nirari I., 242, 243.
Vul-nirari III., 73, 74, 89, 139.

Wall of Nineveh, 87.
Warka, 206.
Waters of death, 181.
Winged bull, 431.
Work to be accomplished, 452.
Works on Cuneiform, 6, 7, 8.

Xisithrus, 167, 177, 212.
    translated, 210.

Yahimilki, Tyrian prince, 329.
Yahuhazi (Ahaz), 263, 286.
Yakinlu king of Arvad, 330.
Yakub's hotel, 26.
Yavan king of Ashdod, 290, 291
Year, 405.
Yedok, 112.

Zab, 49, 67.
Zaccho, 44, 134.
Zaccho pass, 155.
Zaidu, 170.
Zambour, 122.
Zamama-zakir-idin, 251.
Zarephath, 302.
Zibini, 123.
Zidon, 302.
Zirat-banit, 228.
Ziru, 231.
Zoan, 326.
Zodiac, 407.

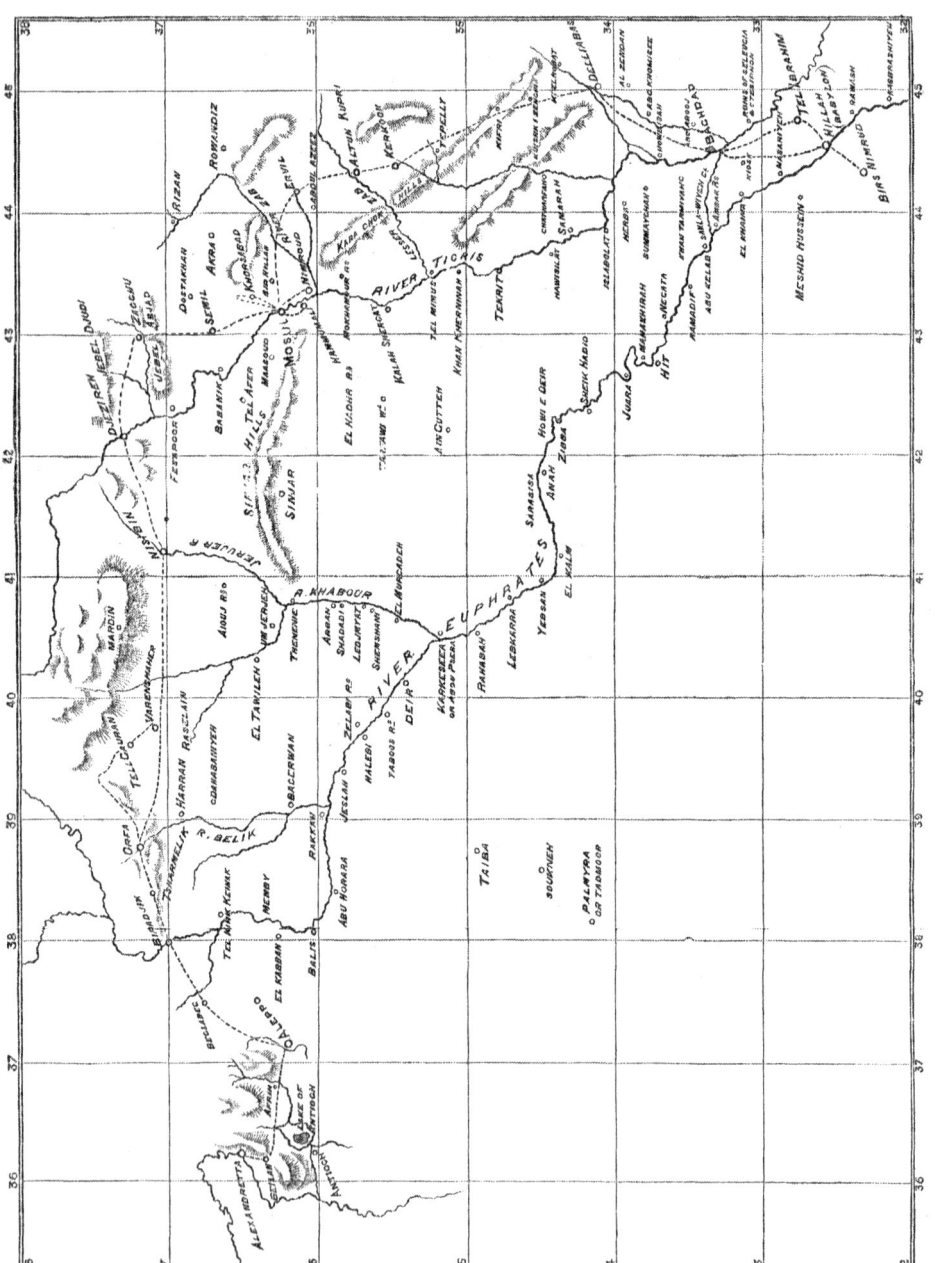

www.ingramcontent.com/pod-product-compliance
Lightning Source LLC
Chambersburg PA
CBHW071221290426
44108CB00013B/1244